# Data Warehousing
# for E-Business

W. H. Inmon

R. H. Terdeman

Joyce Norris-Montanari

Dan Meers

Wiley Computer Publishing

John Wiley & Sons, Inc.

NEW YORK · CHICHESTER · WEINHEIM · BRISBANE · SINGAPORE · TORONTO

Publisher: Robert Ipsen
Editor: Robert M. Elliott
Asistant Editor: Emilie Herman
Managing Editor: John Atkins
Text Design & Composition: D&G Limited, LLC

Designations used by companies to distinguish their products are often claimed as trademarks. In all instances where John Wiley & Sons, Inc., is aware of a claim, the product names appear in initial capital or ALL CAPITAL LETTERS. Readers, however, should contact the appropriate companies for more complete information regarding trademarks and registration.

This book is printed on acid-free paper. ∞

This publication is designed to provide accurate and authoritative information in regard to the subject matter covered. It is sold with the understanding that the publisher is not engaged in professional services. If professional advice or other expert assistance is required, the services of a competent professional person should be sought.

*Library of Congress Cataloging-in-Publication Data:*

ISBN: 0-471-41579-0

Printed in the United States of America.

10 9 8 7 6 5 4 3 2 1

# CONTENTS

# ACKNOWLEDGMENTS

**BILL INMON** would like to thank:

Claudia Imhoff, Intelligent Solutions
Jon Geiger, Intelligent Solutions
John Zachman, Zachman International
Cheryl Estep, independent consultant
Karen Nicosia, SeeBeyond

**R.H. TERDEMAN** would like to thank:

Florence Terdeman, his wife
Michael Terdeman, his son
Colleagues Mike McNulty, Christy Kay, Mack Armstrong EMC
Bandit and Daisy
John and Mary Weis

**JOYCE NORRIS-MONTANARI** would like to thank:

Frank Montanari, her husband
Stephen Aikins, Embarcadero Software
David Allen Spayth, Ascential Software
John Trenary, Ascential Software
Kim Nevins, Ambeo
Lowell Fryman, Independent Consultant

**DAN MEERS** would like to thank his family, old and new for their support. Special thanks to his wife and new arrival (T and T+1) for their understanding. He would also like to acknowledge the help of his friends in the field including: Tom Meers and the members of Result Data Consulting, Barry Smith, Mike Silva, Bill Jellik, Geoff Cole, and Louis and the Genesis Gang. Dan remains deeply indebted to Bill Inmon for his support and mentorship.

E ach new generation must find out for itself that there are certain "universal truths" about technology and information systems. The generation that is responsible for e-business is no exception.

The universal truths about technology and information systems include some themes that continue to be repeated. These themes take many forms and cut across technologies with impunity:

- **Performance is not something that can be bought, but rather must be built into the deepest fiber of the system.** And performance has a huge impact on the usability of the system. If the system does not perform well, the user simply will abandon the system. To complicate matters, the true performance characteristics of the system do not become manifest until the system has grown to maturity. And nowhere is performance more important than the e-business environment.

- **Integration of data becomes a real issue as the number of systems expand and the systems age.** The complications and limitations of a lack of integration do not become apparent until there are a lot of applications and those applications are mature. By then, the seeds of disintegration have long been sown and the weeds have grown.

- **The problems of a lack of integration grow ever worse as the systems supporting the application infrastructure grow and age.** Systems behave one way under a small amount of data and behave a completely different way under a larger amount of data. E-business generates a huge amount of data with its clickstream processing, and these volumes of data present the most serious challenge to e-business.

Unfortunately, in all three cases the real problems inherent to the infrastructure do not become apparent until the e-business applications and systems are mature. And by this time the e-business applications and systems have been cast in concrete. It is expensive and painful to try to reengineer a system or set of applications and systems that have already been built.

E-business developers consider themselves to be a new and separate breed from the developers of the past. It is true that the technology and techniques used by the e-business developers are quite different from the technology of the past. But merely using new technology and techniques does not allow the e-business environment to escape from the universal truths. What would happen if an e-business architect could benefit from the collective wisdom of the past? Is it necessary for e-business architects to repeat the painful learning curves of previous generations?

The answer is that the developers of the e-business infrastructure have a great opportunity before them. There is no need to make the same mistakes that other generations of developers have made when it comes to discovering the universal truths of information systems. This need to build on the lessons of the past, not rediscover them, is especially important in e-business, where the information system is the store. In e-business the public sees and feels the mistakes—openly and nakedly—of the e-business architect because those mistakes are *very* apparent.

What can the e-business architect do? Well, for starters he can be alerted to the fact that there is an infrastructure that has already solved most of the problems that he will run into, so he does not have to reinvent everything. Neither does he have to learn by stubbing his toe in the middle of the night. If the e-business developer will open his mind, there is an easy and elegant way to learn some universal lessons without having to go through the pain that is wrought through ignorance.

This book is about the solid architecture that is available—in one form or another—to the e-business architect. That architecture is called the Corporate Information Factory (CIF), and is an established framework for the management of the information across the enterprise. The CIF has proven to deliver performance, integrate data and processes, and manage large volumes of data. In a word, the CIF delivers *in a state of maturity* on the promises of technology.

Unless the e-business architect actually wishes to bump into things in the night, this book can save invaluable time and can help him lay out a foundation that will serve both the long-term and short-term needs of the e-business.

# How This Book Is Organized

Most topical books are organized in a sequential manner. This may give a good time perspective, but it often lacks content integration. This book has been organized from a business perspective, using a top-down view of architecture. We begin with the business challenges and opportunities and work down toward the technology perspective, allowing for differences in e-business community perspectives. Each segment of the community can see how their particular component is integrated into the whole problem.

Following is a brief overview of each chapter:

- Chapter 1 maps out the new opportunities and business challenges that e-business presents, as well as how they impact the enterprise.

- Chapter 2 relates e-business information to the enterprise's other information, using the CIF model. We demonstrate the value of using a single information model to avoid unnecessary business cost and risk.

- Chapter 3 stresses that the business support infrastructure requires an iterative approach to ensure adequate speed and capacity to avoid negative business impact.

- Chapter 4 takes the reader through the process of identifying e-user groups.

- Chapter 5 helps the reader to understand the need to integrate e-business data with all other enterprise data.

- Chapter 6 indicates the importance of performance in meeting online user expectation. The newly integrated e-business data and traditional data cause an explosion of information.

- Chapter 7 demonstrates how to manage these new volumes of information.

- Chapter 8 shows how to derive value from the new environment by leveraging new applications.

- Chapter 9 takes the user back to a business perspective, encouraging him to explore the data for new business value.

- Chapter 10 cautions the reader that all business and technology lie in a world of constant change and that prudence requires planning for this change.

## Who Should Read This Book

This work will be of assistance to everyone in the organization who creates, supports, manages, or uses the e-business environment. Most works focus on a very narrow band of information pertaining to e-business; this work is focused on a complete view. This book is appropriate for a CEO but equally important for a Web site programmer or designer. A great danger is to read an integrating work with an eye toward a single level in the infrastructure, which will result in a biased view of the world. The CIF model has helped businesses to recognize that no one component is more important than another. For an effective information infrastructure to exist, all components are equally critical to effective business. The authors strongly suggest that you read this book sequentially in order to derive the full value of a comprehensive view.

## Finally

The authors believe that work will help organizations avoid the pitfalls of a myopic view of business. By placing e-business components in the proper perspective, excessive cost and excessive risk can be mitigated. Even more importantly, unrealistic expectation can be controlled. Too often, new technology creates an expectation that can only be met by disappointment. By setting e-business in the context of traditional business, more realistic expectations can be managed to success. Hopefully all readers will use this work as a high-level guide for developing and managing their e-business expectations and implementations.

# CHAPTER 1

# The Opportunities and Challenges of E-Business

E-business seeks to establish an inexpensive, ongoing, and revenue-producing dialog with profitable customers. A properly established e-business allows inexpensive, reliable, and highly dynamic supply chain relationships, which can reduce inventory levels and improve product quality. Many of these opportunities may already be on the strategic map—for example, enterprise resource planning (ERP), customer relationship management (CRM) and enterprise application integration (EAI). But each of these initiatives increases the need for effective data warehousing efforts, and early awareness of that fact is essential to achieving long-term success.

The combination of short-term capital and a "traffic count" mentality spawned the superstructure-without-infrastructure approach to e-business. (The expectation that a traditional information infrastructure was required only in traditional business models was quickly disproved.) The objective of this chapter is to address both the challenges and opportunities that e-business presents, and to demonstrate how data warehousing fits into this new schema.

# From Physical to Electronic Markets

Life before e-business was full of opportunities and challenges that required complex solutions. The advent of e-business has provided new stimulus for investing in information technology; it has also presented a new context for business formation. By expanding our traditional approach to information technology—which emphasizes a layered approach to supporting daily processing and reporting—we can take greater advantage of these opportunities. Table 1.1 summarizes the traditional view of information technology as an enabler of the daily processing and reporting procedures. The target markets are all electronic, as is their infrastructure.

Consider, as an example, the process of analyzing customer profitability in a national bank. There, transactions are processed and summarized across product lines: checking, savings, credit cards, credit lines, and mortgages. Costs are assembled from geographic and product-based lines of business, some allocated directly from known account activity, others allocated indirectly based on volume and other models. Customers view their financial assets based on usage and timeliness; these views are not consistent, which creates disparities in the way customers

**Table 1.1**  Standard View of Information Technology

| INFORMATION SOURCE | INFORMATION USE |
|---|---|
| Transaction Platforms (Legacy) | 1. Process transactions.<br>2. Monitor activity and report. |
| Real-Time Specialized Systems (Client-Server, UNIX) | 1. Process transactions.<br>2. Manage product metrics.<br>3. Monitor activity and report. |
| Groupware Document Management Imaging Multimedia | 1. Support employee interactions.<br>2. Support external interactions.<br>3. Capture transactional evidence.<br>4. Catalog transactions & relationships.<br>5. Store binary large objects. |
| Contingency and High-Availability Systems | 1. Ensure processing availability.<br>2. Provide failover systems.<br>3. Allow rapid application recovery.<br>4. Provide duplicate, near line stores. |
| Archival Systems | 1. Provide worst-case data images.<br>2. Support time-based research. |

use bank products. Many customer product selections are impacted by their holdings in other institutions, often comprising very different portfolios. Because these considerations are not apparent to the bank that is offering the products, and given the plethora of substitutes and the difficulty of factoring in unknown external holdings, analyzing customer profitability is extremely difficult for our example bank.

# The Three Vs: Volume, Velocity, and Variety

Improvements to physical and electronic bandwidth brought with them challenges, most notably, how to deal with volume, velocity, and variety. At the heart of these challenges is the notion that all data is created (as well as stored and moved) equally. Merely digitizing a stream of analog data points cannot create a continuous stream of information. Moreover, since computers came into widespread use for transaction processing, each of these challenges has been presented in different ways, even though the underlying dilemma—of understanding the sources and use of data—remains unchanged.

## Data Volumes

Volume is an indicator of popularity, of customer interest in a product. To accommodate growing customer volume, traditional retailers began to scale their physical infrastructures. Concomitant increases to retail volume likewise prompted businesses to ramp up inventories, staffing, and distribution. Retailers often elected to build more stores or expand existing ones in profitable markets. Necessarily, as increased customer traffic resulted in increased revenue, additional resources were required to support ongoing transaction processing and analysis.

Current growth trends indicate that the distributed storage environment is set to outstrip increases to conventional server processing. Lower-overhead storage alternatives enable faster growth with greater geographic dispersion in support of burgeoning data volumes. Logical management of additional data volumes presents an even greater challenge. E-business data comprises vastly expanded quantities of corporate information, as well as the new clickstream data formats, which will be covered in Chapter 2, "The Corporate Information Factory and E-Business." Corporate information regarding products, customers, and procurement are often replicated into e-business systems in order to

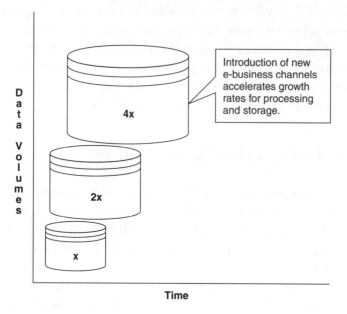

Data Volumes

4x

Introduction of new
e-business channels
accelerates growth
rates for processing
and storage.

2x

x

Time

**Figure 1.1**  Expanding data volumes.

facilitate getting on the Web. Companies with successful data warehouse systems can leverage these systems to provide integrated customer and product information to Web applications. Companies that
lack these resources and that have tried the virtual approach to directly
connect disparate source systems to Web applications have often met
with failure. Consequently, e-business infrastructure providers now
emphasize a hybrid approach, one that utilizes data warehouses to provide integrated information and direct source system connections for
limited transactional purposes. Figure 1.1 illustrates some data volume
sources.

## Data Velocity

Information velocity is a key determinant of overall business growth
capacity, or scalability. In an environment of growing volume, velocity
escalates as well. Velocity is a factor of time: increasing the amount of
activity without increasing the time period necessary to complete that
activity requires that the activity be done at higher speed. An increase in
velocity is first felt in processing activities; whether at the checkout
counter or the general ledger level, transactions have to be processed

faster in order to cope with the increased business volume. But today, velocity refers to much more than processing speed. Greater volumes of data must be exchanged and moved in shorter time frames.

Coping with velocity has been difficult for many local, metropolitan, regional, national, and international networked environments. Data warehousing can offer significant benefits in managing velocity requirements, by creating parallel sources for corporate information. Reporting and analysis components are fed by transactional systems; decision support activities are then offloaded from these sources.

Globalization, too, has dramatically increased the need for velocity, as data sets are often replicated across time zones to support enterprise needs. High-availability systems, disaster recovery planning, and related regulatory requirements have all driven recent expansion of replication and synchronization efforts. The demands of e-business for rapid data access and replication serve to validate the need for robust information architectures that have already been constructed to accommodate business requirements. Figure 1.2 illustrates the pressures leading to increases in data velocity.

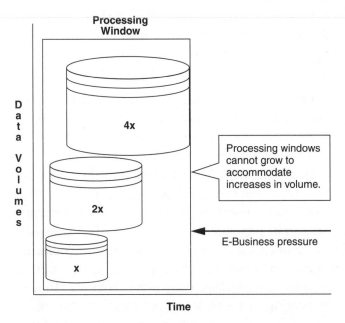

**Figure 1.2**  Increased data velocity.

## Variety of Data Formats

To meet consumer demand for richness and depth in electronic exchange, e-businesses must offer variety. Consumers now require a variety of channels through which to gain access to products. Consequently, channels have evolved to support multiple forms of data exchange. Prior to the advent of e-business, the challenge of offering enough variety was met with various creative solutions: catalog retailers instituted customer support in the form of call centers; facsimile-based order submission became prevalent for just about everything, even lunch orders. Today, however, the bar has been raised higher than ever before. Consumers are not confined to a brick-and-mortar outlet, nor are they restricted by certain hours of service to get their needs met.

Any emerging channel of commerce requires physical- and information-based technologies to support its evolution. Managing media assets was a well-established business activity long before Internet-based selling appeared on the horizon. Previously, imaging and document technologies were most commonly used to manage media assets; soon, digitization and storage of multimedia assets were considered imperative. Hierarchical storage management techniques have been successfully employed in the management of image archives; similar techniques have aided in other archive activities. These techniques have not, however, provided significant success in data warehousing. Therefore, distributed data storage architectures, including near-line and other alternative designs, have merged to support massive data warehouse environments. Figure 1.3 illustrates the sources and uses of enhanced data formats.

Volume in and of itself is not the sole barometer of success. First-wave e-tailers that gained experience by providing electronic richness soon learned that digital richness did not support profitability. It did, however, support interest, and laid a foundation for loyalty. This so-called richness-reach compromise has been well documented, and the success stories, though varied, share consistent themes. Traditional retail firms that established a Web presence, new electronic storefronts, and hybrid models all have had some success in e-business. That success has been shared by business models that embrace and invest in infrastructure commensurate to the overall challenge. Recognizing that volume, velocity, and data variety will increase with success enables enterprise architects to design systems capable of supporting this growth. Of course, there are also success

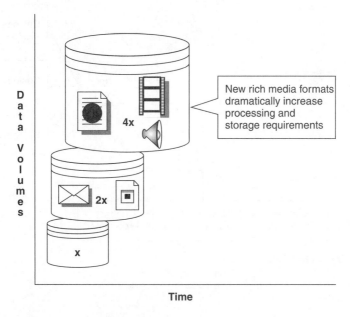

**Figure 1.3**  Enhanced varieties of data.

stories built on failure, for example, overstock.com, which sells liqui-
dated inventories from specialized "dot-bombs."

## E-Business Channels

To succeed, e-businesses must create, then support, electronic dialog.
Business performance relies upon the consistency and tone of this dialog. As electronic pathways—that is, channels—have improved, different views of dialog partners, as well as the context for this dialog, have
emerged. Therefore, aligning transactional and analytical systems to
support these dialog channels has become a major technical imperative.

These channels have been assembled along relationship lines, including:
business-to-business (B2B), which is directed toward commercial and
industrial activity; business-to-consumer (B2C), which is the retail channel for marketing and sales; and business-to-employee (B2E), which is the
expanded internal networks for human resources. Figure 1.4 illustrates
the relationships between these entities and their respective channels.

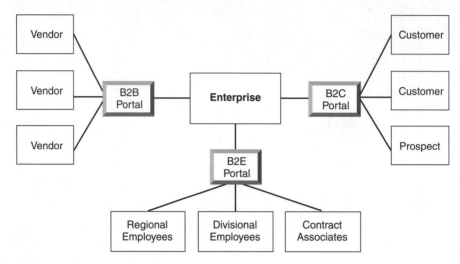

**Figure 1.4**   E-business channels.

# Business-to-Business (B2B): Centralized Exchanges and Emerging Marketplaces

The business-to-business exchange rapidly emerged as a model for the electronic marketplace. B2B exchanges were founded in vertical industry segments, based on shared needs and semantics. Commodity-level goods and services were the first target for this new faceless interaction. But exchanges of any sort require membership, in this case, predicated on the desire of members to find trading partners and to secure consistent supplies. These exchanges were outgrowths of previously formalized trading relationships that utilized private networks. Within the context of a virtual marketplace, centralized exchanges serve to aggregate trading partners, and to act as intermediaries between sellers and buyers, by providing the tools and resources to facilitate complex electronic transactions.

## *Obstacles to Exchange- and Alliance-Based Models*

An obstacle that emerged in response to such exchanges and other alliance-based models came in the form of claims of collusion. Though certainly there is a natural inclination toward price setting and fixing, these were not the primary motivations behind these business models. Nevertheless, balancing the needs of the marketplace with the concerns of regulators became a major obstacle to B2B success. For example, financial services firms attempting to form global currency exchange alliances had to address many levels of concern about pricing, supply, and market control issues. The openness of the model and the willingness of an exchange's members to share information with governing entities are the key factors to assuaging these concerns.

Another obstacle to the success of these models was the result of a new economy precept, which presumed that establishing an online exchange mechanism was a guarantee of success. In practice, however, launching an e-business may have been rewarded with interest, but in many cases, very low levels of commitment from potential members. Locking in trading relationships based upon exchange membership proved unattractive because the exchange itself was not a complete value proposition. Trading partners need several layers of interface and structure to enable supply chain enhancements; they also need tremendous flexibility to support constant changes in economic and industry conditions.

In response to these obstacles, peer-to-peer networking began to emerge as a competing model for exchange-based marketplaces. The peer-to-peer model allows any business to bypass centralized exchanges to find like-minded trading partners. One advantage of peer-to-peer networking is the opportunity to efficiently, rapidly, and securely conduct transactions directly with chosen trading partners. Peer-to-peer networking excels at simple, transaction-oriented exchanges. *Peering portals* link internal inventories and production systems to provide accurate, up-to-date product availability and price listings. A complete approach to partnership management provides answers to each level of need in the supply chain.

## Business-to-Consumer (B2C): The Context of Consumption

Categorizing consumers based upon their purchase behavior is nothing new, but doing so tells only part of the story about customers to retailers. Identifying consumer buying patterns within different product categories tells another part of the story—an equally important part. Consumers make choices about buying based upon the nature of the goods they are examining and how they intend to use them. Therefore, for retailers, understanding the customer pattern of use is a necessary prerequisite when creating an electronic—that is, Web-based—shopping/buying experience for a specific product. Any asymmetries that exist between consumer types and product categories lead to failures in e-tailing, as recent dot-com experiences demonstrate. Symmetry means the products offered by category should align with customer demand by category.

Individual consumers require different degrees of information, as well as different types of experience when shopping online, based on the product being sold. Commodities—here to mean mass-produced or unspecialized products—are relatively easy for consumers to purchase electronically. The more commodity-like the product, the less rich the purchase experience needed to support its adoption. Paper clips are paper clips. Clothing is another matter, because size, quality, materials, brand, and other factors all become issues of concern for consumers. Hence, for more specialized products, gaining customer confidence becomes key to adoption. To consumers, confidence comes from being comfortable with the shopping experience, having brand knowledge, being assured of quality, as well as being informed and assured of fair shipping and return policies. To achieve that level of customer confidence, the product experience must be consistent and predictable, regardless of the delivery channel. Brick-and-mortar retailers have had years to figure out how to meet those goals, whereas e-tailers are still learning how to address these issues, in particular quality of delivery services. An otherwise sustained product quality can be diminished by damages in delivery, as well the dilutive impact of other logistical failures. An example of a logistics failure was when a major toy retailer took orders at Christmas but could not fulfill them in time. Consequently, consumer adoption is also heavily influenced by shipping charges and return policies.

Brand perception is as important to consumers shopping via electronic channels as in the brick-and-mortar world. In fact, in electronic channels that do not undermine brand and quality factors, consumers probably are more conscious of the brand and quality of the goods they are shopping for than of the channels they use to do so. The point is, predictable and reliable adoption experiences build consumer trust; thus, establishing trust is the foundation upon which customer loyalty is built and maintained.

Another factor important to consider when creating an online presence is the level of specialization of the provider. Certain products benefit from enhanced or exclusive utility, for example, banking and insurance. These types of products—and their consumers—benefit from regulatory provisions that ensure the security of their purchase. For example, banks—hence, their customers—can rely on federal insurance to enhance the security of such products as certificates of deposit. Over electronic channels, competition broadens; even large banks with a strong historical presence must now compete with smaller counterparts because all can offer similar security to customers.

## Business-to-Employee (B2E)

Just as the Web has accelerated the business-to-business relationships, the nature of the business-to-employee relationship has also been redefined. This redefinition includes the automation of what was typically a painful paper-based function. An example of this is a firm by the name of Gelco, which provides automated Web-based expense reimbursement. The elapsed time from input to direct deposit in the employee's account is three days. This increased velocity from the old economy of three to twelve weeks to three days has a huge impact on employee satisfaction and productivity. Among the other areas of improvement that have seen immediate impact from the new e-channels are benefits, time and leave, internal education, as well as access to intellectual property within the firm. The entire definition of the business-to-employee relationship has moved from a paper-people–based process to a Web-based process in most large firms. Most employees perceived this as a vast improvement with the elimination of unnecessary gatekeepers between the employee and those things to which the employee is entitled. The result is faster velocity, greater satisfaction, and higher productivity.

## The Impact of E-Tailing

E-tailing is that sector of the online economy directly responsive to customer needs. Until recently, it was the segment of the online economy most familiar to Internet users and the one that had commanded most corporate attention. Business-to-consumer innovations in e-tailing

marked the first-tier technologies in which businesses found it necessary to invest: Web sites, servers, and online transaction processing
were the focal points for the B2C revolution. These technology tools
represented the superstructure of e-business. Unfortunately, too often,
the underlying infrastructure was not designed to support the weight of
this superstructure. E-businesses soon found that learning to use these
"power tools" and understanding how to control them was more chal-
lenging than acquiring and installing them. Quickly they discovered
that producing Web pages was the simplest part of Web functionality—
anyone with a PC or even laptop and some advanced software could create and launch entire Web sites in a matter of hours, though certainly,
the resources for establishing a corporate presence on the Web were
much more advanced.

The problem is that the connections between a Web site and its underlying source systems for processing transactions are tenuous at best. B2C
sites are awash in detailed transaction data, so much so that the very
definition of transaction has changed dramatically. So-called clickstream data indicates transactions taking place but often without resulting revenue. A Web site also makes it more difficult to identify
granularity, periodicity, and relevance, in particular because the volume
of this detailed data flow increases exponentially online.

Small wonder then that the language of e-tailing developed around volume: How many hits did a page or a site receive? How many unique visitors? How many clickthroughs? And for the very fortunate, how many
dollars were spent? It seemed that supporting the Web-based volume of
activity was the only important factor in achieving success with the B2C
systems. This volume-based approach was not promulgated by information technology, but it was the focal point of entire business plans,
which were aimed squarely at venture capitalists. The domestic funding
capacity for technology startups was at an all-time high when Internet
businesses started their funding cycles. After all, venture capitalists are
not paid to fund established companies in need of incremental growth
capitalization; rather, the venture capital formula is built around the
0-to-60 phenomenon—that is, immediate start with nearly immediate
results, as measured by traffic counts and "eyeballs." Venture capitalists
are not generally looking for long-term profitability and stability. The initial public market, particularly in times of economic expansion, rewards
revenue growth with projected acceleration.

# Connecting Customers with Their Transactions

In the physical world, forging links between transactions and customers is not a trivial matter. Big-box retailers struggle just to connect customers to their transactions, much less discover their shopping preferences. Look at the checkout counter at your grocery store: the cash register counts the items you're purchasing, and the credit card scanner processes the payment. See any wires connecting these two systems? The point is, making an after-the-fact connection between customers and their purchases is a difficult task. Even when the cash register is connected to the scanner, neither machine can tell you when the customer came in the door, which aisles the customer visited, or which items he or she might have considered and compared. In the best case, you know who bought what, when, where, and using what form of payment. If source systems don't capture critical connection points, connecting customers, products, and transactions can't be done in the data warehouse.

## *The Affinity Card*

Enter the affinity, or club, card. This is not a specialty credit card; it is not a payment processing component. The affinity card gives customers special discounts on daily market items, and even on their total purchase. It is also used for ancillary services within the complex, for example, video rental. The customer is given an incentive to provide the retailer with basic profile information. The customer's card is scanned upon checkout to ensure discounts are applied. Cash register tapes indicate the discounts given based on the use of the card.

By instituting the affinity card, the retailer is able to immediately link customers to their purchases, payment method, and time of purchase, immediately and accurately. Subsequently, this quality capture technique enables successful warehousing of all related information. The transaction record begins with a unique customer identifier, which makes building the appropriate relationships in the warehouse comparatively simple. Trends—including time of visits, market-basket components, and payment methods—emerge very rapidly from this integrated data. Some elements, which could aid in analysis and marketing, are still missing, however. Physical retailers still can't learn how long their customer is in the store, or which items he or she compared as part of the purchase decision. Neither can retailers know what the customer put into a shopping cart only to remove or replace it later in the visit. Retailers also can't know traffic patterns, the road map the customer followed, through the store.

Clearly, the ability to measure successful marketing campaigns is not limited to sales levels. For businesses that quantify sales at the square-foot level, determining customer attention to displays, specially designed aisles, and other physical marketing elements is essential. E-tailers have the advantage in this regard, because Web site activity is much easier to capture. Of course, what knowing what to do with that information presents new and unique challenges for e-businesses.

## Economics of E-Business

The e-business challenge is to achieve enterprise profitability, one customer at a time—at least, that's the goal among the executive ranks. Closer to ground level, cost allocations and quality management obscure profit perceptions. While aggregating (often called rolling up) transactions by customer, or at least by account, is achievable, allocating profit to those accounts is something else altogether. Why? Profit allocation requires a difficult blend of cost accounting and revenue assignment. A banking example can shed some light on these difficulties. Long before overhauls to banking laws were made, financial services firms were eagerly testing various "online" banking products, including electronic bill pay, pay by phone, and others. Initially, these were seen as convenience features that extended basic banking services. But access limitations and presentation-layer disparities prevented mass adoption of these electronic alternatives. More recently, mandates for a "customer view" of business lines and products have come from newly merged superregional and national banking firms. And increased emphasis on asset management, rather than on traditional transaction processing and lending, add to these demands.

The early drive to create an electronic presence and reap anticipated instant sales rewards has been replaced with a more substantive goal: sustainable performance. Certainly, there is a strong incentive to become more competitive using the Web. E-business does offer distinct competitive advantages in cost structures, turnaround times, and enhanced customer service. On the other hand, it also requires greater investment than most firms contemplated initially. The original goal of climbing the mountain of sales has been replaced by a keen interest in mining the depths of customer profitability. For example, while looking for a sales advantage, a major financial services firm brought its loan offering to the Web. First-quarter results indicated marginal revenue growth; however, data volumes grew 60 percent during the same period. Clearly, ongoing investment in a scalable infrastructure is required to convert that data volume into additional sales.

## Old versus New Economy

In practice, the debate over old economy versus new economy companies has been resolved more by stock market indices than e-business success stories. The growth prospective used to tout these e-businesses to investors was rapidly replaced with metrics such as burn rate, for measuring the pace of cash flow exhaustion. Distinctions between the old and new economies are more about channels, segments, and specialization than they are about completely different business models. Investors now reward old economy companies for adding new economy functionality to their business.

Much attention has been focused on the so-called value of the network, primarily based upon the statistics of node growth and the resulting number of "conversations" that can occur between these nodes. A node is a point of presence (equipment) on the Web. Theoretically, the more nodes, the more robust the network presence. Examples from the physical world are often instructive in evaluating electronic counterparts. In this case, the real estate industry provides a meaningful paradigm. The adage everyone knows from the real estate industry is that land value is determined by three things: location, location, location. What they may not know is that it's not the location of the real estate in question; it's the *locational characteristics* of the real estate. As one very successful real estate developer explained, "People create value; real estate reflects the value of the people who use it." Retail properties are often valued by traffic count, or volume of passersby. Traffic count was an element in the model for e-commerce from the outset.

In the electronic world, too, volume of passersby equates to value, though e-tailers refer to passersby as eyeballs. The analogy is clear: people spend money where they spend time. Attention is the precursor of revenue. Physical traffic becomes revenue when the physical infrastructure satisfies customer requirements—location, access, navigation, and customer service. Whereas physical infrastructure exists to satisfy these needs—it is *responsive* to changes in customer requirements—information infrastructure must be *proactive*. To achieve success with physical infrastructure now requires an integrated approach to information management; and corporate information is the glue that binds physical infrastructure to customer responsiveness. CRM is just one example of the reliance on information to adjust physical resources to customer demand.

The economics of e-business increases the reliance on information infrastructure as a means of satisfying customer needs. E-business relies on information processing and analysis to forge its customer connections. It complements and enhances traditional channels of business for established firms; it provides new economic playing fields for entire classes of e-business startups. As the reliance on corporate information increases, so too does the effectiveness of investments in information infrastructure—if they were made intelligently. Investment cycles are shortened by the coincidental acceleration of economic cycles.

## Impact of E-Business on Economic Cycles

The Internet both enables economic change and is reflective of cultural change. Global connectedness is one result of a maturing telecommunications network; it is a natural outgrowth of centuries of increased global trade. Accumulating, integrating, and indexing information are all tasks undertaken in reaction to the previously identified challenges of volume, variety, and velocity.

Each new wave of connectedness brings with it the need for greater speed, extended business windows, and translation and interpretation. These are forces of acceleration:

- Rapid increases in the need for bandwidth
- Processing and storage capacities
- Development resources as forces of adoption

Forces of adoption are cyclic; they are at the leading edge of economic cycles. Forces of acceleration are continuous; they reflect pressures of growth and increased expectation from generation to generation. That said, adoption and acceleration forces wreak havoc with information technology planning, causing changes in business and technology, usually simultaneously. Table 1.2 describes some of these consequences.

In summary, the Internet has impacted the three key relationships in business b2b, b2c, and b2e by increasing the quantity of information flow and the speed of that information flow. Once people receive a certain level of service, they are unwilling to return to the prior level of service, even when there is a substantial increment in cost. The changes caused by e-business are irrevocable and forever.

**Table 1.2**  Consequences of the Networked Economy

| | |
|---|---|
| B2C | Product selection on the richest site, then mass comparisons based on price, availability, and logistical excellence. Aggregation of functionality (e.g., travelocity.com), "word of mouse" (e.g., Ihatex.com), interest groups and anonymous users (use of specialized e-mail and other identifiers by users and agents), establishment of the daily electronic routine. |
| B2B | Price-making aggregations (commodities), syndications and exchanges, peer-to-peer networks. Ongoing barriers to globalization, intellectual property rights protection, currency and other economic controls, and cultural impasse, all lead to specialized solutions, based on local market domain expertise. Next steps include relationship brokerage due to local contacts and expertise (similar to mutual fund managers). Continued emphasis on domain expertise and presentation. Brick-and-mortar businesses will succeed where they are able to convert domain expertise, brand power, and relationship skills into electronic presentation and execution. Organizational barriers are the biggest risks (fear of dilution of power leads to lack of business ), and their information architecture, data warehouses. |
| B2E | Simultaneous information provision for employees, business partners, and customers. Increased use of knowledge mapping to provide access to knowledge sources, both structured and semistructured. Concurrent use of rich media sets to provide enhanced knowledge exchange (CBT). Evolution of live, interactive media for distance mentoring and training exercises. Increased reliance on wireless access for rapid updates and queries against collaboration support systems. |
| C2C | Creation and support of entire communities of users with shared interests. Massive support networks and resulting dialog for all types of specialized needs. This is where consumers worldwide will realize the "power of the network." Access and content providers will profit by virtue of the conversation level carried on their nodes; they will profit from their infrastructure investment for years to come. Integration will be realized through these communities. Accumulation, navigation, and exchange of the resulting information will require CIF infrastructures, particularly data warehouses. |

1. **Partner discovery and selection.** The process by which new partners not previously known are found and qualified. A great example is the commercial illustrating a Japanese company finding an alternative vendor through the Web.

2. **Partner interaction and support.** The process of assuring a two-way flow of information between the partners to protect the flow of goods and services (i.e., direct access to inventories).

3. **Partner performance metrics.** An agreed-upon set of performance indicators that assure both parties that the partnership is working up to expectation and is mutually beneficial.

# Distinguishing Transaction Cycles from Customer Life Cycles

First-wave customer relationship management (CRM) was focused on collecting pieces of information about customer activities. Call center data, sales force campaign and contact management, and transactional sales data were combined or linked to form a view of customer activity. This was a helpful step forward, but it could not support meaningful analysis.

Next-generation CRM applications and services emphasize a transactional approach to customer life cycle analysis. This is far more meaningful because it enables analysis of purchase considerations and repeat business factors. It also enables the construction of a longer-term view of the customer relationship. Understanding that each transaction cycle is a step in the customer life cycle is critical to constructing a life cycle road map. Using such road maps are not a new idea; they have been used in financial services for years, primarily motivated by regulatory requirements. Life cycle planning is an important tool for identifying suitable and appropriate investment selections. Customer information is analyzed and classified according to age, family status, and overall investment time horizons. Accordingly, for example, high-risk, limited-income investments are avoided for older customers nearing retirement, and who are in need of current income and principal security.

Enabling customer life cycle analysis is one of the priorities of data warehousing. Data warehousing serves as the integration and accumulation

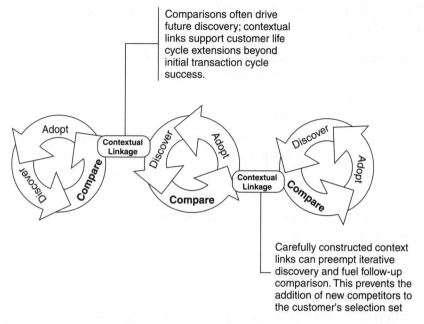

Comparisons often drive future discovery; contextual links support customer life cycle extensions beyond initial transaction cycle success.

Carefully constructed context links can preempt iterative discovery and fuel follow-up comparison. This prevents the addition of new competitors to the customer's selection set

**Figure 1.5**  Customer life cycle as a series of transaction cycles.

point for customer data, making it the logical place to institute the pattern of customer interactions. Establishing a pattern supports all kinds of analysis of customer behavior and classification, thus supporting life cycle management. Figure 1.5 illustrates the chain of value that is derived over the life of a customer relationship. Trust, loyalty, and word-of-mouth advertising are all benefits accruing to the e-business that is cognizant of the need to ensure persistent value via its electronic channels.

## Supporting Partner Relationship Management

Partnership is the process by which two business entities agree to a mutual benefit and risk relationship. Like a marriage, it requires care and nurture; this is partner relationship management (PRM). Prerequisites to PRM include:

- Partner discovery and selection
- Partner interaction support
- Partner performance metrics

The steps in this process are the same for any enterprise wishing to engage in e-business partnerships:

1. **Identify key criteria for selecting and retaining partners.** Is the partner continuing to supply the agreed-upon goods and services at the service levels (metrics) agreed upon prior to actual engagement in interaction.

2. **Define bilateral value components and metrics.** Value components include quality assurance of delivered product, continuous improvement plan, shared benefit from cost reduction, and mutual business practice acceptance.

3. **Identify key information infrastructure components.** These components include site accessibility, communications interchange, data interchange standards, and recovery strategies.

4. **Establish service levels and contingency plans.** This includes outage limitations, automatic failover time expectations, and alternative data delivery strategies (like bulk transfer of transactional data if real time is not possible).

5. **Drive shared understanding and agreement.** Essentially, this means that both organizations have a shared understanding and expectation of the value and limitations of the agreement.

6. **Conduct regular reappraisals of value delivery.** In any partnership, both organizations are in the process of dynamic change. The creation of a standardized expected reappraisal process moves the need for change from crisis to routine business.

7. **Do periodic environmental assessments to discover changing requirements.** Often an infrastructure design for a point in time will not scale in exponential business growth. The entire architectural framework right down the facility level (power, space, air conditioning) needs to be reexamined.

The critical tasks delineated in this list must be supported by the electronic interface chosen for developing peer-to-peer relationships. In the past, attempts to connect links in the supply chain were limited by the electronic interface available. Electronic Data Interchange (EDI) and related efforts to forge concrete links between partners emphasized customer source system interfaces and security. In contrast, the new paradigm emphasizes open standards for connecting source systems across the Internet, which resembles a broadcast, rather than a dedicated, network model. This network model opens a much broader universe in which to discover and recruit business partners. The challenge, of course, is learning to navigate this huge universe of choices effectively. Doing so requires some standards for communicating interests. Enter the registry of potential partners.

## Registries

*Registries* are a tried-and-true means of publicizing the availability of potential trading partners. Phone books, trade directories, and business registries abound, even in electronic form. The problem is that these electronic registries and directories conform to their own formats and content standards, making the search and retrieval of information virtually impossible. Standards bearers emerged to address this problem. Anxious to enable electronic dialog among trading partners, technology providers and users alike have banded together around a common focus: the formulation of standardized presentation and content for business-to-business registration. The presentation layer is constructed in the eXtensible Markup Language (XML); the content is under development. The idea is to present registry content (i.e., entries) in a standard format that categorizes potential partners.

This effort, known as the Uniform Discovery, Description, and Integration Project (UDDI), is supported by technology leaders, which include IBM, Ariba, and Microsoft. UDDI is a model for enabling discovery of business partners in an e-business environment. Figure 1.6 illustrates the directory approach taken by UDDI.

## Meeting the Challenge of the Current E-Business Infrastructure

What is the best way for customers to relate to our businesses? Any way they want, be it to click, call, fax, write, or visit us. The apparent simplicity of these forms of communication enables comfortable, easy ways for customers and enterprises to relate to each other. The key word here is "apparent," because it is the illusion of simplicity that significantly raises expectations for customers and partners. Customers, employees, partners, and stakeholders all are demanding greater access to information

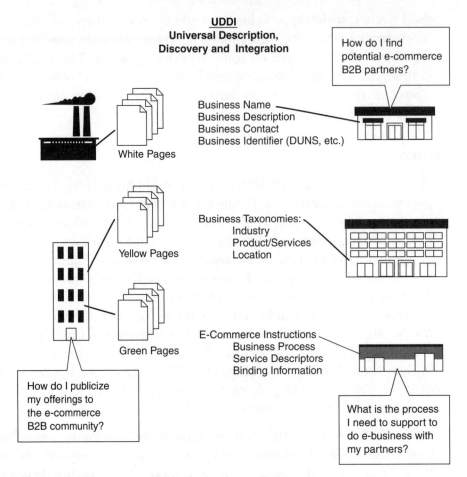

**Figure 1.6** UDDI directory services.

that is relevant to their respective needs and interests. When effectively integrated with an existing infrastructure, enterprise portals can profoundly influence relationships with customers—consumers, employees, partners, and stakeholders—by providing more accurate, timely, and context-sensitive information to support understanding and decision making. Portals leave the information infrastructure open to escalating demands, and heighten the need for scalable infrastructure.

Recent developments in portal technologies are driving enterprises to place a premium on knowledge—knowledge of the many ways customers want to conduct business with them. Strategically integrating information about customers, products, and transactions to establish, track, under-

**Table 1.3** E-Business Evolution

| E-BUSINESS STAGE | CHARACTERISTICS |
|---|---|
| First Generation | Site created with as much content as possible. Branded convenience. |
| Second Generation | Enterprise Application Integration as a means to jump-start e-business. Business exchange participation. |
| Third Generation | Reinvestment in data warehouse technologies to support e-business data volumes and velocity. Adoption of scalable, distributed processing and storage networks. |
| Next Generation | Agent-based activity to increase data volume and support "daily electronic routine." Partner relationship management to prove its value. Information infrastructure viewed as enterprise asset. |

stand, and develop relationships across time represents the opportunity as well as the challenge all corporations face in conducting e-business today. Strategic information integration is not a new challenge.

Initial efforts made by well-established companies entering the e-business arena often fall under the heading of Enterprise Application Integration (EAI). EAI promises fast, easy connectivity among the legacy source systems and their new Web-based counterparts. EAI is very much like a rapid application development effort, although it generally occurs in parallel processes. It is important to note, however, that the benefits of connecting disparate source systems with varying levels of detail and frequency rapidly dissipate when this virtual integration is relied upon for decision support. Certainly, EAI is a valuable tool for connecting source systems to Web-based applications, but it's essential to keep EAI in perspective as a source system function, to greatly reduce the likelihood of architectural failure. To that end, consider the evolution of e-business, some of whose characteristics are described in Table 1.3.

# Infrastructure Opportunity: Warehouse to Web, and Back

Today, business revenue and profit growth potential are driven not just by physical presence, but by information infrastructure. Thus, businesses engaged in electronic commerce require the support of a robust and expandable infrastructure. Various channels require navigation to, and exchanges with, the critical infrastructure components; therefore, global corporate growth is predicated on each layer of this infrastructure.

Once the power and scalability of a data warehouse-based Corporate Information Factory (CIF) are understood, further investments in this solution begin to yield tremendous results. Utilizing the data warehouse as a foundation for e-business success offers immediate and lasting benefits. When the data warehouse is utilized as the integrated source for customer, product, and transaction analysis, e-business initiatives can be implemented much more quickly. Moreover, the data warehouse is the best possible place to integrate newfound customer profile data to support logistical operations and Web-based transaction systems.

## Infrastructure Challenge: Web to Warehouse

Monitoring and capturing outcomes of electronic information exchange is as important to e-businesses as extending information to the user. The rapidity of interactions in all e-business channels requires processing real-time information at the source level, and then analyzing those results in near real time. Finally, feedback must be supplied to the source systems, to support customer knowledge and contextually valid e-business interactions.

These requirements highlight the need for an architectural approach, one that is capable of supporting iterative enterprise growth. That architecture exists in the form of the CIF. The recent addition of mobility in the usage mix adds yet another dimension to the architectural burden. Supporting remotely connected users is not a simple matter of reformatting dynamic screens for different access devices; decisions must be made about how fast to capture, analyze, and update the profiles of e-business users in each layer of the information infrastructure. Usage patterns for Web-based applications are developed based upon both user preferences for delivery channels and content. This conduit distinction is already proving valuable in geographic regions and markets that rely heavily on wireless access.

An enterprise's capability to support these new forms of interaction depend on the maturity of its information infrastructure. "Reaching maturity" is often the result of the way an enterprise chooses to view its use of information technology. Those who view their information systems as an expenditure will lose ground to their competitors who treat their information systems and contents as corporate assets.

# The Financial View of Information

Information asset management is the process of managing hardware, software, and intellectual property as if it were the equivalent of any other capital business asset. Information asset management is an outgrowth of various information-engineering efforts. Product-based functionality aids in the construction, management, and distribution of information. The asset level is generic to all corporate information. Vendors that dedicate themselves to this approach take the first step toward tying investments in their products and process to corporate performance. A more evolved understanding involves classifying information assets in a way that supports derivation of a return on these assets.

The key to understanding information asset value from a financial viewpoint is as a relationship between project-based spending and business impact. The problem with traditional project-based spending is that it seeks to quantify results as a direct result of the project, which is akin to saying that events equal consequences. There is always a translation or execution layer involved when events take place. Interpreting results requires inference and context; results are viewed against selected metrics and within a corporate or technical context. Projects are not completed serially; they are parallel in nature and often span changing economic and business cycles. These factors require a reconsideration of project impact evaluation.

## Project Spending, Corporate Investment

Project-based spending contributes to corporate performance both locally and globally. Local contributions are the general focus for project approvals. There is an obstacle (a pain point) recognized by a project sponsor and addressed by technology and business analysis. E-business project dynamics are designed to alleviate this pain in a tactical manner. Information technology managers are constantly challenged to align these e-business projects with existing standards and planned investment patterns.  Inevitably, compromises must be made, and often they

**Table 1.4** Benefits of Treating Information Components as Assets

| CIF COMPONENT | INFORMATION ASSET VALUE | RETURN ON INFORMATION ASSETS |
|---|---|---|
| Source Systems | Ensures operational efficiency. Reports in real time. | Accelerates revenue growth, operational excellence, customer loyalty. |
| Extract, Transform, and Load Tools | Connects disparate sources, and maps them for integrated use. Translates business rules and processes into working data models. Manages ongoing processes, including change data capture and business/data model maintenance. | Operational efficiency arises from single group of business and data analysts. Profitability increases due to enhanced ability to acquire and deliver new information sources, particularly merged and acquired businesses. |
| Operational Data Store | Updates customer profiles from DW. Supports Web applications with customer profile data. Provides extended applications data availability for operational reporting. | Rapid transit area for integrated data protects profit margins by supporting rapid operational decision making. Prevents redundant spending when adopting e-business initiatives. |
| Data Warehouse | Integrates disparate source data into a "single version of the truth." Accumulates historical data for trends analysis. Improves information quality. | Enhances profitability through reduced overall expenditures, increased availability, and improved information quality. |
| Data Marts | Breaks out line of business or other segmented information that is consistent with enterprise usage. Provides insightful decision support and strategic analytical support. | Improves revenue and profit margins through informed line-of-business decision-making and implementation. Accelerates customer acquisition through rapidly updated marketing effectiveness measures. |

lead to improved views of technology adoption patterns. Recent introductions of distributed processing, storage, and access systems drive many of these compromises.

The core challenge in converting e-business project-based spending into a capital asset. It is only by taking this global viewpoint that a return on information equity can be derived and compared across projects, business lines, and economic cycles. Table 1.4 identifies some of the benefits of this information asset viewpoint.

## Summary

The Internet's capability to directly connect market forces to producers opens new delivery channels and introduces new exchange methods; but it raises some very old problems as well. E-business requires more than bandwidth; it requires infrastructure—physical, human, and technology-based capital investment. Physical connectivity has been improving nationally and internationally for decades, with the long-standing goal to reduce the distance barrier for consumers, who are more likely to visit a closer store. Easier connectivity and/or geographic convenience helps to increase retail volume.

Meeting the challenges posed by e-business requires a long-term approach. Expenditures in information and other technology must be viewed as investments in infrastructure. The vendors and service providers who build these infrastructures must be held accountable for their efforts, meaning that the infrastructure must work well in addition to looking good—an attractive interface is not enough to ensure e-business success. Real success in e-business is measured in terms of scalability, reliability, and sustainability.

The rest of this book examines how the CIF can successfully incorporate an infrastructure that comprises these essential components.

# CHAPTER 2

# The Corporate Information Factory and E-Business

To succeed, e-businesses must be able to adapt to an ever-changing marketplace. By combining the corporate information factory (CIF) and the Web environment, it is possible to create a stable, flexible interface that is relatively simple and inexpensive to maintain. This interface is depicted in Figure 2.1.

This chapter offers an overview of the CIF architecture, followed by an outline of e-business requirements. We will then discuss how the CIF and e-business work best together.

## Components of the Corporate Information Factory

The CIF infrastructure includes the following components:

- Internet
- Corporate Web site
- Firewall
- Corporate operational systems
- Granularity manager

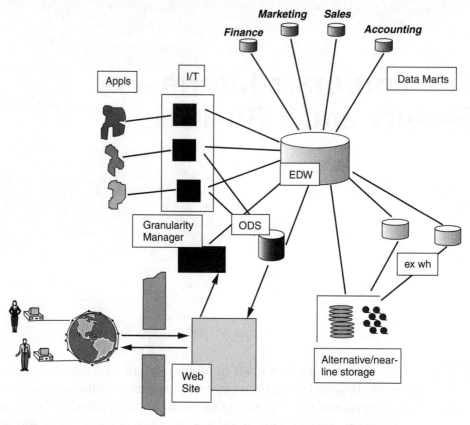

**Figure 2.1** Combining the Web site and the CIF to form a stable interface.

- Enterprise data warehouse
- Corporate data mart environment
- Exploration environment
- Alternative storage/near line storage environment
- Corporate operational data store (ODS) environment

We will examine each of these components as they relate to the needs of e-businesses in the following sections.

# NOTE

This book will review the components of the corporate information factory at a high level. For more detailed coverage of the CIF, please refer to Inmon, Imhoff, and Sousa's *Corporate Information Factory, Second Edition* (John Wiley & Sons, Inc., 2000).

# Defining the Web Environment

When we speak of the Web environment, we are referring to three elements: the Internet, a firewall, and the Web site itself. Using the Internet, businesses can contact other businesses, as well as consumers. The Web site intercepts and manages those activities, while firewalls filter unwanted and unauthorized activity out of the network. These items are not new components to CIF.

## Corporate Operational Systems

The corporate operational systems run the day-to-day operations, usually on a medium other than the Internet, primarily to conduct transactions. These transactions can be submitted directly by the consumer or by the agents (i.e., operators). Usually, these transactions operate in a matter of a few seconds. And in many cases, the activities accomplished by these transactions are legally binding, such as the withdrawal of money from an ATM. Some corporate operational systems are custom-written; other applications are part of a standard application software package, typically with hardware dedicated to supporting their needs on an exclusive basis.

Data is fed through integration/transformation (I/T) programs—also called extraction, transformation, and loading (ETL) programs. They convert the data coming from the many applications into a common format and structure. This transformation of multiapplication data into a single integrated image is very important to the e-business environment because it allows its data to be seamlessly integrated into the corporation. After data is placed in the data warehouse, it can be used in many different fashions, such as reporting, exploration, and data mining.

## The Granularity Manager

The quantity of data generated by and gathered in a typical Web site (much of it at such a low level of detail that it is useless) requires that it be edited for more effective use. The *granularity manager* is software that prepares Web site data for entry into the corporate information factory. The granularity manager organizes the Web site data so that it can be used meaningfully throughout the system. In some cases, this means throwing data away. In other cases, it means combining similar types of data. In yet other cases, data may be resequenced and aggregated. The result is that data exits the granularity manager at a higher level of detail than it entered.

The granularity manager, however, must be used with great care so that it is not misused to destroy or defile data that may be needed later. This task falls squarely on the shoulders of the e-business analyst, who determines what data can and cannot safely be edited and/or merged.

### Enterprise Data Warehouse

The enterprise data warehouse (EDW) is at the center of processing. All data is stored here at one time or another, including:

**Granular data.** This is the lowest level of detail. It can be shaped into different forms and structures. Accounting can look at the data one way; finance can look at the same data another way; sales can look at the data in yet another way. But underlying it all is one stable foundation of data.

**Historical data.** Up to five years worth of data can be stored. The data is available for immediate analysis. A Wall Street analyst or a Washington legislator can call up data immediately, in a manner never before imagined.

**Integrated data.** This is data where the applications bias has been removed. Application bias is where the definition is specific to one application but not universal to the enterprise. There usually are multiple sources of data feeding the enterprise data warehouse, but those sources have their data integrated before entering the EDW. The corporation is able to get a clear and consistent image of data by going to the foundation. Another characteristic of data flowing into the data warehouse is that it can be stored for as long as it is useful. The enterprise data warehouse thus becomes a historical foundation as well as an integrated foundation.

**Corporate data.** This usually comprises large volumes of data that must be easy to access and reshape for reconciliation.

In addition to accepting data from a wide variety of sources, the data warehouse feeds data to other components of the CIF, including the data mart and the exploration warehouse. One of the environments feeding the data warehouse, and indirectly using data from the data warehouse, is the Web environment—which is the focus of e-business.

In a way, the Web environment acts merely as another source for the data warehouse. However, the volume of data, the diversity of data, and the importance of the e-business environment make the Web environment much more than just another source of data for the enterprise data warehouse.

## Corporate Data Mart Environment

The enterprise data warehouse contains very granular, detailed data. Individual departments within a single organization need to see data organized differently, according to their specific needs. As a result, there is a need for physically separate databases—called data marts—that make data easily visible and available to analysts.

The departments that frequently want their own data marts include:

- **Sales.** For sales reporting.
- **Marketing.** To ascertain market potential and penetration.
- **Finance.** To drill-down on expense.
- **Accounting.** To do reporting and correction.
- **Human Resources.** To meet regulatory requirements.
- **Engineering.** To provide product tracking.
- **Actuarial.** To be used in risk management.

These departments may have differing needs regarding:

- Levels of summarization
- Time
- Product structure
- Organizational structure
- Aggregation

## Exploration Warehouse

Exploration processing involves the user searching data for important and previously undiscovered patterns of business activity. The user searches for relationships that exist between events and people, in the hopes that the discovery of any patterns will lead to insight. Exploration processing is vastly different from data mart or other data warehouse-related processing. Typically, exploration queries take up huge amounts of resources.

As long as only a small amount of exploration processing occurs, it can be done in the data warehouse environment. But once the corporation starts to do a significant amount of exploration processing, the resources consumed by this activity start to become a real burden for the data warehouse. Therefore, after the corporation begins to mature as an experienced exploration user, it will need a separate structure called an *exploration warehouse*. The exploration warehouse allows the explorer to do as much exploration processing as desired without having a negative impact on the other users of the data warehouse environment. Data from the Web environment finds its way into the exploration warehouse by passing through the enterprise data warehouse.

The exploration warehouse is very important to the Web user because it is through exploration processing that new trends are detected. When there is a change in business patterns, it is first, and most clearly, detected in the exploration warehouse. For this reason alone the exploration warehouse is very important to the Web environment.

### Alternative Storage

The enterprise data warehouse almost always sits on classical high-performance disk storage. For many reasons this choice of technology makes sense. But two things happen that quickly make high-performance disk storage a less than optimal medium for the storage of data:

- The volume of information in the enterprise data warehouse increases at a very dramatic rate. This is especially true for the e-business environment that hosts thousands of visitors a day.
- Data separates into two categories: highly used data and very seldom used data.

Because of these two factors, the organization discovers very quickly that if it is to accommodate the volumes of data that appear in the Web-enabled enterprise data warehouse environment, it will be necessary to extend the EDW to media other than high-performance disk storage.

The storage media that makes the most sense to use to extend the enterprise data warehouse is alternative secondary storage. Alternative storage is inexpensive and slow; near-line storage exists on robot-controlled tape cartridges. In both cases, the media is much less expensive and much more effective than high-performance disk storage. By moving infrequently used data to alternative or near-line storage, the enterprise data warehouse is extended.

There are many factors to consider before implementing alternative secondary storage. Some of those considerations are related to performance: What is the performance impact of moving data to alternative secondary storage? If the data that has been moved is in fact used less frequently, performance will be enhanced by moving it away from high-performance disk storage, and cost will decrease. There is no question that the cost of data warehousing is reduced significantly when secondary storage is introduced. When data warehouses are extended to secondary storage, the level of detail at which data can be stored at the warehouse is its lowest, most granular level.

By extending the data warehouse to alternative or near-line storage, the Web site can effectively generate an infinite amount of data—there is no limitation to how much data can be generated and used by the Web site.

## Operational Data Store

Online transaction processing is never run against a data warehouse, for a whole host of reasons, including workload. Because of the extreme mixture of processes in the data warehouse workload, trying to achieve very high performance is difficult while maintaining update integrity. Normally, updating is not done in the data warehouse; but where it is allowed, overhead is incurred, in most cases, significant overhead, depending on the volumes of data. The volumes of data found in the enterprise data warehouse are so vast that searching them efficiently is difficult to do.

High-performance processing not done in the enterprise data warehouse is handled in a special structure called an operational data store (ODS). The ODS is where the amalgamated, refined results from the enterprise data warehouse are stored. Once stored there, the results become available to the Web environment at a millisecond's notice; therefore, the ODS is one of the most important structures of the corporate information factory as far as the Web environment is concerned. It is from the ODS that the Web environment draws the majority of its data. (Figure 2.2 shows the positioning of the ODS.)

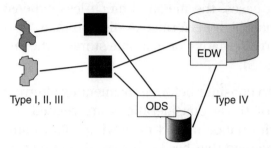

**Figure 2.2** The ODS enables high-performance processing on the Web site.

The ODS is characterized by a need for an operating system and a database management system (DBMS) that can handle a mixed workload. Consequently, online transaction processing (OLTP) technology is typically found in the operational applications environment. The data mart environment is serviced by OLAP multidimensional technology. The enterprise data warehouse environment requires industrial-strength, large-scale DBMS strength, with the capability to manage very large amounts of data. The exploration environment often uses token-based processing. And the alternative storage/near-line environment requires database technology that can manage very large volumes of data on a nonhigh-performance disk storage medium.

### The Two ODS Types

There are actually two operational data stores in the Web environment:

- The Web ODS, which is inside the Web environment, and has a modest-sized computer at its heart.

- The corporate ODS, which is inside the CIF, and has a very large computer at its heart.

The two serve very different purposes. The corporate ODS is a true "industrial-strength" processor; it can hold much more data than the Web ODS. The Web-based ODS serves only the transactions originating inside the Web server; thus, it is a "local" ODS. The corporate ODS contains truly corporate data, which is available to a wide variety of processing; thus, the corporate ODS is a global server. The Web-based ODS sits within the site and administers that environment. It is integrated with the corporate ODS at different intervals throughout the day. The Web ODS usually does not reside on the same server as the CIF or cor-

## Server Components

Though it is possible for all CIF and Web components to reside on the same server, it is not necessarily a good idea, especially when the volume of data and the number of transactions grow. As long as there are only a few transactions and a small amount of data, a single server may be viable. But once the environment matures, multiple servers will be needed.

There are many reasons for using separate servers for the Web and CIF environments. For one, in the CIF itself there will be multiple servers for the different components. Other questions to ask when considering multiple servers are:

- How do you optimize the environment for transaction performance?
- How do you handle the volumes of data?
- How do you handle the different kinds of activities?
- How do you handle the different kinds of users?

A server can be optimized for one kind of processing or another, but it is very difficult to optimize a server for different kinds of processing all in the same server.

porate ODS because of performance and throughput issues. For instance, it is not a good idea to mix response-sensitive queries and batch reporting with data structures for real-time processing, as such mixing slows performance for both the Web and corporate ODS.

The ODS can accommodate different levels of data granularity (Level 0, Level 1, and Level 2) via the granularity manager (these levels will be described in detail later). By using the three levels in the environment, data updating and summarizing can be accomplished successfully. The levels of granularity require different data models based on the different levels of summarizations and actions taken during interaction with a Web site visitor (See Chapter 5 for details on data models).

Integration and consolidation of customer information can be accomplished in the corporate ODS. Integrating and consolidating customer information from all corporate systems and the Internet is what gives CRM the data it needs to succeed. In this environment, the following can be brought together in a data structure that enables quick response times and reporting capabilities for the business community: Web site information (clickstream data), customer order history (buying behavior), customer demographics, and customer campaign information (from analysis in a data mart within the data warehouse). Then, using the customer profiles that are formed, specific customers can be targeted appropriately for tailored marketing campaigns. Moreover, the sales channels can become quickly aware of the opportunities in the ODS via mobile or Internet access within the corporation.

## Putting It All Together

The preceding discussion addressed some of the more interesting aspects of the components of the Web environment. Here is where we put it all together (see Figure 2.3).

Detailed, historical data is found in the enterprise data warehouse, the EDW. Deeper historical data is found in secondary storage. Summarized and aggregated data is found in the data mart environment. Integrated, up-to-the-second, accurate data is found in the ODS; and detailed, very

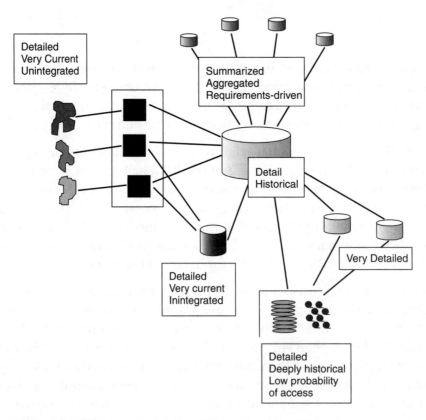

**Figure 2.3** Differences in data found throughout the CIF.

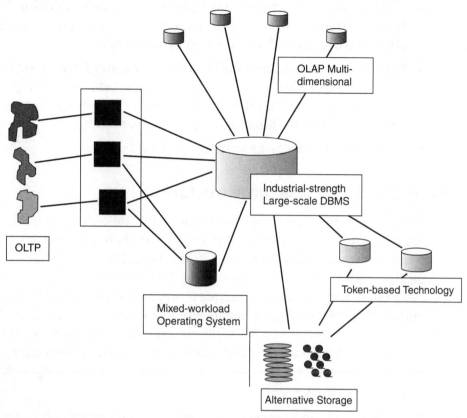

**Figure 2.4** The different technologies used in the CIF.

current data that is not integrated is found in the operations application environment.

Another way to examine the big picture is to ask which technologies are found where. Figure 2.4 shows the different technologies that are found across the CIF.

# Defining E-Business Architectural Requirements

To understand the architectural requirements of the e-business environment, it is necessary to be able to answer the following questions:

- What is the e-business infrastructure?
- What is clickstream data?

- What actions and activities take place during the interaction of the Web user and the Web site? How do these actions and activities affect the overall architecture and data models?

- What are the information and meta data transfer languages? How does the use of the eXtensible Markup Language (XML), Hypertext Markup Language (HTML), and (eXtensible Hypertext Markup Language (XHTML) affect data and metadata transfer?

- How do we handle large volumes of data?

## Building the E-Business Infrastructure

During the initial stages of creating an e-business environment, a company typically will start with one or two servers to support the Web site. It may even start with an Internet service provider (ISP), sharing configurations with other companies. (An ISP alleviates the upfront costs associated with creating a private corporate configuration during the initialization phase of the e-business.) For small companies, an ISP may be more than adequate. The server(s) contain much of what is needed for the e-business environment, such as Web logs, content information, personalization programs, product ordering programs, and clickstream collection mechanisms.

Early in the creation process, Web pages include mostly descriptive and static information—what the company does; when the company was established and by whom; and product or service description: dimensions, colors, weight, quantity. Layouts, ads, and banners are changed frequently to capture and hold the interest of visitors. Email addresses are prominently displayed so that users can inquire about the company and its products; later in the design, the capability to order products or services online is added, to cut down on the volume of incoming emails.

As the business expands, multiple, or larger, servers are required to support its online environment. Multiple servers are used to collect the Web log information (i.e. clickstream) and to deliver any type of content to the user. (Content may be defined as data or information on any subject or product, supplied by the company's marketing group and delivered to the users of the company's Web site. See the "Content Information and Content Servers" sidebar.) As the Web site grows, it may start to experience data "glut," at which point a single ISP may not be able to handle performance and capacity issues that arise. For example, the ISP

## Content Information and Content Servers

Content information refers to textually described and/or graphically illustrated product and/or service materials. A derivation of general content information is personalized content information, which is sent to the user based on knowledge derived from personalization engine software, which can be purchased off-the-shelf or programmed in-house. This software is used to generate a profile of a customer, which consists of a description of his or her buying habits and demographic information. From this profile, content (ads and banners) are presented to the user.

Such software programs must be able to interface with customer-content profiles to deliver the correct content to each Web user. After the Web user has responded to a profile inquiry or has participated in a promotional campaign, the personalization engine software, which sits between the Web page and the content server, and interfaces with the customer profile, identifies the information to be supplied to the user at subsequent visits to the site. Let's say, for example, that a customer regularly purchases a number of books from an online bookseller. After the user's third visit to the Web site, the personalization software extracts information from the content server; and based on information culled from that third visit, it delivers a 10 percent off coupon to the customer the next time he or she visits the Web site. Personalization content enables the e-business to offer, and the e-customer to enjoy, a unique online experience.

A content server is a database formatted to store information. Current content information can be stored within the realm of the distributed ODS. Content information is usually on its own server, which makes it easier to exchange components within the environment. Content server(s) may be considered part of the distributed ODS. In other words, content servers are used by both the Web ODS and the corporate ODS. A content management server makes it possible to update data without having to update the Web site. The Web site will use the content to dynamically build the Web site pages, based on customer preferences, buying habits, and navigational attributes.

may not have an operations group to handle such day-to-day activities as monitoring performance and memory allocation.

To meet the growing Web site needs, the e-business managers will probably begin to consider setting up an online environment that is controlled by the corporation itself. One of the first steps in this process is to consider moving to a *proxy server*, a computer that is placed between the Web page interaction and the servers within the e-business corporation. A proxy sever is used to reduce the load on other servers within the Web environment and deliver information to the Web user faster. The proxy server is also used to cache content information, reduce the load on the content servers and/or network. The proxy server can also be used to store routing information or to redirect page requests to a different content server.

Of course, as the Web business grows, additional servers will be required to handle specific areas of the workload. The company may also discover that it needs to install servers globally or centrally. Accordingly, the Web site may be *centralized* or *distributed*.

### Centralized Web Sites

A centralized Web site's servers are contained in one place, certainly in one city, and usually within the same room. The centralized functions for these servers may be maintained either by company personnel or outsourced to an ISP.

A centralized Web site is how most Web companies set up initially, but it's rarely their final architecture. Though the centralized Web site makes it easier to make changes and conduct maintenance, it has performance limitations, as growth naturally adds complexity to the environment. More "horsepower" can be added to the centralized Web environment, but separation of proxy server, content server, and the personalization engine will be required to attain maximum performance levels (e.g., page retrieval speeds for some e-companies is less than 400 milliseconds). Separating processing activities serves to streamline maintenance, and gives the Web company the flexibility to exchange functionality as the environment grows.

### Distributed Web Sites

A distributed Web site has a collection of servers that do various tasks within the Web environment. As the company grows, so does the demand on the processors, hence more servers will be needed to separate functionality; for example, placing different content onto multiple servers to efficiently handle the demand for more pages of information. Multiple content servers may also be required as Web site volume grows. This raises two important issues: how to synchronize the log data from the additional servers, and how to maintain them. Compatibility between the various vendors' software and platforms is another issue, though using standard languages (such as XML, HTML, and XHTML) for transferring metadata and data between applications can help.

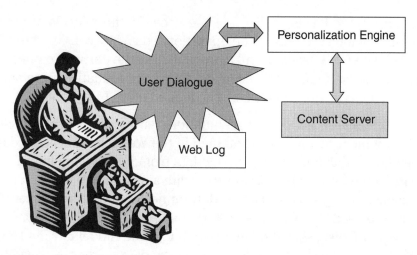

**Figure 2.5**  Distributed Web site.

As the number of "hits" to a site increases, some rearchitecting may be necessary to manage the performance of the environment efficiently. Functionality within the corporation will change many times. In response, the company may consider using global Web servers to accommodate international growth, or multiple Web servers, each to do one task very well. A global Web environment may, for example, have a server for content, a server for navigational activity (i.e., the Web log), and a server for collecting information for future use within the corporation (i.e., the operational data store and/or the data warehouse). Data collection from global servers must be synchronized at specified times during the day. In this way, the global servers seem to function as a single unit in a single place, though they actually exist in various places around the world. Figure 2.5 shows what a distributed Web site might look like.

## Understanding Clickstream Data

The data contained in the Web log is known as *clickstream data*. It is data generated by users during their interactions on a Web site. The Web log contains the Web user's unique online identifier or Internet address, where online the user came from, and which query he or she used to launch the site. The Web log is used in conjunction with the summarized and integrated corporate data.

There are three levels of Web log use—that is, three levels of granularity—all of which are part of the operational data store. Level 0 resides in the Web site ODS; levels 1 and 2 are placed in the corporate operational data store. Together, the three levels form the foundation for a successful e-business environment. Each is defined more fully here:

**Level 0.** The lowest level of granulation, represented in the e-business environment by the data contained in the Web log. This is the data used for immediate analysis. The data from the Web log interacts with personalization software to create a customer profile. In turn, the customer profile is used to determine content to be delivered to the Web user. The Web site ODS is small, fast, and transactional. (Chapter 6 discusses the Level 0 Web log data models.) Data from the Web log can be stored for later use in the data warehouse, usually at intervals throughout the day. (Chapter 4 goes into more detail on the data found in the Web site ODS.)

**Level 1.** Contains simple aggregation from the Web log (i.e., Level 0). The simple aggregations are created during integration with other corporate data, such as shipping, billing, and general ledger data. Integration from the source systems and Level 0 into Level 1 data takes place at least once a day.

**Level 2.** Contains tables that are aggregated or summarized. Summarized and aggregated tables are used for reporting purposes in the corporate ODS. Under normal operations, Level 2 tables are created once a day to aid in query performance and to improve ease of use in the business environment. Reporting tools are used extensively with Level 2 summarized tables to create an easy querying environment for the business user.

Data from the Web log can be used in multiple ways:

- *As a basis for immediate analysis.* With every keystroke or combination of navigational keystrokes (action), an activity is triggered. The trail of the activity that is triggered might be an event such as a new banner that promotes a new product at a special price, or an email coupon that is sent to the Web user after he or she has logged off the Web site. The activities to be analyzed may be decided through a personalization engine or program based on preset rules or a combination of rules using the Web site ODS. The rules are determined by the business users and determine "usability" of the information.

- *For less-than-immediate analysis (15 minutes to one hour after the Web log(s) have been collected).* The data can be *Propagated into the Level 1 data model.* This entails aggregation and summarization of data. If there are multiple Web logs to be gathered, the time required to collect and process the log data will dictate the content of the data models. For instance, a company might have three logs, average size 100 megabytes each, to collect every 15 minutes throughout the day. They would need to be integrated and sorted by IP address for analysis by a program to determine which e-mail message to send to the Web user. A 15-minute window is not much time to collect, merge, sort, and analyze three Web logs. The last step is the integration of the merged log with the Level 1 data. Without much time left, the Level 1 data model must be very simplistic. At this point, a choice must be made to integrate the Web logs once a day instead of multiple times throughout the day.

- *Analyzed to gain additional knowledge about the customer of the Web site.* Information gathered during this analysis will be used to interact with the Web user the next time he or she visits the site. Some of the Level 2 information will be propagated into the data warehouse once a day. This information is combined with marketing information (customer profile) from the data warehouse or a data mart to determine the next campaign to launch to encourage customer loyalty to, and need for, the company's products or services.

A typical clickstream log content is shown in Figure 2.6.

**193.250.220.68 - - [01/Feb/2001:00:05:15 –0800] "GET/help.index.xpml? Rf=1.1:6.0 HTTP/1.1" 200 13057 "-" "Mozilla /4.0 (compatible; MSIE 5.0; Windows 98; DigExt)" "br=93873889143716236; userid=8600529976; Sessionid=5000428992"**
152.164.189.67 - - [01/Feb/2001:00:05:16 –0800] "GET/panel/thanks.xpml HTTP/1.0" 200 14770http://eval.somebookstore.com/team/p_rategen.pl "Mozilla/4.0 (compatible; MSIE 5.0; AOL 5.0; Windows 98;DigExt" "br=04004524300399199; userid=8542895610"
**209.240.200.22 - - [01/Feb/2001:00:05:17 –800] "GET /reg/login. xpml? lr=login&url=/merchant/merc_frame.xpml?mid=17439&rb=30pct HTTP/1.0" 200 12576 "http://somebookstore.com/merc_frame.xpml?mid=17439&rb= 30pct" "Mozilla/3.0 WebTV/1.2 (compatible; MSIE 2.0)" "userid= 8501474737; sessionid=5000427550"**

**Figure 2.6** Web log.

Clickstream data is simplistic in nature; it is easy to understand, capture, store, and format. Information in most Web logs includes these forms of identification, usually in columnar (field) format:

**Client IP address.** Identifies the location of an Internet user. The IP address may also have information about a proxy server. A proxy server redirects and caches information in the Web environment. An example of a client IP address is: 192.54.222.77

**Customer or user identity.** Identifies a Web site user. This information is usually captured when a user registers with a Web company. Most Web sites require a user to register prior to purchasing a product or service. This column normally contains a dash (–). If a user has not yet purchased a product or service, information about the Web site and a unique user identifier is placed on the user's computer. This information is known as a *cookie*. This action is possible through a Web browser, usually either Microsoft Internet Explorer or Netscape. A user cannot make a purchase unless there is a cookie on his or her computer.

**Authorized user element.** The secure user ID. Used when a secure logon is required, and is filled in only when the user has correctly transmitted a secure server logon. The column usually contains a dash (–). (Note: The authorized user element attribute is being used more often today, in response to increasing breaches of computer privacy over the Internet.)

**Date and time stamping.** Date and time when the Web server responded to the request. An example of date and time stamping is: [01/Feb/2001:00:05:20 – 800].

**Server request information about the Uniform Resource Locator (URL).** A request in the form of a GET or POST command; for example: GET /merchant/top.gif HTTP/1.1.

**Status of request.** A three-digit code returned by the server to the browser. The two most widely used products are the Apache Server and Microsoft Internet Information Server (IIS). Currently, Apache, an open server, is in widespread use in Web environments. It uses status codes, from 100 to 505 (other Web servers use similar codes) to identify activities, for example:

| | |
|---|---|
| 100 | Continue |
| 101 | Protocol switch |
| 200 | Good and Okay |

| | |
|---|---|
| 201 | Created |
| 202 | Accepted |
| 203 | No authority information |
| 204 | No content |
| 205 | Content reset |
| 206 | Part of the content |
| 300 | More than one choice |
| 301 | Permanently moved |
| 302 | Temporarily moved |
| 303 | Other |
| 304 | No change |
| 305 | Use proxy server |
| 400 | Bad request |
| 401 | Not authorized |
| 402 | Payment needed |
| 403 | Forbidden |
| 404 | Not found |
| 405 | Method not allowed |
| 406 | Unacceptable |
| 407 | Time-out requested |
| 408 | Conflict |
| 410 | Gone |
| 411 | Required length |
| 412 | Failed precondition |
| 413 | Requested entity too big |
| 414 | Request-URL too big |
| 425 | Unsupported media type |
| 500 | Internal server error |
| 501 | Not implemented |
| 502 | Gateway bad |
| 503 | Service unavailable |
| 504 | Time-out on gateway |
| 505 | HTTP version not supported |

**Number of bytes sent.** The number of bytes returned from the server to the browser, for example: 4578 bytes.

## Using Prior Site Information

Prior site information is as the term implies: a Web log entry that indicates where the visitor was before coming to the current Web site. Prior site information contains:

- URL of previous site
- Host name at previous site
- Path or file name of previous site
- Documents of prior site
- Query string; that is, information to the right of the question mark (?). This field usually contains information from the query engine; for example: ?mid=812&rb=8pct.
- Browser and operating system version information, to determine features needed for support; for example: Mozilla/3.0 WebTV/1.2.
- Cookie information, which includes the name of the cookie, the string value to be stored, expiration date and time, domain name of servers that read the cookie, domain path name, and whether the transaction is secure or not. An example is: 800fBanner flowers%5Fcom www.1800flowers.com/flowers  0 1885936896 29388024 * In this example, the domain name is "flowers"; the connection is not secure; the path name is *flowers*; there is no expiration date; and two domain servers can read the cookie information.
- Session and user identification, unique cookie information about the Web user; for example, sessionid=49494903.

It should be clear from this discussion that though clickstream and cookie data are simplistic, they are extremely important. Clickstream data becomes the foundation upon which the process of collecting information about the Web site visitor is launched. When clickstream analysis is required at near real-time frequency, the data structures and analysis resemble those created in a transactional system.

## Working with Operational Data Stores

The Web CIF environment has two operational data stores. The first, the Web site ODS, is lean and mean, and contains Web log data. As already

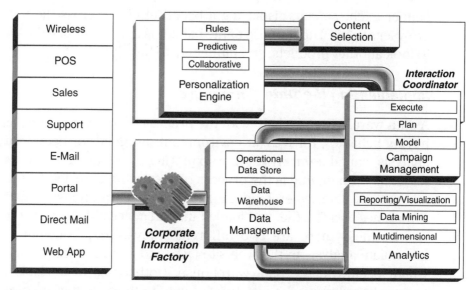

**Figure 2.7** Personalization engine, content server, and CIF and Web.

explained, personalization engine software or programs are required to act on Level 0 clickstream data for this ODS. Sets of clickstream records will be analyzed by the personalization software. These records are based on the information retrieved from the content server. The second ODS, the Corporate Information Factory Operational Data Store (CIF ODS), which usually resides on a different server and integrates corporate data with Web site information (Level 1), is almost always larger than the Web site ODS. The CIF ODS does not carry immediate transactional data as does the Web site ODS; it carries profile data. Figure 2.7 shows the interaction between the Web, the personalization engine, the content server, the two operational data stores, and the data warehouse.

Based on rules or an algorithmic statement, personalization software processes and analyzes low-level clickstream data, and then delivers specific content to individual users as they interact on the site. Algorithmic statements are usually in IF-THEN-ELSE form, and are based on input from marketing and knowledge gained from the analysis of navigational and demographic information. When navigational activities occur, such as a combination of keystrokes (clickstream data), a programmatic activity is triggered that changes the appearance of the Web page to be more appealing to the visitor. A good example of this type of interaction is a Web site such as www.flowers.com. While a user is looking at bouquets, a banner might appear, displaying a beautiful plant across the top of the browser screen. The purpose of the banner is to try to entice the Web user to look at other products, and ultimately to buy them.

### Implementing the Data Warehouse

A data warehouse can help with the process of understanding customer buying behavior, for it is an environment designed for heavy-duty data analysis, called *data mining*, or exploring navigational correlations of the data. Data mining is the process of extracting knowledge from large amounts of data, whereby data from the data warehouse is extracted, sometimes to a flat file, and loaded into an accessible format. Basically, in e-business there are two different analysis requirements, one for immediate analysis in the Web site ODS and one for analysis over time, which occurs in the data warehouse. Both types of analysis can be accomplished using the constructs found in the architecture of the CIF. (See *The Corporate Information Factory* by W. H. Inmon, Claudia Imhoff, and Ryan Sousa [John Wiley & Sons, Inc., 2000]).

As defined earlier, there are three levels of log information, shown in Figure 2.8. The volume of data at Level 0—the Web log—grows quickly as activity on the Web site accelerates. Level 0 data is integrated with Level 1 data at least once a day. The volume of data at Level 1 is smaller, due to customer activity consolidation into fewer records. Level 1 data is summarized for reporting, hence, it usually becomes smaller in volume. When business requirements are gathered and understood during the development iteration, customer information such as buying behavior, navigational information, and demographics can be collected within the ODS. Information can also be integrated in the CIF ODS with other corporate data. Data is eventually propagated to the data warehouse in a more summarized fashion, usually on a daily basis. Summarization and aggregation of data takes place in Level 2 of the CIF ODS. (Chapter 7 discusses archival and storage of large volumes of data.) Low-level clickstream data may be kept for long periods of time, thus requiring large amounts of either offline or alternative storage. This leads to a number of the most important questions e-businesses must answer: how much clickstream data to keep, where to keep it, at what level, and for how long.

The short answer is that clickstream data is stored until it is no longer useful to the organization. Consider a company that has just launched

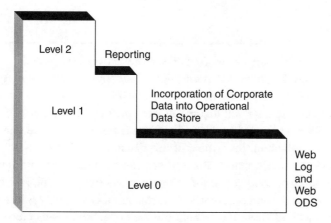

**Figure 2.8**  Levels of log information.

its Web site, let's say to sell ski equipment, ski tickets, and bargain vacations (www.Uski4Fun.com). Over the first six months, the company's Web logs are processed four times a day to extract customer and purchase information. The customer and purchase data is updated in the corporate ODS, and integrated with shipping and billing information once a day. The data is now stored redundantly in the ODS, the Web log, and the billing and shipping systems. Once a month, customer sales information is propagated to the data warehouse. In month seven, company managers realize that data storage is reaching its limits. They decide to move the first six months' of Web log information to alternative storage (with the understanding that no program will be able to go back earlier than six months) and to keep the current month's logs where they are easily accessible to the business users. At the end of each month, a month's worth of logs are moved to alternative storage; the oldest month in alternative storage is deleted. In this example, the emphasis has been placed on integration and propagation of relevant information to the data warehouse.

# Interpreting Information Using Meta Data Transfer Languages

Communicating between systems has always been a challenge due to differences among platforms, networking, programming languages, protocols, and other elements. Technology advances so quickly that developers

## Types of Web Sites

Many Web sites are created to sell services or products; many others are created without any profit motive, including personal, medical, and government Web sites. The latter tend to be informational in nature and rich in content. Of course, deciding how best to analyze and store Web site data will depend in large part on the type of site under analysis. Chapter 1 defined the broad divisions of site types, but we review them here, so that you can consider them in the context of this discussion—data analysis.

**Business-to-business (B2B) environment.** The B2B environment may host different products for different suppliers or companies; for example, www.Flowers.com, which advertises flowers, gourmet foods, and other gifts. Advertisements there may reference another company (e.g., www.GoodFood.com) to help the Web user who needs more information. Based on the search criteria, information about the product and/or supplier may be displayed to the Web user. When the Web user decides to purchase a product, www.flowers.com is responsible for relaying the order and shipping the requirements to the vendor. Links to the supplier Web site may be part of the program, but usually the business takes the order and transfers it to the supplier.
Some banners and ads for similar or complementary products will be continually displayed while the Web user is logged on to the Web page; others may not appear until the user logs on at a later date.

**Portals.** Companies that supply products or services may choose to have their Web sites available through a portal, which is essentially a window into the Web environment. A portal is an easy-to-use front-end tool, fashioned after some search engines (e.g, www.Yahoo.com, www.Excite.com, and www.Infoseek.com). The portals are created using robust searching capabilities based on keyword searches. Portals are also capable of running background activities and managing complexities such as links to other Web sites. These background activities are hidden from the users. Some companies are represented on many B2B portals.

**Business-to-commerce (B2C) environment.** In this environment, the e-business sells directly to the consumer, for example, www.amazon.com and www.disney.com. Sites in this category change their look and product mix frequently to keep the customer's interest high.

**Consumer-to-consumer (C2C) environment.** In this environment, individuals are linked as a point of Web processing. A point of Web processing is a logical connection between two users. C2C may include the definition of relationships within the extended household, usually found through mining the data. It is important to manage and maintain these relationships. The assumption with C2C is that the structures are in place and can be easily built and torn down as business dictates. The business users define the meaning of relationships. The term C2C was first coined in *Building the Customer Centric Enterprise* by Claudia Imhoff, Jonathon Geiger, and Lisa Loftis (Wiley, 2001).

are constantly struggling to find easier ways to integrate data. In the e-business environment, it is extremely important to move data as soon as possible so that analysis and integration can take place. The faster the data is analyzed, the faster the company can respond to the customer's future needs.

# Enterprise Application Integration

Enterprise Application Integration (EAI) is an interface that works with different platforms and software to bring data together into one store of data. It creates the "feeds" necessary for applications to interact. The EAI strategy requires software that comes in three forms:

- Application switch technology
- Data transformation technology
- XML, HTML, and XHTML technology

We will discuss each EAI strategy in turn.

## Application Switch Technology

Application switch technology uses adapters to communicate. Each application has a different technology and access mechanism, and it is up to the software vendor to create an adapter (connector) to them. The software provided by the vendor interacts with each platform and pulls the data together based on the meta data setup within the product. For instance, IBM offers Data Joiner and Data Propagator to communicate between products on different platforms. Oracle offers a connect product line, as well as all the middleware and gateway products that enable connectivity.

## Data Transformation Technology

Data transformation technology uses messaging software to trigger data transfer and consolidation. Examples of messaging software are IBM MQSeries, Neon, or Tibco. Messaging software seamlessly connects disparate systems through message transfer that can take place in near real time or as fast as technology will allow. E-businesses use messaging software to transport data from the Web site to the ODS and/or the CIF ODS in real time. Following transfer, data is analyzed and messages are sent back to the Web site for interaction with users. Because data transformation technology requires synchronization and careful programming, extraction, transformation, and loading (ETL) vendors are working with messaging vendors to create an easier environment to set up and administer.

## XML, HTML, and XHTML Technology

XML, HTML, and XHTML are three markup languages that allow for a standard way of interacting using flat files. The flat files are interpreted and analyzed as soon as they are received from the Web site. Information in one of these languages is sent back to the site for customer support or to identify a very important customer. Let's examine these languages one at a time.

### Hypertext Markup Language

HTML is used primarily to create Web pages. It uses tags (words surrounded by angle brackets—< and >—and attributes (in the form name= "Value"), and often includes text between tags to show how the data will look in the browser-displayed page. HTML defines the page layout, graphic elements, fonts, and links to other documents, all within the tags. For instance, to display some text in boldface, the command would look like this:

```
<B> BOLD THIS TEXT <B>
```

HTML has some prespecified formatting tags, such as bold, italics, and underlined, which makes it very easy to use.

### Extensible Markup Language

XML development started in 1996; since February 1998, it has been a World Wide Web Consortium (W3C) standard. XML was designed to organize data exchange, as opposed to formatting it into some predefined way, such as that required for a database. Similar to HTML, XML is a language that makes exchanging data or metadata in an e-business environment much easier.

XML is becoming the standard that most software companies use to communicate among products. It can be used to integrate metadata from disparate systems, as well as to transfer data between products. Like HTML, XML uses tags and attributes; however, it requires all data in the file to be enclosed in tags, and each file can have only one set of top-level tags. XML leaves the interpretation of the data to the application that reads the XML. A misplaced tag or forgotten attribute will make the

XML file unusable to the application, causing an error (in contrast to HTML, which forgives such oversights). When the error occurs, the application will stop until the XML file is fixed. Fortunately, line breaks and white space are ignored, thereby making parsing much easier.

A document type definition (DTD) in XML describes the tags for the document. A DTD will include optionality (i.e., which tags are required and which are not). The DTD is written in XML, which shows the different uses of this language. Not only is XML used to organize the data for transfer from one product to another, but it is also used to interpret the XML file. Most metadata repositories can create XML for transfer to other systems, but this capability is of little use if the receiving system does not know how to use the data passed by XML.

### Extensible HTML

XHTML is the reformulation of HTML as an application of XML, based on three document types that correspond with and extend HTML to new devices and applications. On January 26, 2000, the W3C reformulated HTML 4 in XML 1.0. XHTML is designed to work in conjunction with XML, and is intended to be used as a language for content, and to be viewed, edited, and validated with standard XML tools. XHTML also makes it possible to target the data to any device, such as a hand-held computer or cell phone.

## Summarizing Languages

All of the EAI strategies described here require an organized implementation plan for the interfaces within the Internet environment. XML, HTML, and XHTML are becoming standards for the transfer of data and meta data between systems, but advances to technology will continue to drive which format will be used in the future.

Rapid technological changes make it difficult to choose an interface and exchange mechanism that will be stable over time. As technology evolves, any data and metadata exchange strategy must be capable of adapting or of being absorbed.

## Understanding the CIF and E-business Interface

Successful e-businesses have Web environments that:

- Quickly load, analyze, and query.
- Identify metadata for the Web user.

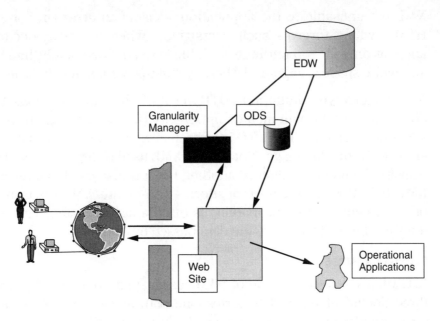

**Figure 2.9** The interfaces between the Web environment and the CIF.

- Establish repeatable processes acquisition and delivery of data.
- Have the capability to handle large volumes of data.

The interface between the Web environment and the corporate information factory, shown in Figure 2.9, illustrates that the Web environment and the corporate information factory environment only directly meet in three places:

- The point at which the Web environment sends transactions to be executed in the operational environment
- The point at which the Web environment passes data to the enterprise data warehouse through the granularity manager
- The point at which the Web environment receives data into the Web server through an ODS

The movement of transactions from the Web to the operational environment appears as just another transaction. The Web environment must format the transaction in the structure required by the operations application, then route the transaction to the operations environment. The fact that the transaction came from the Web environment is transparent to the operations application. Once the application executes the transaction, the results of the transaction are made available to the Web environment. Typical transactions executed include:

- Placing an order
- Scanning a catalog
- Inquiring as to the status of an event
- Verifying an activity

The second major interface between the Web environment and the corporate information factory is the movement of data from the Web site to the CIF. A whole host of data is moved in this direction, typically including clickstream data. From the clickstream data, other information is derived, such as data gathered as Web activities occur: new customer registration, product examination and product purchase, and so forth. The volume of data that can come through this interface is tremendous. The third interface to the Web site is the flow of data into the Web from the CIF through an ODS. The ODS is capable of providing subsecond response time. As such, the ODS becomes the place where the Web site goes to get detailed information. The Web queries the ODS as a regular part of Web page management, and on an interactive basis with the expectation of very fast response time. The queries the Web makes are for small, very detailed pieces of information. The Web might ask the ODS such things as:

- Is this customer known to us?
- Do we have any more parts in stock?
- What are a customer's likes and dislikes?
- Where is a shipment located right now?
- What is the status of an order placed yesterday?

The three interfaces to the CIF are shown in Figure 2.10. The speed of the interfaces is very different. The operational interface is used on an as-needed basis; if no orders come in, the interface is not used. If an order comes in at 10:15 A.M., then the order may be sent to the operational environment that afternoon. The interface to the data warehouse is usually exercised once a day (but under special circumstances, it may be exercised more frequently). Once a day, all the clickstream data is unloaded and passed through the granularity manager. The passage of data is done in a batch, sequential manner.

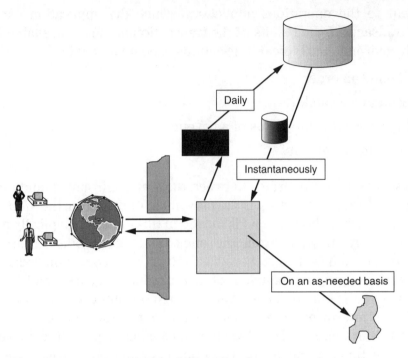

**Figure 2.10** The speed with which the interfaces are used.

# NOTE

**The interfaces described in this section can be termed the "regular" interfaces, those used on a regular basis. But there are also so-called irregular interfaces between the Web environment and the CIF. On an irregular basis, you will need to get data from the data warehouse or the exploration warehouse into the Web environment en masse—for example, when an analyst has discovered a new classification of customers. After the analyst creates a subset file of customers of this particular variety, the results are loaded into the Web environment as a special promotion. The load is only done once. This is an example of a special interface to the Web environment from different components of the corporate information factory.**

## Sending Transactions to the Operational Environment

The operational interface is made so that the operational environment is undisturbed by the creation of the Web environment. Figure 2.11 shows that transactions are created, formatted, and routed from the Web environment to the operations environment.

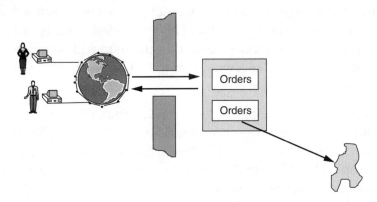

**Figure 2.11**  In response to a direct need for access to the operational environment, a transaction is created and formatted in the Web site, then routed to the operational environment.

One important benefit accrued from the creation of transactions inside the Web environment is that the operations environment is unaware that the source of the transaction is other than what is normal. This means there is no need for changes to the operations environment to accommodate the needs of e-business; therefore, the operational environment can be kept separate from the Web environment. This means that there will be fewer complicating factors as the environment grows.

## Data Passing through the Granularity Manager

The granularity manager is the point at which the Web places data inside the corporate information factory. The most important function of the granularity manager is to offload data out of the Web environment. This offload function is very important because it keeps the Web environment lean and mean. Without the offload capability, the Web environment would either grow very, very large or would be forced to jettison data. Obviously, neither option is ideal. But with the capability to offload data, the Web can function in a normal and efficient manner and still generate as much data as is needed.

The granularity manager also condenses data—especially clickstream data—as it leaves the Web environment. This is a vital functionality, because there is much extraneous data in the clickstream environment.

The granularity manager reads the data, determines what is needed, and passes on only the necessary data. The unneeded data is either discarded, or, if there is a remote chance that the data will be needed later, it will be summarized or otherwise aggregated. In short, the granularity manager acts like a data sieve.

Finally, the granularity manager acts as an ETL tool, integrating and converting data into formats that are consistent and compatible with the other corporate data. Figure 2.12 shows the usage of the granularity manager as an ETL tool. Like ETL tools, the granularity manager assures consistency and does transactions.

It is worthwhile noting that the granularity manager draws from many different parts of the Web environment. Clickstream data makes up the largest volume of data found in the granularity manager, but other data passes there as well, including transformed partially cleansed corporate data.

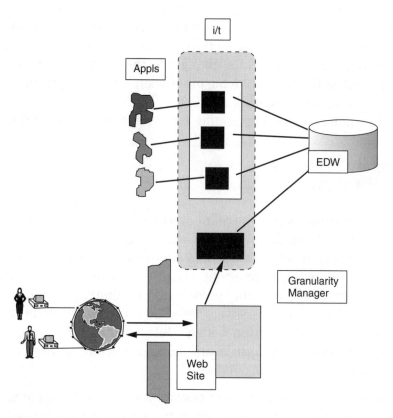

**Figure 2.12** The granularity manager is used to integrate data much as ETL programs are used for the application environment.

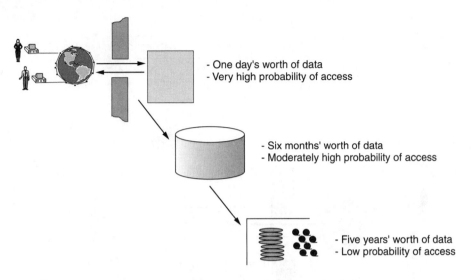

- One day's worth of data
- Very high probability of access

- Six months' worth of data
- Moderately high probability of access

- Five years' worth of data
- Low probability of access

**Figure 2.13** Data at the different locations in the CIF has very different properties.

A good way to think of the overall Web data structure and the CIF environment is to consider the length of time the data resides in a component and the corresponding probability of access to the data. Figure 2.13 shows this important relationship.

Figure 2.13 shows that data that has a very high probability of access and data that is not very old resides in the Web environment. Data that has a modest probability of access and up to six months of data is found in the data warehouse. And data that has a low probability of access and data that is up to five years old resides in the alternative storage/near-line storage component of the corporate information factory. A "cascading" effect takes place as data ages and as volumes of data grow with regard to the placement inside the Web and CIF environments. This cascading effect enables efficient use of resources (which in turn leads to high performance). Theoretically, an infinite amount of data can be stored in the architecture.

## Data Passing through the ODS

The ODS is the vehicle that allows the Web environment to access data from the corporate information factory. The ODS provides very fast response time for the Web request. The ODS is a classical type IV ODS, whereby the data is fed from the enterprise data warehouse (EDW). Once in the ODS, the data is organized so that it can be optimally

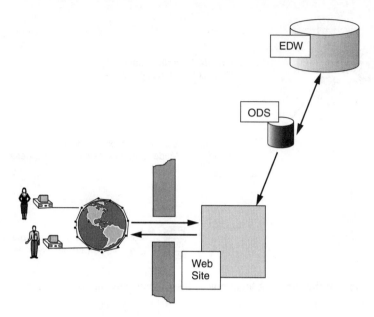

**Figure 2.14**   An ODS from the data warehouse.

accessed by the Web environment. Figure 2.14 shows the positioning of the ODS versus the Web environment.

The data in the EDW is read and then is analyzed to produce the analytical results needed by the Web environment. Figure 2.15 shows the analytical program that sits between the EDW and the ODS. The analytical program examines and analyzes data warehouse data in a freeform manner, meaning that the processing is unstructured; hence, the analyst is free to prepare the data for the Web environment in any manner desired.

Typical analytical processing done here might examine:

- Highest-volume customers
- Most profitable customers
- Products with the longest shelf life
- Most price-sensitive products
- Days most traffic expected
- Anticipated results of having a sale
- Profit margins for a product

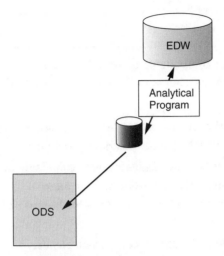

**Figure 2.15** The analytical program feeds the ODS from the EDW.

Generally, analytical processing will read and analyze a large amount of data and condense it into a small amount of detail. For example, of all the information gathered about a customer's past activities, payment history, and so forth, the analytical program might condense it into a single parameter, such as: this customer is highly profitable/moderately profitable/break-even/unprofitable. This enables the Web environment to access data in a very efficient manner.

To envision the role of the ODS and the granularity manager, consider what happens when a customer enters the Web environment. If the Web site has no prior knowledge of the customer, a standard set of HTML pages are sent to the customer to begin the dialogue. Upon completion of the dialogue, the clickstream data is sent to the granularity manager, whereupon it arrives in the enterprise data warehouse. At the EDW, a historical record is created for the customer, reflecting the date of entry, the activity, and other information. The customer data is analyzed, and a record is written in the ODS. When the customer enters the system at a later point in time, he or she is now known. When the Web site queries the ODS about the customer, the ODS acknowledges (in split-second timing) that the customer is known to the corporation, and returns any predictive information about the customer based on the analytical processing conducted in the enterprise data warehouse. The Web environment can then start to tailor its response to the customer. When this interaction with the customer is complete, the results of the interaction pass to the granularity manager. The historical record

## Privacy Issues

Privacy requirements vary across the different components of the CIF. The Web components add additional privacy considerations. Some of the security considerations on a component-by-component basis are:

- Web environment: Internal and external exposure, DBMS technology and firewall technology available, very vulnerable to hacking and virus data warehouse

- Internal exposure: DBMS and network technology available, very vulnerable to in-house analysis going to wrong place alternative/near-line storage internal exposure, application security available, not particularly vulnerable because of difficulty of hiding access and analysis ODS

- Internal exposure: application, network, and DBMS security available, very vulnerable to unauthorized in house access data mart

- Internal exposure, network, and OLAP security available, low level of vulnerability exploration warehouse—internal exposure, DBMS, and application security available, not vulnerable due to difficulty of hiding access and analysis operational applications

- Internal exposure: DBMS and application security available, not vulnerable due to difficulty of understanding legacy applications

in the enterprise data warehouse is updated with the most current information, and the ODS record is refreshed.

This, then, is how the different components of the Web environment and the CIF interact. At first glance, it may appear that the data in the EDW and the ODS are redundant. To some extent, this is true, especially after the first interaction. But after many interactions, the differences between the EDW and the ODS become more apparent. The EDW contains historical data, while the ODS contains the most up-to-date information and the results of analysis of other information. Note that the ODS reflects a consensus of opinion. The consensus is reached by the analysis of data found in the data warehouse. In summary, the more entries there are in the enterprise data warehouse and the more the data warehouse data ages, the less the two environments look alike.

# Summary

This chapter introduced the need for a mature, stable infrastructure for the e-business environment, a structure known as the corporate information factory. Each component of the CIF is important to the success of the e-business environment.

This chapter also explained the importance of flexibility to the e-business environment, pointing out that flexibility also makes the e-business environment hard to manage. By, using such standardized markup languages as XML and its derivatives, it is possible to create repeatable processes that will enable the e-business to meet the growing demands of its customers.

One must remember that requirements change over time; all components are subject to the iterative process covered in the next chapter.

# CHAPTER 3

# Building an Iterative E-Business Infrastructure

Requirements for an e-business infrastructure will change over time; therefore, the development of the e-business environment should be iterative—a process described in the first section. As in any system development, by implementing a methodology, it is possible to design processes that can be used repeatedly. By gathering the correct business requirements for each development stage, and by creating a flexible environment that can be easily enhanced and changed to accommodate future requirements, the result will be a successful implementation. This chapter explains how to build such an environment, using the iterative approach methodology.

## Taking the Iterative Approach to Development

By its nature, the e-business environment undergoes constant change. Take, for example, campaign management. An Internet marketing campaign will be run on the Web site until it has been determined to be successful—or not. The campaign will be measured over time, its statistics will be analyzed in the data warehouse and will be adjusted within the corporate and Web site operational data store. In this ever-changing environment, taking an iterative approach to develop the programs and data structures is crucial.

What do we mean by iterative in this context? In iterative development, some—not all—requirements are gathered from a facilitated session, after which a formulation for the implementation of the requirements is made; ultimately, the result is moved to production. After the first iteration—that is, implementation—is placed in production, the usage and effectiveness of the system is monitored. Subsequent iterations will follow the same steps, except that their development will be done based on a different set of requirements. In this way, each development iteration builds upon the previous iterations. When iterative development is not used, each portion of the environment is created with no thought to future module reusability. Over time, the noniterative approach generates overhead, both in maintenance and human resources. Eventually, that overhead becomes impossible to manage, as there is no way of understanding the redundancies inherent to the various iterations of development.

## The Importance of Meta Data

Meta data—data about data—is very important to iterative development in e-business. The *where-used* analysis shows all the jobs, program modules, data models, and front-end software where a change could cause conflict in the environment. For instance, let's assume that a specific program module must be changed to include a new data item. Where-used analysis conducted with meta data can show exactly where this module is used and which job(s) might be affected by the change.

Another important feature of meta data relates to "lineage"; starting from a parent program or module, the meta data shows the sequence of steps required for a process to complete—its lineage. For instance, if a job has five steps, Step 1 has to finish prior to Step 2; Step 3 must finish before Step 4 fires, and so on. Meta data can also show the prerequisites necessary before any given step can start processing. Many of the homegrown e-business infrastructures created in the online economy's early days are now experiencing maintenance difficulties for the following reasons:

- Where-used analysis is difficult to attain.
- Lineage information is difficult to attain.

- Code is documented and the key personnel who wrote it have left.

- Too many programs must be changed when new requirements are defined.

- Infrastructure changes are difficult to implement due to a lack of a foundation, such as the Corporate Information Factory (CIF).

In those e-business environments created without an iterative approach—therefore, without repeatable processes—individual activities were created differently. For example, reports may have been created in Perl—a text- and string-manipulation programming language developed in the late 1980s by Larry Wall for NASA as a reporting language. Database acquisition and population probably were implemented using C—a general-purpose programming language originally designed on the UNIX operating system. Perl and database utilities may also have been used for extraction, transformation, and data loading, and as a procedural language with SQL extensions for propagation of data to form the corporate ODS to the data warehouse. Not only are such environments difficult to change and maintain, but very little meta data is available that reflects the content of these modules; certainly there is no integration of meta data.

## Creating an Iterative Cycle

To create an iterative cycle, review the following, *before* each new iteration begins:

- Existing data structures and models
- Programs and procedures created in earlier releases
- Reusability of processes and steps within earlier releases
- Determination of change required in earlier releases based on the current iteration's requirements

Most of this information can be captured and managed within the meta data environment. As Figure 3.1 depicts, the meta data component of the CIF spans the entire architecture. Meta data can encompass project information, acquisition program information, delivery program information, deployment and release information, as well as definitions of all the source and target objects.

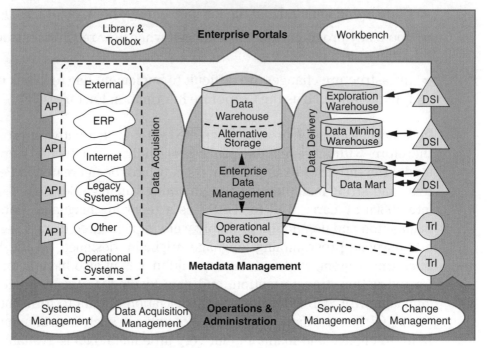

**Figure 3.1** Meta data in the CIF.

# Implementing Your System Using a Methodology

To be successful in the development of any system, you should use a methodology to establish a framework for the various development activities. You must first, of course, understand the e-business environment, as described in Chapter 2, "The Corporate Information Factory and E-Business"; upon that understanding you impose a set of rules, your methodology, to guide the creation and implementation of an e-business system. The project manager and architect are responsible for making sure the projects interact successfully.

A number of packaged methodologies are available for purchase. Each has elements that are useful in the creation of the e-business infrastructure. Conversely, each methodology also has elements that may not be so useful. Therefore, the e-business team should assess the development methodology and assemble the elements that best fit the enterprise under development. Four major e-business areas will be impacted by methodology:

- *Program management.* This involves the coordination of all activities within the decision support environment. Program management includes strategy development, individual project management, and administration and operation. Strategy development, which is part of program management, is the design of a road map or plan that shows where the enterprise wants to direct future development iterations.

- *Project management.* This refers to the day-to-day coordination of activities necessary to the implementation of a development iteration. A program may have many projects (iterations).

- *Administration and operation.* These areas include the activities that support the environment and ensure smooth daily operations. They include the following:

  - System management ensures that the environment is maintained while upgrades and new development iterations are being implemented. Smooth and seamless changes in the core technologies are the goal.

  - Data acquisition management is the set of processes that define, implement, and manage the processes used to capture source data. Data acquisition management also entails the preparation for loading the data into the CIF.

  - Service management is the set of processes for promoting user satisfaction and productivity within the CIF. Service management includes the processes designed to define, implement, and manage the creation and population of data marts.

  - Change management is the set of processes for employing changes to tools, data, hardware, and software.

- *Data management.* This e-business area consists of processes that manage data within and across the CIF. Data management includes processes for backup and recovery, partitioning, creating standard summarizations and aggregations, and archival and retrieval of data to and from alternative storage.

As Figure 3.2 shows, five major activities occur within project management:

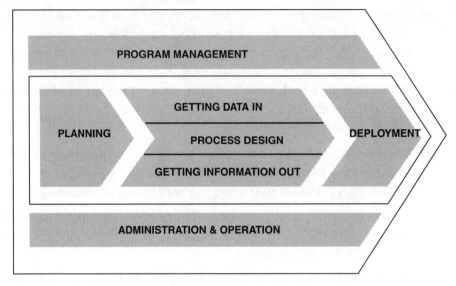

**Figure 3.2**  Methodology for iterative development.

**Project planning.** This includes starting the effort, forming a team, assessing the environment, and establishing standards.

**Getting data.** This involves gathering the business requirements, creating the data models, setting up the physical environment, and designing the processes.

**Process design.** This includes creating processes and activities for analysis of clickstream data within the Web site and corporate ODSs. Processes to move data from the data warehouse or data mart to the ODS, propagation of data to the data warehouse from the ODS, and integration of other data sources with Web data are also part of this construct.

**Deployment.** This includes prototyping front-end and managed queries for the business users. They use the methodology and the iterative approach for the next development iteration.

**Administration and operation.** This includes monitoring the effectiveness of the applications and performing ongoing system tuning.

The following sections describe each activity and the steps required for development in a Web environment.

# Project Planning

Project planning, the startup phase, begins by assessing the environment. The assessment entails gathering information about the current state of affairs in the corporation, including conducting interviews with current employees; reviewing the current systems, platforms, and software; and identifying strengths—and weaknesses—within the corporation. Prior to doing an assessment, the core team should be formed.

## *Organizing the Team*

The next step is to organize the team, which includes identifying the project sponsor, project leader, architect, data analyst, business users, data acquisition and delivery programmers, application specialists, business analysts, and support personnel. All of these roles are crucial to the success of the infrastructure.

The project sponsor is responsible for obtaining management commitment and support, to prevent what is called "scope creep." Without this commitment, people have a tendency to continue to change the parameters of project's scope. An environment suffering from scope creep rarely gets much accomplished. The project sponsor also assists in obtaining the funding for this and future iterations.

The project leader manages the development iteration on a daily basis. He or she is responsible for the activities leading up to and including the delivery of the iteration according to the aforementioned scope. Ideally, the project will be delivered on schedule and within budget.

### Assessing the Environment

Conducting the assessment is an integral part of providing a base for a successful project. The assessment is separate and distinct from gathering functional requirements. An assessment is a "readiness" analysis of whether the organization is prepared to support the application. Some of the issues include: Is the organization prepared to use the output from the project? Is there technical expertise in the platform of choice? Is there expertise in the software of choice? Is there adequate connectivity? An even more critical cost is whether the organization is prepared to cope with the hidden cost and can they actually exploit for value the output of the project? All these issues need to be surfaced in the assessment.

**Standards**

The assessment stage is the perfect time to establish standards for the project. These standards include all of the factors cited in the previous section as well as meta data standards. The creation of standards by the core team will dramatically speed up implementation and keep the subsequent team members from engaging in "interesting diversions." The previously mentioned periodic reassessments are the appropriate time to open technology inquiries, not during project implementation. With standards in hand, the team can move on to the business requirements gathering phase.

## *Gathering the Business Requirements*

Generally, a meeting is held to identify the business requirements. It begins with a discussion of the corporate mission statement, including future objectives. The group assigned to gather the requirements should be small, usually not more than 10 people. This makes it easier to control the meeting and to keep attendees focused. Members from the development team who are in attendance should be observers only; they should not participate in the discussion. In some cases, it may be more effective to have the meeting facilitator be someone from outside the company. Professional industry facilitators are readily available—but make sure you use someone that comes with good recommendations.

The venue for the requirements-gathering session should be away from the work environment, preferably at a facility designed specifically for such meetings. Ideally, the room should be U-shaped, to ease interpersonal interaction. Tape, flip charts, and markers will also be needed. A scribe should be assigned; this is the person responsible for monitoring the flow of discussion. Issues raised that are not within the scope of the session underway are written by the scribe on a page called the "Parking Lot," and taped on the wall. This becomes the list of issues to be taken up at a later time or as part of a later iteration. The scribe also prioritizes requirements based on importance to the corporation. Only those requirements that are considered a high priority by the group will be addressed during development. Budgeting for the development iteration will be addressed based on the requirements; obviously, the more requirements met in the development iteration, the more it will cost.

Gathering business requirements for the Web environment can be difficult, because what needs to be captured and measured will change over time. The best place to start is by using sample metrics such as

- Top 10 requested pages by day
- Page dwell time—how much time did the user spend on the page?
- Banner campaign effectiveness—did this cause ser to go to that page?
- Top number of referring sites—primary referral source
- Top number of referring search engines—primary referral search engines.
- Top entry pages—where in the Web site did the user enter?

Then, to the sample metrics just listed, get the answers to questions such as

- Is frequency of visits important?
- Is knowing the last time a customer visited the Web site valuable?

### Technical Team Roles

The architect is responsible for the overall connectivity within the infrastructure. The architect is also responsible for determining which tools, databases, platforms, networks, and security software work well together. The architecture must be modeled to encompass at least two-year's of growth in the corporation, and it must be reviewed with every business change and at every new development iteration. For instance, suppose the corporation has decided to add another server to the environment to offload an existing server. The architecture diagram and document would have to be changed to reflect networking and software enhancements. The architect is also responsible for synchronizing programs and modules. This includes optimization of the software used to program interfaces, summarizations, and propagations to the data warehouse.

The data analyst helps gather the business requirements, and relates them via business rules with a data model. Both business and technical definitions are agreed on during this process. The definitions are reflected within the modeling software. For instance, the business definition of a customer may be "a prospective or current user of the company's services or products," whereas the technical definition of a customer may be "an account or unique customer identification within the customer subscriber system." A customer may also be defined as someone having made zero, one, or many purchases from the company's service or product offerings.

The e-business users are responsible for conveying their requirements to the development group. The business users and development team will work very closely during prototyping to refine these requirements. A mechanism for collecting and coordinating requests for change in the environment will have to be set up.

## Establishing the Physical Environment

Setting up the physical environment requires coordinating the technical team, vendors, and purchasing and receiving departments. The physical environment should be selected early on in the project, as delivery can take from one to two months. A development environment, as well as the production environment, should be set up prior to the start of development.

Selecting hardware and software is an important and time-consuming part of setting up the physical environment. It involves these elements: platforms, storage, software, a personalization engine, an ETL tool, a front-end product or managed query tool, and a clickstream analysis tool. The selection of components is a team decision based upon the assessment.

### Platforms

A computer platform is the combination of hardware and database software. It could be IBM, Sun, Hewlett-Packard (HP), Dell, Compaq, Sequent, AlphaBlox, NCR, or Sony, with the combination of a database management system (DBMS) such as DB2, Informix, Oracle, SQLServer, Sybase, Tandem Non-Stop SQL, or Teradata. The operating system could be IBM MVS 390, UNIX, LINUX, Microsoft NT, VMS, or Windows. (Benchmarks for these platforms can be found at www.tpcd.org.) No one platform or DBMS is inherently better or worse than any other; each has its advantages and disadvantages. The choice should be made based on what works best in your environment. Answering the following questions will help to guide the decision-making process:

- How much and what kind of training will our group need?
- Will the team be self-reliant after knowledge transfer from the vendor?
- Does the team have the required skill set?

- Can the vendor provide at least three references?
- Is long-term vendor support assured?
- What type of partnering does the vendor want with the corporation?
- What is the cost of acquisition and operation?
- What is the capacity and throughput?
- What is the vendor market share?

You also must ascertain the extensibility of a platform: Will it be capable of handling future development iterations? If the platform is not sized properly during the first iteration, there could be problems down the road, such as inadequate "horsepower" to cope with increases to the volume of data. Bringing in bigger servers, more processors, and additional storage units could cause havoc in the environment.

The decision to replace a platform should be made at the beginning of a new iteration. Therefore, monitoring the environment over time is very important to ensure that you are not caught unawares. Gathering growth statistics on a weekly and monthly basis is very useful when it comes time to prepare for future iterations. Questions to answer in regard to platform extensibility are as follows:

- Do we have enough storage to accommodate the next development iteration?
- How fast is our Web site growing?
- Based on the past growth, will we have enough processors and storage for the future?

After answering these questions, approach the decision-making process in an organized fashion, using either monitoring software or database administrator (DBA) and system administrator routines. These routines are either supplied vendor programs or written language routines to monitor system utilization.

### Storage

Though we address storage in depth in Chapter 7, "Data Storage Technologies for E-Business," it is a major aspect of the up-front decisions you must make regarding a platform, so it deserves mention here. You will have to make the storage decision prior to the start of programming based on your estimate of how much data you plan to keep from the web logs, and for how long. This estimate will alter as the business grows and changes, so you will have to review it before every iteration. Detailed data, usually large amounts of clickstream data, can cascade from the Web site to the data warehouse. If it is not currently needed for analysis in the data warehouse, it can be stored in alternative storage. This viable architectural solution to the problem of managing and storing data should be addressed early in the project development. Early e-businesses that did not institute storage and data management strategies have suffered for it. Consequently, some e-businesses now invest in hardware and software solutions that can manage and store vast amounts of detailed web data.

### Software

Software evaluations should be completed early on in the project. The following list describes the different types of software that must be purchased or created especially for the project, including criteria used to make buying decisions. Return on investment for these products may not be realized up front, but during later iterations, especially when maintenance is required, their value will become clear.

**Personalization engine.** The personalization engine, described in detail in Chapter 2, interfaces with customer information to create a profile of each customer on the Web site. You will have to decide whether to purchase a personalization engine software package or to create one. If you decide to buy from a vendor, the following are some to consider: BEA, Broadvision, e.Piphany, Interwoven, and Vignette. (For more on personalization engines, as well as for a more extensive list of vendors, go to www.personalization.com.) If you decide to create the personalization functionality in-house—the programs, interfaces, and synchronization routines—the suite of tools should include

- Campaign management (to track marketing initiatives)
- Content management (a repository of all forms of content delivered to the Web site)
- Clickstream analysis (a mechanism for capturing all interactions at the Web site)
- Rules engine (standards that dictate interaction with a customer)
- Predictive engine (action is taken automatically based on standard patterns of use)
- Collaborative filtering (a form of automatic learning behavior)
- E-mail response (creation of automated response by parsing incoming e-mail)

**ETL tool.** As explained in Chapter 2, extraction, transformation, and load (ETL) products give the user the ability to create programs that can extract data from the source systems (whether DBMSs or flat files), move it to the target environment, then transform, integrate, and load it into the target database. These products are very graphical and usually have very robust functionality. An ETL tool is required to create repeatable processes, encapsulate all the meta data, and enable enhancements and changes to be completed in a timely manner.

**Messaging software.** In the e-business environment, messaging software may be required to transport clickstream data and to execute complex algorithms quickly (for real-time analysis). Messaging software can be used in the personalization process. For instance, suppose a person had logged on to a Web site for the first time, and based on some navigational predictive model, a certain ad campaign was sent to the customer. Messaging software could transport the clickstream data, retrieve the response from the content server using the ETL program, and deliver the campaign information to the Web site user. Messaging software can also be used to move data from the data warehouse to the corporate operational data store at preset intervals. ETL programs are required to work with messaging software; currently, ETL vendors are working with messaging software vendors such as IBM, Neon, and Tibco to offer integrated tools.

**Front-end product or managed query tool.** Selecting the front-end product or managed query tool is an important and somewhat complex process, as, typically, each person in the business group will have his or her favorite tool or preconceived notions about a specific tool. Therefore, selection of this tool should be organized well, and must include the business users from the outset. Furthermore, the company must be prepared to support multiple tools over time as the skill level of the user increases. Note that some of these tools are more administrative, and will require training for the administrators, as well as the business users. E-businesses would be wise to establish a curriculum to follow during user training sessions, which should be conducted in their own environment. The training curriculum should include instruction on using the current toolset, as well as instruction on the use of meta data.

**Clickstream data analysis.** Web log collection may take place anywhere from every 15 minutes to multiple times throughout the day, based on Web site size and activity level. For instance, a new company may need to pick up the logs only once an hour. As the Web site becomes more popular, log collection may need to be done more frequently, driven by the size of the log and immediacy of analysis of the information. At 15-minute intervals, a Web company might pick up the log, analyze the activity (to determine which pages a specific customer visited, whether the customer bought anything, and if so, what), and save this information. The next time the customer logs on to the Web site, the customer can be welcomed by name, and offered a custom item based on his or her last visit to the Web site.

Web analysis activities are changing as vendors and Web site personnel learn more about how to use personalization information gathered on the Web. But there can be no doubt that real-time customer profiling is a must for e-businesses. The goal of most e-businesses is to understand their customers' buying habits and behaviors in as close to real time as possible can.

### Creating the Data Models

Data models are necessary for identifying redundancy within the system. Data models also represent the corporation and its information needs in the form of a picture that helps identify the complete scope of a project. By synchronizing the data model with the scope document and business requirements, it is possible to spot any discrepancies or deficiencies within the project. The data models also enable you to see where additional data should reside within the e-business environment.

Typically, it is the data analyst who creates the data models, using data modeling software. Chapter 5, "Integrating E-business and Corporate Data," contains more in-depth coverage of data models.

## Process Design

The data acquisition and delivery programmers are responsible for creating repeatable processes that capture, cleanse, integrate, transform, and load the data that comes from the Web site servers and other data sources to the Web site Operational Data Store (ODS), corporate ODS, and data warehouse. The programmers are also responsible for mastering the ETL tool and creating the as-needed modules to direct the outcome of analysis from the data warehouse or data mart to the ODS, in order to reflect campaign or promotional changes. Programmers also acquire the meta data, and use it extensively to evaluate future changes and enhancements.

### Creating Processes in the Web Site ODS

Within the Web site, you will need to create the following processes:

**Web log collection (Level 0 data model).** Global collection requires synchronization; the more logs that must be gathered, the more difficult they are to synchronize. As explained, ETL tools can be used to collect logs. Specific collection intervals can be scheduled with most tools; for instance, a schedule could be set to launch the same job—say, to collect the web logs—multiple times a day.

**Collection of customer behavior data for immediate (real-time) analysis.** Based on the number and type of clickstream data collected within the log, this data will come either from the data warehouse or the corporate ODS.

### Creating Processes in the Corporate ODS

Within the corporate operational data store, you will need to create the following processes (see Figure 3.3):

**Propagation of detailed web log information to the corporate ODS data model (Level 1 data model).** This is done multiple times throughout the day, if possible, using an ETL tool. The ODS update records new information about a customer, including any new items purchased since the last update. New products that a customer has purchased throughout the day can be included in the corporate ODS via an ETL process, to eventually be passed on to the data warehouse.

**Processing of web logs into higher aggregated path (Level 2 data model).** Rollups, or summarizations, may take place once a day within the corporate ODS. Once a day, rollups are re-created, and hold only a day's worth of history. The summarized rollups are used for reporting, as well as for tactical analysis, and can be placed in a path cube structure or Online Analytical Processing (OLAP) product. (Chapter 6, "Performance in the E-Business Environment," includes sample star schema data models, with summarized data.) An ETL process can be created to launch once a day to generate the summarized data.

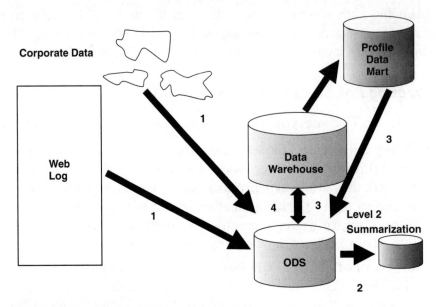

**Figure 3.3** Optional Level 2 summarization.

**Acceptance of data from the data warehouse or the data mart.**
The data may need to be integrated with other corporate ODS data,
therefore an application will likely be required to complete the task
of bringing meaning to the two sets of information. An example is
past customer product purchase information that should be
integrated within the corporate ODS and fed to a personalization
software product.

**Propagation of data to the data warehouse.** Snapshot information
about the activities in the operational data store, such as customer
purchases, may be of use in the data warehouse. An analyst can look
at the purchase history over time to determine subsequent marketing
approaches to the customer. ETL processes can be created, for
example, to provide the following customer snapshots over a month:
number of products, product types, amount spent, and number
of visits. The data would subsequently be propagated to the data
warehouse for storage. Such customer buying information
contributes to the determination of whether the customer should
be declared as a very important person (VIP). VIP indicators are
set in the corporate ODS customer data.

# Deployment

The application specialist is responsible for developing the process that filters, formats, and delivers data in a form that the business user can access from the ODS, data warehouse, or data mart for analysis. The process requires writing programs that can summarize and transfer data to the designated business user's platform.

The application specialist also creates a user-friendly front end for the business user. The front end may be as simple as a managed query product directed at a summarized table, it may be a reporting product that combines the information in many tables, or it may be a product specifically developed for web analysis. A number of these products are currently available on the market, offered by vendors such as Business Objects, Brio, Seagate, Knosys, MindSmith, Platinum, Oracle, SAS, and many others. The functional capabilities of these products vary, but may include query performance when executing SQL statements, visual formatting capabilities, security, and administration. The business analyst provides input on content, data quality, delivery, and the interfaces within the e-business environment. He or she is involved in all aspects of the e-business infrastructure, identifying meta data and ongoing processes required by the Customer Relationship Management (CRM) specialist.

## Prototyping Queries in Deployment

Prototyping queries are usually designed based on the business questions raised during requirements-gathering sessions. The objective of prototyping queries is, essentially to fine-tune the requirements-gathering effort. During prototyping, the end user will naturally ask for changes based on the information presented, so be prepared to tear down the prototype and rebuild it in a short amount of time. Try to limit this effort to a two-week period, explaining to the end user that the information gathered during the sessions will be implemented in the production environment. And keep in mind that the production environment will change, too, as new business requirements are discovered.

## Integrating Data During Deployment

Billing, inventory, general ledger, and call center data may reside on different systems on different platforms. To get a complete view of the customer, this corporate information may be integrated with the web data in the operational data store. This is usually done once a day, though it may be integrated more frequently. ETL products are used extensively to complete this process. Only through integration of data does a comprehensive customer view begin to emerge.

### Deploying the Development Iteration

Deploying the development iteration into a production environment requires mapping a production rollout plan, which consists of the following:

**Reviewing any change management requirements.** The development iteration must be documented and formalized in the company change management system. All interested parties should be listed in the change management record.

**Notifying users via e-mail and project web page update.** All users should be notified when the project is going into production. They should also be supplied with a mechanism for asking for changes or enhancements to the e-business environment.

**Synchronizing the human resources, hardware components, and software products involved in the implementation.** All synchronization activities should be clearly delineated during the change management meeting, along with scheduling and planning implementation events and sequences.

**Estimating the shakeout period (usually not more than two weeks).** During the shakeout period, you will have to closely monitor processes and activities. Emergency changes are sometimes required, so a procedure to handle such changes should be established in the rollout plan.

## Administration and Operation

The support personnel will include those who have knowledge of existing systems. An example of a support person is someone who has knowledge of the billing system and can add value to the creation of the CIF. Operations and technical support personnel will be required to schedule and execute the jobs placed in production, as well as to monitor the performance of the programs. These people must be included in preparing the scope document.

### Preparing the Scope Document

*Scoping the effort* is the act of taking the requirements, prioritizing them based on business needs, and setting the boundaries each development phase; this is a team effort. This is easier said than done! Usually a scope document is written soon after the business requirements have been gathered. A scope document should be simple, and composed at a high level of abstraction. Too much detail will convolute the requirements for the development iteration. Keep the scope document to three to five pages, leaving space to discuss future iterations.

The scope document should contain information about the business needs, possible ways to meet those needs, strategy, and benefits. For each project, define the objectives, benefits, organizational structure, critical success factors, and measures of success. Include what each iteration does—and does not—comprise. Attach sample business queries, as well as expected follow-on project definitions. Keep an eye out for the aforementioned scope creep, adding requirements that are beyond the scope of the development iteration. This often occurs during prototyping or the construction phase, when other requirements surface. Evaluate each change request to determine whether the request should be addressed in the current iteration or included on an enhancement list for the next one.

### Developing the Project Plan

Developing the project plan is a tedious task that can take anywhere from three to five days. The objective is to manage the project based on the project plan, and not to let the project plan manage the team. Consider starting this task by listing the major categories of the methodology, and then detailing each one. Figure 3.4 shows an example of some of the major categories of a project plan. Any task in the project plan that takes more than a day may need to be broken down into smaller tasks.

### Monitoring the Effectiveness of Applications

During the first month of implementation, monitoring the application is critical. This includes tracking the following:

**Load response times.** Monitor the time it takes to complete any of the load processes. The load times should be kept in the meta data repository for analysis. Adjust load times based on the analysis.

| ID | Task Name |
|---|---|
| 1 | **Initiation** |
| 2 | Start effort. |
| 3 | Form team. |
| 4 | Assess environment. |
| 5 | Establish standards. |
| 6 | **Planning** |
| 7 | Define scope. |
| 8 | Develop plan. |
| 9 | **Effort** |
| 10 | **Strategy Development** |
| 11 | Analysis |
| 12 | Design |
| 13 | Construction |
| 14 | **Getting Data In** |
| 15 | Analysis |
| 16 | Design |
| 17 | Construction |
| 18 | **Process Design** |
| 19 | Analysis |
| 20 | Design |
| 21 | Construction |
| 22 | **Getting Information Out** |
| 23 | Analysis |
| 24 | Design |
| 25 | Construction |
| 26 | **Deployment** |
| 27 | Rollout Planning |
| 28 | Education |
| 29 | Production Implementation |
| 30 | Rollout |
| 31 | Support Initiation |
| 32 | Post-Implementation Review |

**Figure 3.4**  Major categories in the project plan.

**User response times.** Monitor daily user response times, and follow up with users who called in an unacceptable response time. Provide users with a mechanism, such as a help desk, for reporting unacceptable response times.

**User query pattern recognition.** Implement monitoring software that enables pattern recognition—such as the same group of users executing the same query multiple times throughout the day. Based on an analysis of this information, create a summary table to enable better response time for multiple users.

**User follow-up.** It's a good idea to hold weekly meetings with the business users; start this with the first iteration and continue it throughout the life of the project. Use these meetings to help users address any problems they have with the environment.

**System resource tuning (memory and paging).** The system administrator should use system utilities to aid in the collection of tuning statistics, which are used to improve the system.

### Performing Ongoing System Tuning

This process includes the following:

**Tracking data usage.** Usage tracking information includes who is using the data, as well as how often the data is accessed or selected. Based on usage tracking information, you can refine the environment—for example, determining that some data is never used, which will enable you to regain disk space.

**Monitoring performance levels.** Based on the information from the monitoring processes, you can resolve performance issues that involve the system, ETL processes, and memory changes.

**Setting up a mechanism to handle user request changes or enhancements.** Request coordination can be automated or manual. A manual process may require a change request form to be filled out and submitted for approval, whereas in an automated system an e-mail form can be used.

**Archiving data.** Archival routines can be set up to move data that is no longer useful to alternative storage. The archival routines can be set up using an ETL tool or archival software.

### Using the Iterative Approach for Next Steps

Before beginning a subsequent development iteration, the team should discuss mistakes made and lessons learned during the previous one. At this review meeting, encourage a candid but tactful exchange among team members. From this review, you will generate a plan that precludes making the same mistakes. Let's say, for instance, that in the previous iteration, having two logical data modelers and no physical data modeler caused concern during the creation of the database schema.

Therefore, during the meeting, the team decides to make sure one of the data modelers is a physical modeler during the next iteration. Or, let's assume that during the first iteration, the programming of the ETL product was outsourced to a vendor, who left after implementation, and knowledge transfer to the team was not complete. During the next iteration, you can plan to ensure that knowledge transfer is done on an ongoing basis.

## Summary

Building the e-business infrastructure requires the completion of a specific set of activities, including following a development methodology that will produce repeatable processes. As stated, changes to an e-business environment are inevitable, so the ability of the team to accept and deal with change is crucial to the success of an e-business infrastructure.

# CHAPTER 4

# Identifying E-Business Users

T o develop satisfying relationships with the different types of users and groups that rely on the CIF, it is necessary to understand how each of these groups use the CIF as their source of information and processing support. Whereas operational systems are generally transaction-centered, data warehouses are the systems designed to support a customer focus. Data warehouses are designed relationally, that is, to map relationships between customers, products, and transactions. Consequently, companies with a data warehouse-centric CIF are well positioned to establish systems that enable enterprisewide sharing of all data and information.

The ability to share information about relationships benefits employees, business partners, and customers alike. When customer-centric warehousing is implemented, it reduces the cost of making customer relationship data available, and makes it possible for a broader range of employees to make informed decisions (because they have deeper knowledge of each customer). Employees can identify the most profitable customers and take appropriate measures to enrich the relationships with them. Armed with this more comprehensive understanding, businesses can better customize marketing to these valuable customers, providing them with products and services tailored to their needs, expectations, and preferences.

# Identifying Internal User Groups

Identifying different groups of users is a critical first step toward understanding their individual needs and expectations. A needs assessment reveals distinct interest groups and provides insight into who is tapping CIF resources and how the CIF support their work. The results can be used to determine infrastructure requirements necessary to support the timely delivery of relevant information in appropriate formats through preferred channels. Internal users can be broken out into two broad categories: analytical users and simple end-user groups.

Consumers are interested in product and sales information that helps them evaluate, select, acquire, and use products. Business users are both internal and external and include suppliers and partners. Business users are interested in production, inventory, and delivery information, as well as sales and marketing information, anything that helps them forge and maintain business relationships. Internal users are interested in information that helps them to answer questions, uncover trends, make predictions, or test hypotheses. Internal users form overlapping communities that include analytical users, work groups, project teams, and practice communities, all of which have both distinct and common interests and needs.

## Analytical Users

Foremost among internal communities are the analytical users. Analytical users consist of five broad types: farmers, explorers, tourists, miners, and operators. These loose groupings help identify different patterns of use, anticipate user's needs and predict their demands on the CIF. Table 4.1 summarizes the key activities and CIF requirements for each of these five types.

### Farmers

Farmers are frequently found in management and business-planning groups. They are familiar with the environment, and conduct frequent analyses. Farmers have consistent, well-defined requirements with

**Table 4.1**  CIF Requirements of Internal Users

| INTERNAL USERS | INFORMATION USES AND ACTIVITIES | CIF REQUIREMENTS |
|---|---|---|
| Farmers | 1. Track data and create reports for key performance metrics.<br>2. Monitor budgets and reports. | OLAP, DSS, reporting, and data visualization |
| Tourists | 1. Track key performance indicators.<br>2. Conduct keyword searches for clarifying information, to confirm intuition about key indicators.<br>3. Determine quality of available data. | Query, reporting, EIS, OLAP, and intranet/Internet |
| Explorers | 1. Identify patterns in data.<br>2. Identify relationships in data.<br>3. Generate and test hypotheses.<br>4. Determine conditions surrounding notable events.<br>5. Determine predictability of conditions. | Specialized exploration data warehouse (if available), OLAP, query, business intelligence with embedded data mining, data visualization, and DSS |
| Miners | 1. Classify information in sets.<br>2. Estimate values for variables.<br>3. Predict future behaviors; classify records.<br>4. Place records in affinity groups.<br>5. Cluster data in heterogeneous groupings.<br>6. Describe complex database to increase understanding of underlying data. | Data warehouse, specialized data mining mart (if available), statistical languages, query, and data visualization |
| Operators | 1. Track and report day-to-day, weekly, or monthly performance for key metrics. | OLTP, ODS, and operational applications |

well-known schedules, media, and display formats. They track patterns and trends to forecast key performance metrics, and make immediate decisions based on the data at hand and by inference of the data that is missing.

## Tourists

Tourists are usually management- and executive-level users. They query based on intuition, therefore, their needs are difficult to predict and to plan for. Tourists submit queries that support analysis of unstructured data. Typically, they have a broad business perspective, coupled with deep knowledge of at least one aspect of the industry or company. They tend to use key performance indicators such as profitability or sales volume as the foundation of their analyses. And though tourists are adept at finding information, their use of advanced decision support system (DSS) features is unsophisticated.

Tourists are aware of different types of data and meta data, but focus their attention on formal meta data because it describes both the content and structure of the data it summarizes. Formal meta data is enterprise sanctioned and defined descriptions of the meaning of data elements.

## Explorers

Explorers are unconventional thinkers who use trial-and-error (that is, heuristic) strategies to analyze detailed historical data in an iterative manner. Their business requirements reflect this unconventional viewpoint; hence their architectural needs tend to be difficult to satisfy. Explorers look for patterns and relationships as a guide to understanding conditions surrounding events. Their activities are characterized by random queries and unconventional procedures. They use data to create and test hypotheses, which are passed to data miners for confirmation. After confirmation, explorers form predictable queries, which are given to farmers. Among explorers you will find marketing analysts, actuaries, and strategic analysts.

## Miners

Miners delve into extensive, highly focused data sets to determine the truth of a hypothesis and the extent to which the data supports it. They are skilled in statistical techniques, and typically extend the analyses launched by an explorer. Miners also share the results of their analyses with explorers as part of a collaborative effort. Miners use specialized tools, and their patterns of use are predictable.

### *Operators*

Operators are the most common users. They schedule reports composed of current, detailed information using standardized queries. Operator needs are specific, and their expectations high, because they require detailed, subject-oriented operational data for business management, which they must analyze rapidly in order to be able to take immediate action. The data they need must be current, tactical, and integrated, and they must be able to access it quickly, with current performance metrics pushed or published. The word "pushed" means that changes in the data are automatically sent or forced to the user's attention.

## End User Groups

E-businesses can thrive only when they have the requisite knowledge they need to do so. To that end, diverse group strategies—work groups, customer- or product-focused business units, cross-functional project teams, and practice communities—are increasingly being organized to cultivate and accumulate organizational knowledge. Understanding the individuals who populate these groups, what their various functions are, and how they work is the first step to knowing how to support them.

The work performed by these groupings is inherently of a collaborative nature. Collaboration increases communication and the exchange of a broader range of information, formats, and document types. These groups rely upon the CIF for structured, quantitative data and information; increasingly, they use context-rich, unstructured information to build knowledge, understand problems, and fashion solutions. By accommodating and nurturing the exchange of knowledge among these user groups, it is possible to institute a new context upon which the information infrastructure can be built. Consequently, one role the evolving CIF plays is that of support mechanism for teamwork and innovation.

These internal user communities include analytical users, who use many of the same business intelligence tools; however, the collaborative character of their work also requires other tools, formats, and channels. These channels and tools include Web sites, bit streaming data, and telemetry. These forms constitute unstructured data. Group processes typically include setting goals and objectives, and planning, monitoring, evaluating, and analyzing risk. These processes in turn require activity tracking through qualitative information—anecdotal information and case studies—that document successful strategies from which the users can establish best practices. Once the best practices have been established, enterprisewide learning can take place, in order to include the development of strategies to implement those best practices.

## Work Groups

Work groups are typically formed by managers to deliver a product or service; thus, they share job responsibilities and common goals. These groups stay together until their mandate changes. Group members tend to draw on CIF resources, including data marts, operational data stores, and exploration warehouses. Because their responsibilities are limited in scope, a distinguishing feature of work groups is that they tend to engage in fewer of the knowledge-building and -sharing activities of other teams and communities. Figure 4.1 illustrates the relationships typical of these work groups.

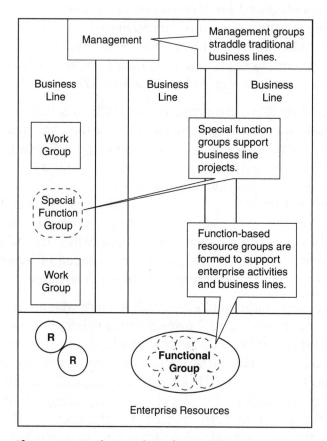

**Figure 4.1**  Business unit work groups.

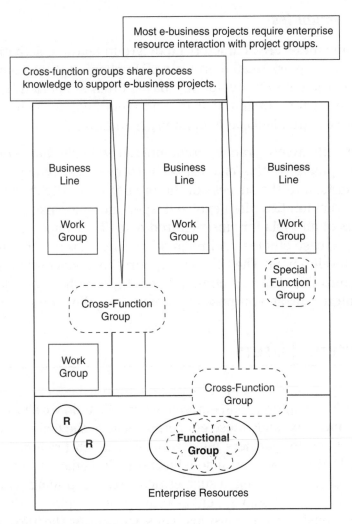

**Figure 4.2**  Cross-function project teams.

Liaison teams are formed within work groups to complete a specific task or a circumscribed set of problems. Senior management typically chooses the team members. Project milestones and goals bond these teams, a bond that is usually dissolved after the project is completed. Project teams are frequently multidisciplinary, composed of "experts" from different units within an organization, to take advantage of their diverse strengths and expertise. Project teams may include members of the organization's partners. Figure 4.2 illustrates the cross-functional nature of project teams and their members.

### Practice Communities

Practice communities are characterized by group learning activities, by sharing a focus on work-related problems. Members of these communities usually participate on a voluntary basis, often supported by management. Passion for, commitment to, and identification with, mutual objectives drives attendance at community "gatherings."

To work more effectively, practice communities typically share common language and practices; this enables them to more easily develop the capabilities critical to the success of the organization. Highly functioning practice communities often evolve deeper, more sophisticated uses of, and forms of analysis for, unstructured data. They implement anecdotal evidence, case studies, and related learning materials to support meaningful development. The CIF can support the needs of this type of learning organization. Practice communities stay together for as long as there is an interest in, and purpose for, maintaining the group.

# Identifying External Users

Traditionally, questions around security and appropriateness drove the distinction between internal and external users: What do we share? With whom? E-business expands these concerns because the dialog between the enterprise and its partners must address a much broader base of information. Furthermore, because e-business also enables automated and systemic decision making in such critical areas as pricing, availability, and support, it often supplements—or may even replace—the traditional dialog of business relationships. Thus, supporting the information for this dialog to ensure that it reflects the nature and importance of these relationships has become a critical task of the CIF.

External users can be broadly classified as business partners or consumers. Understanding the needs and importance of these two groups is necessary to support e-business initiatives.

## Business Partners

Effective e-business partnerships (that is, B2B) center on comprehensive, customized services that include personalized interfaces, specialized pricing, extensive customer support, technical information, software updates, product configuration tools, troubleshooting support, and online training and certification courses. Buying and selling are the paramount reasons for establishing trading partnerships; and price, quality, timeliness, and customized support are the building blocks for trust. The organizations with high online profiles—including such leaders as Cisco, Dell, and Granger—understand the importance of working the business-to-business landscape. They efficiently, effectively, and creatively provide a diverse range of services that enhance value and significantly reduce the complexity of buying, using, and supporting their products. Customer-centricity is evident throughout the diverse communication channels that they provide for developing and deepening relationships.

Business-to-business users differ markedly by market or industry; however, patterns of common use can be found in their research, procurement, support, and learning activities. To satisfy the complex demands made by the B2B community—in particular, the need for integrated information updates and analysis—the CIF is constantly expanding, both in terms of scale and complexity. The CIF provides support for expanded transactional processing, particularly in the web environment. These processing systems are directly linked with the other components of the CIF to provide timely and accurate information flows. The inherent scalability of the CIF further supports these complex processing and analytical demands.

## Consumers

Clearly, businesses must focus on satisfying customers if they expect to build mutually satisfying relationships that lead to customer loyalty. E-businesses must gather and analyze data to construct profiles for each customer, profiles that are composed of the customer's interactive habits, interests, modes of connectivity, preferred formats and channels, and buying patterns. Customer profiles are emerging as an effective means for interpreting needs, interests, and preferences, in order to create a personalized context for researching, buying, using, and supporting products. Profiles are used to coordinate customer relationships, to provide information tailored to their interests, to identify the time to send "teasers" for related products, and to offer special discounts. However, applying the knowledge gleaned from customer profiles, in order to make decisions about product offerings for mobile consumers, can only be done effectively in real time.

As with internal and business users, understanding the customer's requirements, interests, and preferences is a prerequisite for the delivery of relevant and timely information at the *point of need*. This effort is complicated by the fact that the point of need continually shifts as options for mobile and remote connectivity open new channels for reaching consumers. As consumers become connected and mobile in more ways, the implications for business intelligence, marketing, and strategic partnerships become clear: The CIF must grow to address expanded communication channels, diverse presentation formats, and automated decision support processes in order to provide a context for delivering appropriate information at the changing point of need.

## Categorizing Consumers

E-business consumers can be categorized as researchers, shoppers, buyers, and/or community members. Each of these consumer types accesses the various web delivery channels with different expectations, all of which significantly impact the CIF. Let's examine them each in turn.

### Researchers

Consumers classified as researchers rely on product information, technical data, and other seller-provided data to analyze product/service features and options, to identify desirable qualities, to compare competing products, and, ultimately, to make informed decisions about product fit. Researchers are interested in uncovering details about product and service information. They tend to be among the most computer-literate, focused, and tenacious of consumers. Researchers use a much broader range of sophisticated search strategies, and know how to match those strategies to the context of the search. Researchers thrive on detailed technical, pricing, and service-related information. They commonly seek additional information beyond what is presented, therefore, it is often valuable to researchers to be able to accumulate result sets for further comparison and analysis. In this way, researchers behave similar to analytical internal users, in that query results often mark the beginning of their analysis. Researchers rely on the CIF to provide a continuous stream of analytical results. They also become reliant upon increasing levels of personalization over multiple sessions to shorten their search patterns.

Most suppliers provide a range of support services that aid customers who are in the role of researcher. Customers are commonly given self-serve access to frequently asked questions lists (FAQs), as well as to more complex query tools, which they can use to identify and solve their own problems. Field engineers, call centers, and other technical support personnel use similar tools, in conjunction with more advanced resources to facilitate the configuration and use of their products. Researchers also can make use of semantic and taxonomy-based search tools to narrow result sets. They use iterative patterns to identify similar information for comparable products. Customizing the research landscape involves providing access to rich data sets, appropriate search tools, and automated features that ease the search and the research processes. The CIF can support researchers by developing robust profiles and maintaining a placeholder on their progress to date.

### Shoppers

Computer literacy of shoppers can range from novice to intermediate. Shoppers tend to have limited patience and focus, and they can be easily frustrated. As a result, shoppers require more structure, less complex navigation features, and succinct displays. Shoppers are driven primarily by factors of price and product availability. They do not request, nor drill down to, in-depth information. They use less sophisticated, iterative search methods, and can become overwhelmed easily. As a result, shoppers require broad categories of information that have been filtered before presentation.

The data warehouse may contain information on 30 different products that tend to meet the needs of the shopper. These 30 must be narrowed to a field of not more than five "best fits" for any single shopper's needs. The CIF, then, not only must contain and update these selections, but must also filter and present them in accordance with individual user needs. All of this filtration helps to engage a customer's attention, extending his or her visit to the Web site, and preventing site hopping in search more focused results. The process of site hopping, or site-level comparisons is illustrated in Figure 4.3.

### Buyers

Buyers can be defined generally as more focused, motivated shoppers. They tend to be more technology-literate than shoppers, hence know how to impose their own structure on context; they prefer a "shortest distance between two points" navigation style. Buyers are purposeful and strategic, and employ a complex, but narrow, search pattern. Buyers

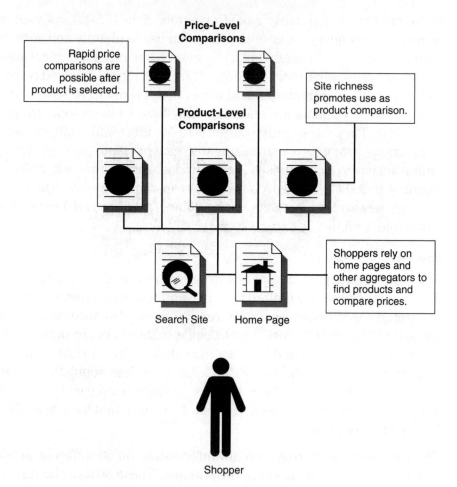

**Figure 4.3** How shoppers utilize Web sites.

are driven by both product availability and price. They know what they want and typically do not request, or search for, additional information.

The net effect of buyers on the CIF is less search traffic with smaller results sets. Data quality and meta data pointers for search functionality are especially important to provide meaningful results for buyers. Buyer purchase patterns are illustrated in Figure 4.4.

## Communities

At their best, communities create a sense of affinity and trust that carries over to product offerings. These communities provide members with a powerful context in which to discuss ideas and share experiences

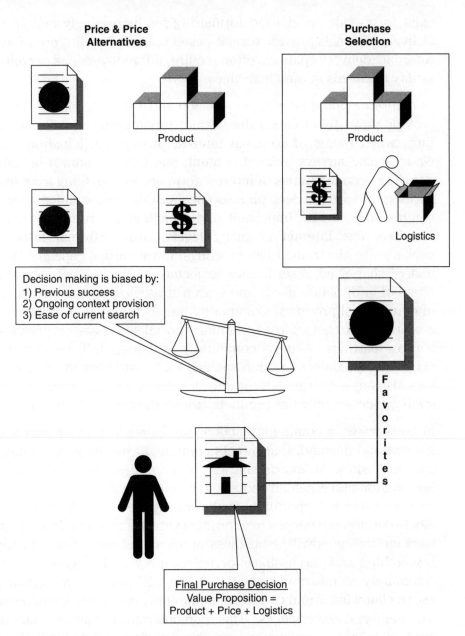

**Price & Price Alternatives**

Product

**Purchase Selection**

Product

$

Logistics

Decision making is biased by:
1) Previous success
2) Ongoing context provision
3) Ease of current search

Favorites

Final Purchase Decision
Value Proposition =
Product + Price + Logistics

**Figure 4.4**  Buyers develop purchase patterns.

and information about products and services. Community members commonly look to the community for information to make product decisions. The community context also helps users associate information needs with retrieval opportunities by providing a framework for relevant searching. In addition to these context providers, delivery channels exist to provide specialized formatting for increasingly mobile users. Delivery channels provide format-based context for all types of access. Alternate delivery channels often require different versions of content to satisfy the needs of mobile devices.

Content-rich portal sites, from Amazon and Yahoo! to sites in between, provide powerful contexts that attract broad audiences. Communities form when issues of personal interest prompt participation through e-mail, chat, surveys, related content, and other channels of information. These communities of interest form around anything from graphic accelerator cards to deep philosophical issues of race and gender. Such communities are an important and meaningful forum for exchange. Members can interact at many levels, from informal information exchange to electronic town meetings. In this broad capacity, the context of shared interests frames expectations for content relevance in terms of information needs and search strategies, as well as availability of commercial products. Community members are also shoppers, buyers, and researchers. Most community portal sites have corporate sponsors or partners. A deep community affiliation influences purchase decisions by conferring upon sponsors a "trusted brand" status. Sponsors also enjoy a "friend-of-the-site" loyalty, especially where marketing strategy successfully ties products closely to community interests.

In these ways, a community acts as an aggregator, or intermediary of interest and demand, that directs community members to commercial sponsors' sites. As intermediaries, communities can provide valuable information and essential context to community members. Such knowledge serves as an opportunity for leveraging the goodwill of the community to develop and deepen relationships with its members. To successfully leverage this goodwill, e-business applications must frame shopping, researching, and purchasing experiences in a way that is consistent with community members' expectations. The CIF provides the capacity to use the knowledge and context of community memberships to personalize members' experiences. This personalization includes ambiance, product offerings, navigation, search strategies, and delivery channels. The impact of personalization on the CIF is significant, in terms of real-time processing and the capacity to analyze, identify, determine, and deliver relevant, personalized content based on community memberships. The process of aggregating and redistributing communal interest is illustrated in Figure 4.5.

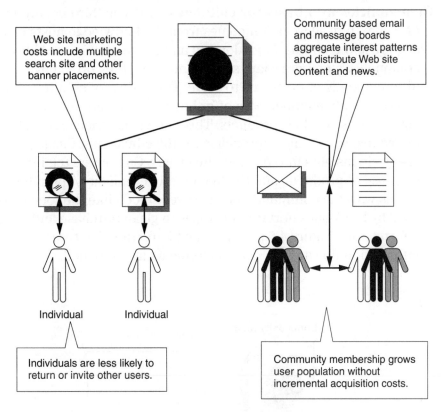

Web site marketing costs include multiple search site and other banner placements.

Community based email and message boards aggregate interest patterns and distribute Web site content and news.

Individual

Individual

Individuals are less likely to return or invite other users.

Community membership grows user population without incremental acquisition costs.

**Figure 4.5**   Community aggregation and redistribution.

Aggregating individual interests and activities is only the first level of community benefit. Here are two others:

**Communities as a target for CRM.** The aggregation of community membership and its interests brings enhanced attention from e-business hosts, who are eager to aid in attracting members. The community offers the e-business host the opportunity to identify user interests in a broader context. Identifying complementary purchase options is easier when customers are grouped by interest. The purchase patterns of these groups can be analyzed in near real time. This analysis then becomes a basis for managing a community-based relationship. Supporting community interests with consistent value increments leads to the development of loyal and consistent usage patterns. Value increments include push- and pull-based techniques.

**Communities as a basis for collaboration.** The third benefit level of community aggregation comes from the knowledge hosts can acquire about community adoption and usage strategies. Although community members share similar interests, they often have different kinds of problems to solve. The variety of solutions found by community members can offer hosts new insight into actual customer use of their products. This knowledge then can lead to innovative marketing approaches for the e-business. Usage patterns also yield insights into product life cycles. Customers tell hosts about their use of products, and the likelihood of replacing/upgrading them. In this way, the community behaves very much like the focus groups used by brick-and-mortar enterprises to glean purchase and usage information. Figure 4.6 portrays the bidirectional nature of information flows when value increments are provided.

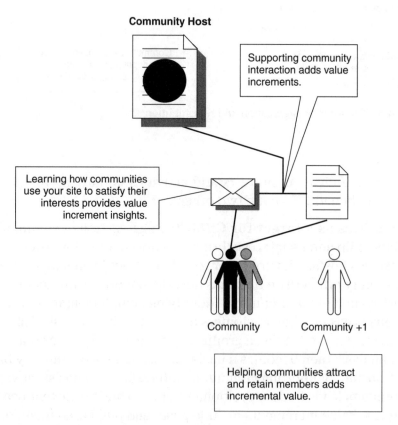

**Figure 4.6** Value increments drive information exchange.

One disadvantage of the community structure is that e-businesses come under increased pressure to get things as right as possible the first time. Nevertheless, these communities offer tremendous value for e-business hosts interested in developing their value proposition.

# Procurement

Streamlining business processes is a central focus of e-business. Procurement is the process of obtaining goods and services to run the enterprise, and offers one of the richest payoffs for these streamlining efforts. Automating the B2B interaction is one of the key target project areas. Benefits of automation accrue to early adopters in stages. Initial success of the project stems from the expanded delivery of information. Buyers are investing in supply chain automation to reduce costs and time frames.

Business users focused on procurement differ from their consumer counterparts in three critical ways:

- *Purchase priority.* E-business buyers have immediate needs. Whether accessing an exchange or using marketplace collaboration tools to find suppliers, these buyers need products now.

- *Custom functionality.* E-business buyers need to customize their purchases, either by specifying assemblies and combinations or by constantly tuning quantities and shipping and return mechanisms.

- *Range of options.* E-business buyers must be able to rapidly narrow a result set of product options based upon intelligent search criteria. The business buyer will not wade through 50 or more "matching" products for a given specification.

These requirements make procurement processing a very different activity from e-tailing. The payoff on both sides of these transactions is potentially huge, but can be limited by the capability of the seller's information infrastructure. Rapid, contextually valid product matches and configurations, coupled with logistical excellence spell big success for business-to-business players.

## Partnerships In the Supply Chain

The benefits of forming partnerships in the supply chain are tied to the value propositions advanced by each partnership. Finding the best possible partners and crafting beneficial alliances consumes much of the attention of business procurement groups. Enabling prospective partner discovery and framing relationship structures and metrics is the domain of B2B software applications and industry specifications. The complex and dynamic nature of these relationships precludes complete automation, but it is not a barrier to rapid discovery and comparison processes. Business buyers utilize iterative attempts to identify prospective product sources, and then focus their efforts on developing a relationship. Comparisons can be made as utilizing industry standard (UDDI) specified information browsing. Results help buyers narrow the field of potential suppliers so that more attention can be paid to developing relationships with the best prospects. In this way, the shopping process benefits from rapid iterations of predefined search patterns.

## Supporting All Users

Users of all types face some similar challenges. Navigation, search methods, and contextual help are at least as important in web-based clients as they are in traditional applications. The interconnectedness of web technologies such as hypertext, component-based applications, and portal-based integration brings an order of magnitude increase in possible uses. Therefore, supporting users through search process requires a number of common elements on the electronic landscape.

The complexity of usage does not always reflect the respective user's sophistication or competency. The electronic dialog can rapidly spiral beyond the control or understanding of consumers and business users alike. Multiple navigation attempts, semantic search variants, and iterative query instances can accumulate without an apparent road map back to the point of origin. Supporting interactive usage requires information-mapped interfaces that maintain an awareness of the location of the information assets upon which users rely behind the scenes.

The portal interface is a layer of abstraction; users rely upon this presentation layer to intelligently map their access to information. Information is housed and delivered via multiple channels from a variety of assets. Mapping the CIF assets for rapid and contextually valid access is the only way to provide architectural support to portal-based users.

# Knowledge Management and the CIF

Knowledge Management is re-emerging as a way to identify and navigate enriched information sources in the CIF. Knowledge management (KM) is the process of documenting in a structured manner all the intellectual capital of the enterprise regardless of form. Knowledge management is offered as a means of supporting e-business access to corporate information that is dispersed across many systems and formats. The focus of these projects is to connect to as many source systems and formats as possible in order to provide an enterprise access point for consumers and business users. While this approach raises many problems, it is often utilized in first and second enterprise portal attempts.

## Knowledge Mapping

Knowledge management is supplemented by knowledge mapping, an extended form of information mapping meant to bridge relational, informal, and multimedia stores for expanded access. The problems inherent in providing access to nonintegrated information stores are prevalent in this approach. These problems are, however, often mitigated by the business value of enhanced access and simplified navigation tools provided to employees and consumers. Figure 4.7 illustrates the unstructured portal approach.

The primary focus of these knowledge-based approaches is the construction of maps and search functions that lend themselves to the needs of users. Various indexing, cataloguing, and personalization functions are provided to simplify and automate access patterns. The value of these tools is that they provide users and their hosts with an accelerated means of answering questions and sharing information. Mapping information sources in the CIF offer additional benefits to users and hosts by identifying appropriate sources of content and context. One of the business benefits of data warehousing is the provision of a single enterprise view. Providing portal users with appropriate access to the data warehouse assures analytical consistency.

Many business intelligence tools are Web-enabled, thus they can provide web output of query result sets. More robust tools provide interfaces for portals to extend these results, seamlessly, to their users. It is these

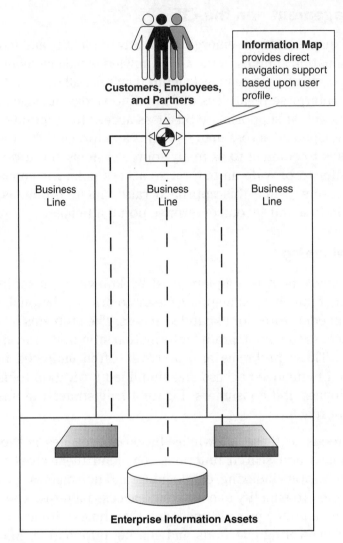

**Figure 4.7** Information mapping.

tools that extend the success of the data warehouse environment. The effects of a structured information map are illustrated in Figure 4.8.

## Training and Education

Information mapping also provides a foundation for the exchange and transfer of knowledge. Electronic training is the simplest form of knowledge transfer because it involves very low levels of interaction. Elements of successful electronic training include the following:

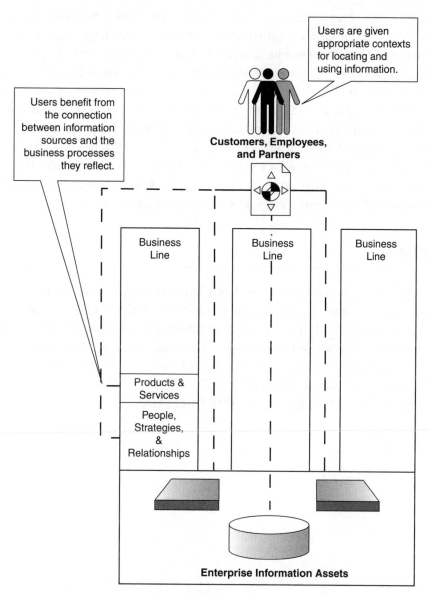

**Figure 4.8** Benefits of mapping information access.

**Intelligent curricula.** These adjust to the performance of the trainee, adapting to increase difficulty based upon testing performance.

**Rich media sets.** Rich media is defined as unstructured data, such as pictures, movies, and audio. These have been shown to extend attention span and increase retention.

Intelligent curricula and rich media sets also support educational efforts, although to a more limited extent. Learning occurs within the broader context of social interaction and acquired experience. Information assets can foster learning by mapping the knowledge components necessary to the learning experience and by capturing learning outcomes in a form consistent with search and retrieval. Experience is a key learning catalyst, whose outcomes constitute a powerful knowledge transfer agent for shared learning. It is important to note that many of these information assets exist anecdotally; they do not lend themselves to database capture and cataloging. The use of alternative media provides capture of outcomes, consequences, and context.

## Summary

Relationships among users, both business and consumer, increase in importance and complexity as e-business evolves. Users require consistency, clarity, and immediacy to form relationships with their e-business partners. The depth of these electronically linked relationships is often limited by the context and variety of delivery mechanisms supported. Context provides a landscape against which to view the transactions or search results that users generate from session to session.

# CHAPTER 5

# Integrating E-business and Corporate Data

You will need to integrate Web site data with the rest of the corporate data. To support the integration process, you will use a number of data models, each of which plays a major role. They include:

- Subject area model
- Corporate logical data model
- Data warehouse and data mart model
- Web site ODS model
- Corporate ODS model

## Levels of Granularity

To accommodate the analysis of the vast amount of information you will gather from the Web log, and to enable you to integrate that data subsequently with the remaining corporate data, you will have to deal with different levels of data granularity (see Chapter 2 for definitions of these levels). Recall from Chapter 2 that the Web log itself is at the lowest level of granularity in the e-business environment. The log is retrieved from the Web site environment at intervals throughout the day. Usually, the Web log(s) are retrieved every 15 minutes, 30 minutes, 60 minutes, or 3 to 4 times a day.

The Web log is loaded directly into the database management system (Level 0) in the Web site ODS. For instance, if the Web log is switched every 15 minutes, a copy of it is loaded into the database management system (DBMS). The Web log can be loaded into the DBMS programmatically or with a utility program. From level 0, the data is integrated with the corporate data in the corporate operational data store (Level 1). Customer information obtained from the Web log (e.g., IP address, purchase information, and navigational information) is integrated with customer information in the corporate ODS. An example would be a star schema with customer, product, amount, and shipping information created and populated for quick access by the business analysts. Finally, the daily data for one or more days in aggregated (Level 2) within the ODS for quick reporting access. Each of the three levels of granularity requires a data model.

## The Role of Data Models

A data model helps the business user understand the end result of what is being created, by helping the user envision how all the parts and pieces fit together; a data model also ensures that builders and requesters have the same expectation of the delivered product. Using a data model helps lower the incidence of redundancies, which the model will highlight for the developer to remove. In these ways, data models can help reduce the overall risk of the project.

An example will help demonstrate the value of using data models. A data model for an e-tailer such as www.Uski4Fun.com, (which sells ski equipment, garments, ski tickets, bargain trips and novelty items) would show the relationships between a customer, product, promotion, supplier, and an order. Building the relationship within the constructs of the DBMS ensures that the integrity of the data will be maintained. The data model, then, becomes an abstraction of the information needs of the business.

Conversely, when data models are not implemented, or there is resistance to their use, e-businesses find it difficult to extract the Web log data and integrate it with other corporate data: more interfaces will be required to launch development iterations. Without data models, corporations are hard-pressed to manage data as an asset.

# Defining Data Models

This section introduces the following data models:

- Subject area model—to better understand areas like product categories.
- Corporate logical data model (enterprise data model)—to associate disparate subject areas like customers and products
- Data warehouse and data mart model—to meet tactical operational needs like sales reporting.
- Web site ODS model—to leverage Web site log path
- Corporate ODS model—to integrate Web and other corporate data

## Subject Area Model

A subject area data model is a high-level conceptual model that encompasses the information needs of the entire corporation. Typically, data naturally congregates around the following subject areas: customers, products, transactions, and financials.

Figure 5.1 shows the subject area data model for www.Uski4Fun.com. It has five subject areas. A definition is constructed for each subject area, along with the candidate entities (entities that may reside in the subject area) for the enterprise logical data model:

**Customer.** Comprises legal entities that acquire services from the company. Candidate entities include prospect, consumer, and account.

**Product.** Includes goods and/or services supplied to the customer. Candidate entities include product, component, and service.

**Supplier.** Refers to the producer of goods and services supplied to the company for a fee. Candidate entities include supplier, supplier address, and distributor.

**Order.** Refers to a specific instance of demand for a product, and a means of obtaining products from the company. Candidate entities include purchase order and payment.

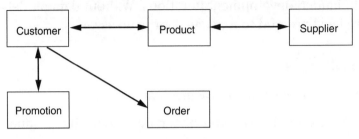

**Figure 5.1** Subject area model for Uski4Fun.

**Promotion.** Comprises all forms of marketing campaigns to sell goods or services to a prospective or active customer. Candidate entities include promotion type and promotion.

## Corporate Logical Data Model (Enterprise Data Model)

The subject area data model will help you develop the corporate logical model, a process that can take years. Corporate models can take years to create due to their size and complexity. In this model, each subject area can be defined to a higher level of detail, to include all attributes about the candidate entities. Subject area data models typically have anywhere from 12 to 20 subject areas for a given corporation, depending on size.

The corporate logical data model can be used to design the data warehouse and ODS data models. If you don't develop a corporate logical data model, you will have to create the areas required for the development iterations. Each iteration adds to the corporate logical data model, until, eventually, it approaches completeness.

A long-term strategy should be instituted to dictate how all the data models will be kept up to date. All changes and updates should be part of the project plan for each iteration of development. The corporate logical data model may not exactly match all the computer systems created for the corporation; that is, the logical model may not represent exactly how the systems are physically implemented. Rather, the corporate logical data model represents a paradigm (see Figure 5.2, which shows a partial corporate logical model for www.Uski4fun.com).

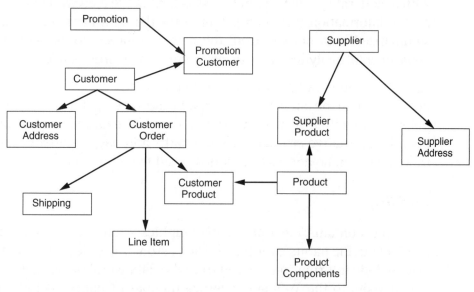

**Figure 5.2**   Corporate logical model.

As with all models, each entity and attribute within the corporate logical model should be defined. These definitions are a form of meta data, hence should be stored within the modeling tool—and elsewhere if there is a distribution of meta data. Figure 5.2 depicts only the sections needed for the current iteration.

# NOTE

Some generic data models that may be useful as starting points are available for free. Some of these are available at www.billinmon.com. Each business is unique and will require modification.

## Data Warehouse and Data Mart Model

The data warehouse is a subject-oriented, integrated, nonvolatile, time-variant collection of data that is used to support strategic decision making within the enterprise. To continue with our e-business example of www.Uski4fun.com, we'll assume the data warehouse model is made up of a low level of granularity: promotion, customer, product, and supplier information is kept over time. Low-level clickstream data from the Web log with a moderate probability of access is kept in the data warehouse—after profile information has been gathered for the data mart (customized or summarized data derived from the data warehouse to support specific departmental analytics in the decision support environment).

After Web log data has been determined to have a lower probability of access, it can be stored in alternative storage. Later still, it can be deleted altogether. At www.Uski4Fun.com, for example, when data has been in alternative storage for six months and usage statistics indicate there has been no access to it, it is deleted from the system.

## Profiling

A profile contains customer demographics (contact information and product buying habits over time). The customer profile star schema may also include information derived from the data warehouse, such as number of visits to the Web site, average number of pages visited prior to making a purchase, dollar amount of purchased item(s), and number of purchases to date.

Figure 5.3 shows the data found in the data mart that is stored in a star schema modeling format to depict customer profile information. The denormalized structure of the star schema is optimal for accessing the data by all the users of the department. Aggregate customer profile information is kept over time in the data mart according to the needs of

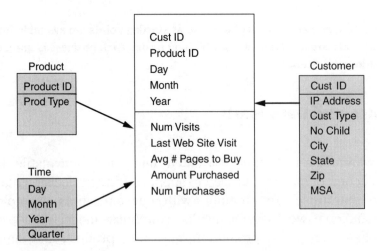

**Figure 5.3**  Customer profile in the data warehouse or data mart.

the department. Profile information is transferred back to the corporate ODS and Web site ODS on a daily, or more frequent, basis. As Figure 5.3 shows, there is other information about a customer that is of interest to the Web site.

## Web Site ODS Model

The Web site ODS, sometimes called the local ODS, is part of the interactive environment of the e-business. The local Web ODS services transactional requests from the Web site directly within the site. The local Web ODS works with the personalization engine or programs, as explained in Chapter 2. It also interacts with the personalization engine based on the customer profile information.

To demonstrate, let's say, for example, that a user logs on to www. Uski4Fun.com for the fifth time. The personalization engine, upon reading the local Web ODS customer information, recognizes IP address 10.4.29.299, and notes that this is the fifth time this customer has purchased products from the Web site. Consequently, it executes program "Fifth Purchase," pulling the appropriate information from the content server—in this case, let's say it offers to the user a 20 percent discount on rooms at the Breckenridge ski area in Colorado between February 2 and February 15.

To understand the local Web ODS, you must first understand the data found on the Web log itself. To reiterate, the Web log is considered Level 0 of the data models; that is, the lowest level of detail within the Web site. The Level 0 portion includes those portions of the customer profile needed for the activities or triggers for processing incoming customer information.

Figure 5.4 shows the Web site ODS customer profile. Note that it does not have many dimensions and can be updated quickly. In the example, when IP address 10.4.29.299 makes the fifth purchase from www. Uski4Fun.com, the information pulled from the Web site ODS customer profile comprises the number of cumulative visits and specifies whether the customer is high volume and profitable. The information from the Web site ODS interacts with (is passed to) the personalization engine, which sets off the chain of events that follow, whether in the form of an e-mail message or a 20 percent discount coupon.

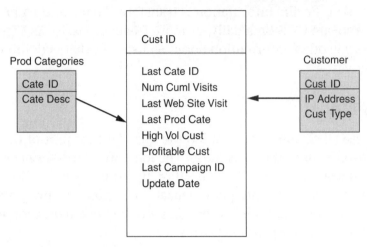

**Figure 5.4** Web site ODS customer profile.

### Level 0: The Web Log

As stated, the Web log can be gathered at regular intervals throughout the day. At Uski4Fun, we'll say the logs are collected every hour. The Web log triggers an event or activity based on user keystrokes or clicks. Based on the host IP address, user ID, or any cookie information coming from the local PC, an activity or trigger can prompt the lookup of information from another table within the local Web site ODS. For instance, programs on the local Web site ODS can trigger a lookup on the Web site ODS customer profile table to see if the customer logging on to the Web site has purchased products five times, and so is eligible for the "Fifth Purchase" campaign initiative. (Recall that the Web site table contains customer profile information that has been created from the corporate ODS and the data warehouse. The Web site customer profile table can be a subset of the information held within the corporate ODS, or information that is never found at the corporate level.) Figure 5.4 shows a typical customer profile for a Web site. The corporate ODS may include additional demographic and psychographic information about the customer, as shown previously in Figure 5.3.

The local Web site ODS should have only a few dimensions or update times, otherwise the table won't be able to support heavy Web traffic. As new customers log on to the Web site and order products, the local Web site ODS customer profile should be updated. Suppose, for example,

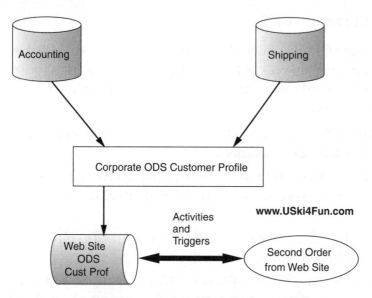

**Figure 5.5** Updating the Web site ODS customer profile.

that a customer logs on to the www.Uski4Fun.com Web site and orders a pair of gloves. Normally, the product would be shipped in 24 hours. But now suppose that, two hours after purchasing the gloves, the same customer decides to log back on to www.Uski4Fun.com, to order a pair of goggles. The information for the first order had already been sent to shipping; both inventory and the corporate ODS were updated (because it's done on an hourly basis), and the Web site ODS was updated at the same time. Therefore, upon the second logon, the customer was greeted by name at www.Uski4Fun.com. Thanks to the interactive nature of the e-business environment, the customer's second order could be included with the original order, thereby saving the customer a second shipping charge. The customer was notified of the interaction while checking out with the second order. Figure 5.5 shows the interaction between the Web dialogues, the source systems, the corporate ODS, and the Web site ODS.

## Corporate ODS Model

The corporate ODS (or "global" ODS) is an integrated and subject-oriented structure. Unlike the data warehouse, the corporate ODS is time finite and contains a limited amount of historical data. In the e-business environment, the corporate ODS is considered to be at Level 1 of granularity.

## Level 1: Corporate ODS

The corporate ODS is updated from the source systems (Web site ODS and traditional business systems) and from the data warehouse or data mart. In other words, the corporate ODS is a combination of operational data store *classes:*

**Class I ODS.** The corporate ODS is a Class I ODS if source system data is integrated instantaneously.

**Class II ODS.** The corporate ODS is a Class II ODS if the source system data is integrated with the ODS at intervals throughout the day.

**Class III ODS.** The corporate ODS is a Class III ODS if the source system data is integrated once a day.

**Class IV ODS.** The ODS is a Class IV ODS if it is updated from the data warehouse or a data mart as required. In other words, it is updated from the source systems at least once a day and from the data warehouse or a data mart as required.

The complexity of the corporate ODS environment can be overwhelming. Figure 5.6 shows all the flows from the source systems and the data warehouse or data mart.

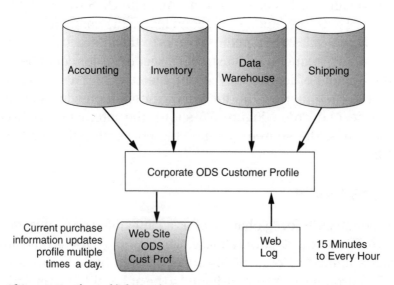

**Figure 5.6** Flow of information.

At our example site, www.Uski4Fun.com, it is imperative that the source systems update the corporate operational data store on an hourly basis (Class II ODS); the Web site ODS must be updated immediately thereafter. To meet that requirement, the programming staff at www.Uski4Fun.com has created an update program with an ETL tool; it updates the corporate ODS and the Web site ODS at the same time with the same data. The corporate ODS feeds the Web site ODS, so that some processes can be run together, to take advantage of the parallel structure of the platform and the ETL tool.

# NOTE

If a company does not own an ETL tool, a database trigger can be created to fire and update the Web site ODS when customer data in the corporate ODS receives new records or is updated. Integration with other source systems is accomplished once a day.

### Customer Information in the ODS

The Customer entity within the corporate ODS is very important to the e-business environment. At www.Uski4Fun.com, the information about a customer's most recent purchase is kept in the corporate operational data store. From there, it is taken to the data warehouse once a day. Figure 5.7 shows a partial data model for the Customer entity in the corporate ODS.

### *Level 2: Daily Aggregation*

In the corporate ODS, information can be aggregated once a day for reporting purposes. A report might include campaigns that were run during the day, plus how effective they were; the number of hits for the day; types of products purchased, totaling how much; and so forth.

The daily aggregations are modeled in star schema format, based on reporting requirements gathered during facilitated sessions with the users. Figure 5.8 shows a corporate ODS rollup configuration in a star schema.

## Relationship among the Models

Figure 5.9 shows the relationship among the data models, reading from bottom up and top down. When a change is made at the system level, all

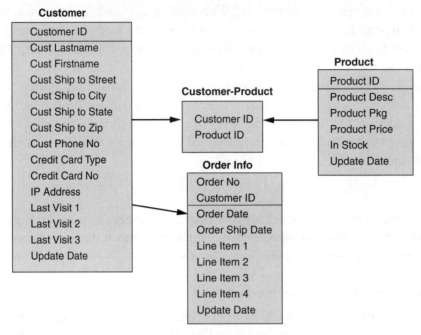

**Figure 5.7** Customer entity in the corporate ODS.

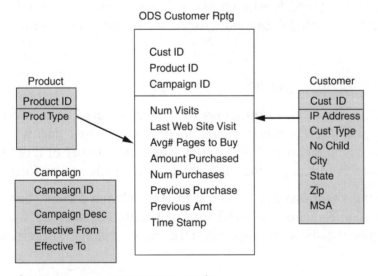

**Figure 5.8** Corporate ODS aggregation.

models above it must be addressed to accommodate the change. For instance, let's say www.Uski4Fun.com has purchased a gourmet food catering business that sells yummy food items online. Though the sub-

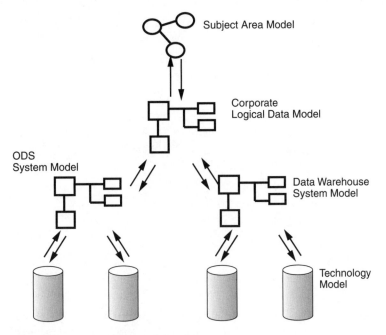

**Figure 5.9** How data models relate.

ject area data model doesn't change, and the corporate logical data model may not change, the data warehouse and ODS models will require alteration. Each model, at each level must be addressed when there has been any change.

## Summary

Daily, weekly, or monthly data from the corporate ODS may be placed in the data warehouse. The determination of which data to move to the data warehouse is based on how much information is stored in the warehouse and for what time period. Our sample e-business, www.Uski4Fun.com, has determined that data will be brought from the corporate ODS to the data warehouse on a daily basis. This gives Uski4Fun more detailed data with which it can more effectively manage customer relationships.

.com

http://

# Performance in the E-Business Environment

http://

http://

O bviously, performance is essential to the e-business environment. Simply put, no customer shopping online today will be willing to wait a long time to complete a transaction or even for pages to load while browsing a company's Web site. Online customers expect good—if not outstanding—response times; it's one of the reasons they prefer shopping online, as opposed to going to brick-and-mortar establishments. The message to e-businesses is clear: If you expect to succeed in the online economy, you must conduct your enterprise according to high-performance standards.

## Building Performance from Day One

At first, most e-business environments provide good response times; this is not difficult to achieve when only a small number of customers are logging on to the system, and there isn't much data to manage. But when the Web site becomes popular, performance often degrades. Very quickly, an e-business can lose the attention of current and prospective customers; and this impact may be felt for the long, as well as the near, term, because people remember sites that perform badly as well as they remember those that perform exceptionally.

This of course raises the question: How do you build a Web infrastructure that will provide good performance today and tomorrow?

## The Fundamentals of Performance

The secret to building good performance into the Web environment is to begin by understanding the fundamentals of performance; that is, you must understand how response times are measured, and how they are relevant to the performance level goal of an e-business.

To begin, it's important to recognize that there is a hierarchy of speeds—electronic, mechanical, manual, and wait. Let's look at each:

**Electronic speeds.** The electronic speeds of certain parts of the computer are measured in nanoseconds. The internal memory of a computer operates at nanosecond speed; programs are executed, logic is followed, data is moved in memory, all at very high speeds measured in nanoseconds (one billionth of a second).

**Mechanical speeds.** The mechanical speeds in a computer—typically used to measure reading or writing data to a disk and to other record reading devices—are measured in milliseconds (1/1000 of a second). When a programmer issues a read statement in a program when he or she wants to fetch some data, the programmer has caused the computer to slow from electronic speeds to mechanical speeds. The act of reading or writing from a computer to a disk is called an input/output (I/O) operation. The I/O is one of the basic building-block operations of computing; so knowing how to manage I/O operations is essential to achieving good performance.

**Manual speeds.** Manual speeds are the speeds at which an individual user enters data, measured in seconds. The time the computer waits for a human interaction are also often measured in seconds.

**Wait Speeds.** Wait speeds—when a user is unable to continue his or her interaction on the computer—are measured in seconds. There are many reasons why a computer is unresponsive to a user: a device may be disabled; a server may be overloaded; the network may be down; power may have failed somewhere along the line; and so forth.

To achieve good and consistent response times, the e-business developer must learn to think and operate in terms of nanoseconds and milliseconds.

## Achieving Optimal Performance

To ensure good performance in the e-business environment, the developer first has to understand that each interaction with the computer through the Internet is like a trip with numerous stops along the way. As an example, let's consider a hypothetical trip that a passenger (we'll call him Joe) takes from Los Angeles to Tulsa.

- For the first segment of the trip, Joe takes a commercial airline to fly from LA to San Francisco.

- In San Francisco, Joe hikes to San Jose.

- In San Jose, Joe takes another airline to Denver, where he rents a car and drives to Salt Lake City.

- At Salt Lake City, Joe boards another plane and flies to Dallas Love Field.

- From Love Field, Joe hikes again, this time to Dallas-Fort Worth, where he takes another jet, finally arriving in Tulsa.

Clearly, this trip would take days; and certainly it is anything but the most efficient route, so we can assess performance as terrible. How could Joe make this trip more efficient? Get a ticket on faster jet airplanes? Well, a jet that flies 800 miles per hour as opposed to 500 miles per hour offers only very marginal performance enhancement. If he were really serious about improving performance, he could make sure that he didn't have to hike anywhere. For the surface legs of the trip, he could simply drive rather than hike. That would greatly enhance performance. And therein lies the first principle of performance: optimize the slowest, not the fastest, part of the trip.

But looking at the trip strategically, we have to ask another question: Is it really necessary to make all of those stops? Does Joe really need to go via Denver? Salt Lake? Dallas? Obviously, to really optimize the speed of the trip from Los Angeles to Tulsa, Joe should take a nonstop flight from Los Angeles to Tulsa. The second principle of performance, then, is that we need to minimize the number of segments in the trip.

In summary, to achieve optimal performance, we need to:

- Improve the speed of the slowest parts of the trip.

- Eliminate any unnecessary legs of the trip.

# Transaction Processing and Performance

The performance principles summarized in the sidebar hold true for any kind of transport, including e-business transactions. Take a look at what's involved in processing e-business transactions in Figure 6.1. As

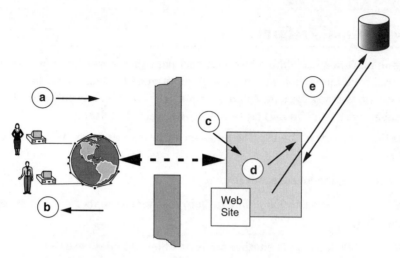

**Figure 6.1** The elements of performance in the e-business world.

you can see, there are five stages that a transaction may pass through in the e-business environment. Those elements are

- From the user over the Internet into the Web site
- From the Web site over the Internet back to the user
- Through the firewall into the HTML manager
- From the Web site manager into data contained in the Web site
- From the Web site to data external to the Web site

These are the standard paths that a transaction can take. Some may simply involve an (a)-(b) or an (a)-(b)-(c) transaction; others will be more complex. We'll look at these transactions in more detail in the following subsections.

## Simple Transactions

The simplest e-business transaction is an (a)-(b) transaction, as shown in Figure 6.2. Here, all that happens is that the transaction goes out and verifies that the Web site is there. Though dull, this illustrates a basic activity that every transaction goes through.

The transaction shown in Figure 6.3 is more interesting, as it more comprehensively represents activity taking place over the Internet. It shows

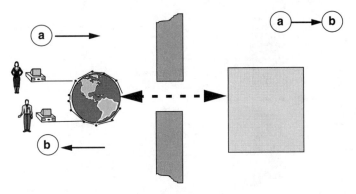

**Figure 6.2**   Connecting to the Web site—up and down the line.

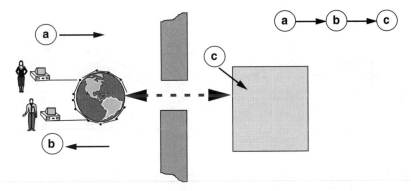

**Figure 6.3**   Connecting to the Web site and grabbing an HTML page.

that a transaction goes across the Internet, enters the Web site, finds an HTML page, and returns that page to the user. Such an activity occurs countless times a day.

## More Complex Transactions

An even more interesting transaction is one that goes beyond grabbing an HTML page; it looks at data stored in the Web as part of the transaction. That data may be displayed as part of the HTML page; in other cases, the data may simply be used to determine which HTML page should be displayed. Figure 6.4 shows the transaction.

Figure 6.5 shows another transaction of similar complexity. Instead of looking inside the Web site for data to enhance the HTML sent to the end

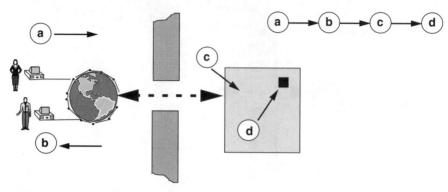

**Figure 6.4** Connecting to the Web site, grabbing an HTML page, and getting data from inside the Web site.

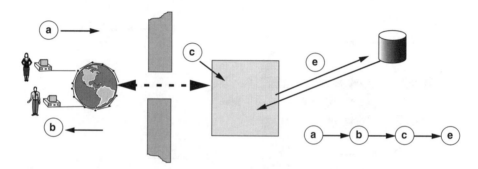

**Figure 6.5** Making connection to the Web site, grabbing an HTML page, and getting data from outside the Web site.

user, it uses data located in a corporate ODS for analysis and input to the HTML itself. In this case, corporatewide data interacts directly with the Web site to produce a powerful transaction.

## Transaction Summary

Each of these transaction types has particular performance characteristics, summarized here:

- The (a)-(b) transaction goes over the Internet; it does nothing else. Transaction speed over the Internet is often very slow—measured in seconds or longer.

- The (a)-(b)-(c) transaction has the same performance profile as the preceding, except that access to the HTML page is very fast, measured in nanoseconds.

- The (a)-(b)-(c)-(d) transaction has to access data inside the Web, and its speed depends on whether the data is accessed in memory or requires disk access—memory access is much faster than disk access.

- The (a)-(b)-(c)-(e) transaction assumes disk access to an ODS, which also is slower than memory access.

# Managing Web Site Performance

The speed at which a transaction travels over the Internet is a function of the equipment being used, including the telephone lines that link the various Internet components. Therefore, the speed achieved over the Internet is not the responsibility of outside vendors managing the Web site. If a company chooses to install a slow-speed telephone line to transmit bulk quantities of email, for example, poor performance cannot be blamed on the Web manager. The performance responsibility of the Web manager begins after the e-business transaction has arrived at the Web site.

Once it has arrived at the Web site, a transaction can process in one of two ways: it may process inside memory; or it may process in memory, and require one or more I/Os. The goal of the Web administrator/designer is to create transactions that do not require numerous I/Os. The reason is that, when transactions begin to arrive at a high rate of speed, and any one transaction requires many I/Os, a queue will quickly begin to form, thereby causing performance degradation. So it is not just a given individual transaction that must be considered; it is the transactions that are not currently being executed, but that may be waiting to execute that must be accounted for. Figure 6.6 shows this process.

## The ODS and Performance

Based on the previous discussion, it should be clear why access to the data warehouse for purposes of analysis is not a normal activity: directly accessing the data warehouse from the Web site will result in many I/Os, which can severely degrade Web site performance. Therefore, access should be made via the ODS instead. Recall that the ODS is created by reading and analyzing the contents of the data warehouse. By "preprocessing" the data warehouse, its data can be aggregated and finely condensed inside the ODS, thus making the ODS a very efficient place from which to access data.

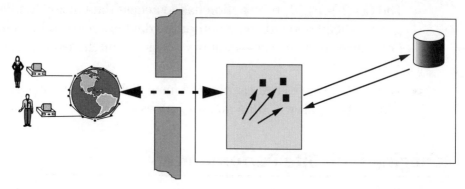

**Figure 6.6** Managing the e-business environment.

For example, let's say the Web designer wants to develop a customer profile, to consist of these factors:

- The customer's demographics: name, address, and so on
- The total amount of money the customer has spent at the Web site in the last year
- The number of times the customer has been to the Web site in the last year
- The cost of the individual purchases made by the customer during that time

The Web designer could go to the corporate data warehouse and get some or all of this information, but doing so would require that a lot of reads be issued to the data warehouse. Instead, the Web designer generates a profile record in the ODS. This the designer can arrange to do by accessing data in the data warehouse in the wee hours of the morning, when there is no traffic on the system. This is a more effective and efficient use of time and resources—and, more important—it doesn't cause performance slippage to the Web site. Subsequently, when the Web designer needs to see the profile of a specific customer, the profile can be accessed quickly from the ODS, as only one I/O is required to get all the information, because the data has been already collected and is stored there.

Another good reason for the Web designer to access the ODS rather than the data warehouse is that he or she must consider the queue of transactions—many potentially quite large—that probably are also waiting for access. Though the query to the data warehouse may well take place quickly and efficiently, if it must wait in line for an answer, that efficiency becomes moot.

In summary, the ODS is built using data from the data warehouse. All of this so-called back-end processing in the data warehouse is done on a separate machine from the Web server. Once the ODS is loaded, it is then made available to the Web server, thereby ensuring an absolute minimum number of I/Os, and consequently, very high levels of performance.

## Monitoring the Web Environment

Another sound practice for achieving high performance in the e-business environment is to monitor Web server activity. There are two types of Web monitors: a passive monitor, and an active online Web monitor. Both are necessary, as each performs a different function.

Monitoring should be done:

- At the firewall
- In the Web environment
- At the data warehouse
- At the ODS

Transaction activity and data content and growth both need to be monitored. Figure 6.7 shows where different monitors are required.

### Passive Monitoring

The feedback a Web designer/administrator looks for from the passive Web monitor include such factors as

- Nature of the workload being run
- Most active users
- Lengthiest transactions
- Most popular transactions
- Most active time of day, week, month, year
- What queues are formed and are they parameterized?
- Nature of data being accessed

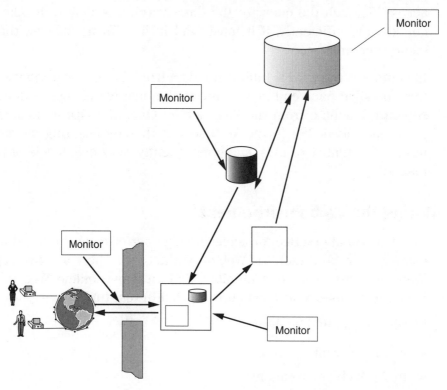

**Figure 6.7** The Web/CIF environment needs to be monitored in several places.

- Average response time
- Number of I/Os

The passive Web monitor generates a lot of data, so it is important that it be run efficiently. Every monitor requires overhead, but to be used successfully, it cannot consume so many resources as to become its own bottleneck.

## NOTE

A third approach to workload management is to interactively monitor the transaction workload. In this case, an online monitor tells the Web administrator exactly what is happening to the Web site in an online mode. This monitor is slightly different from the monitor mentioned in the earlier section in that this is an online interactive monitor. Like a blood pressure device, it only reports the current-moment state of the site.

### Active Online Monitoring

The online activity monitor tracks such factors as

- Currently executing transactions
- Resources required by each executing transaction
- Current bottlenecks
- Current response time

#### Service-Level Agreements

A proven performance technique, one that goes hand in hand with an online systems monitor, is the establishment of service-level agreements (SLAs). (SLAs are applicable only to online transaction processing.) The purpose of the SLA is to set a standard that is acceptable to both the technical staff and the end user/business staff, against which performance can be measured. An SLA might, for example, specify that 75 percent of all transactions execute in 5 seconds or less, or that 10 percent of transactions execute in from 5 to 10 seconds, and so forth.

Service-level agreements can be tailored in any number of ways. They can be set to apply only to certain hours of the day and certain days of the week, or to a class of transactions. Moreover, SLAs can be established for both performance and system availability. For example, an availability SLA might state that the system be up and available 97 percent of the time.

The online systems monitor, then, not only tracks the transactions passing through the system, but the performance of the system as well, according to the standards set in the service-level agreements.

## High-Performance Database Design Techniques

There are other techniques for designing and achieving performance in the Web environment, including

- Generating indexes based on data usage patterns.
- Creating data arrays.
- Merging data tables.
- Generating redundant data when access patterns mandate.
- Summarizing and aggregating data according to the predominant pattern of usage.

# Indexing Data

An index is used to pave a very efficient path to data. For example, an index on a customer database may be set up by name, account number, or order number. By creating an index, the data can be accessed directly and efficiently. The more indexes there are on a table, the more directly data can be accessed. An index is a direct path the system can take to data, and a direct path is almost always faster than an indirect path.

There are, however, some performance trade-offs to consider when using indexes:

- Indexes must be loaded. For large amounts of data this load time can be considerable.
- Indexes require their own space. The more indexes, the more space required.
- Updating indexes in an online update mode can be troublesome, and can cause performance problems. This is due to the additional I/O required to update indexes.

### Sparse Indexes

One option for working with indexes is to use a specialized form called a sparse index. A sparse index provides index entries for only some of the data being pointed to. For example, suppose there is a database of people in many professions, one of which is medicine. A sparse index may be created to point only to the doctors in the database. Using a sparse index in this way can be much faster than using a common index to which every profession has a pointer.

Sparse indexes, however, also have their drawbacks, hence are not useful in every case. Some DBMSs do not support sparse indexes. And a sparse index may require special maintenance. This includes creation and update by writing application code.

# Using Data Arrays

A data array makes it possible to physically gather data so that it can be accessed very efficiently. For example, let's say a Web designer has one record for a customer's January activity, one for February, March, and so forth. But now let's say the designer discovers that the data concerning the customer's annual activity is regularly accessed; in this case, it makes sense to create an annual record, to include space for the individual monthly data as well. In doing so, only one I/O is necessary to get a year's worth of data rather than using 12 I/Os to get each month's data.

## Merging Tables

Merging tables is a very good idea when the tables are used together regularly. For example, suppose there is an order table, a shipment table, and a parts table, and that numerous processes access all three tables on a regular basis. In this case, it is much more efficient to merge the three tables based on a common key structure, to allow the system to physically access all three tables at once. Kept separate, unneeded I/Os are forced on the system, thus degrading performance.

## Instituting Redundant Data

In many cases, there will be data that is used in many places by many transactions. For example, suppose that in a manufacturing environment the data element Part Description is used in many places. When that data element exists in only one place, it must be accessed every time it is needed, each time requiring an I/O. A better approach is to make Part Description redundant to the many tables where it is used.

## Aggregating Data

When data is accessed at the lowest level of detail, aggregates and summarizations are created. If the same aggregate and/or same summarization is being created repeatedly, then it makes sense to create the aggregate and/or description once, and enable users to access the aggregated/summarized value.

## Splitting Transactions to Minimize I/O

So far, the discussion has focused on minimizing the number of transactions that execute numerous I/Os as a method of improving Web site performance. But what can the Web designer do when there is an absolute need for the execution of a transaction that requires access to large quantities of data? The answer is to break the transaction into smaller components.

This technique has long been known to have a very beneficial effect on performance. As an example, consider the airlines reservation environment, which is famous for being able to execute numerous transactions at a high level of performance. To maintain that status, among other things, the airline reservations environment requires that long-running transactions be broken up into a series of smaller, related, fast-running transactions. This principle can be applied equally well to the Web environment.

As an example of how a Web e-business transaction might be split, consider the following scenario. Suppose that a user submits a Web transaction that, to execute, must examine the various parts a company sells. One way to do this is to look at the individual parts by their ID numbers; in this case, the user enters the part desired, and the information appears. But the user can also look at parts generically. The user enters XYZ, to see all parts whose ID numbers begin with XYZ. In some cases, there may be only a few parts to be displayed. But in other cases, there may be many generic parts. For example, for part XYZ there may be

XYZQWE1

XYZQWE30

XYZWET01

XYZWER002

XYZTRW0091

XYZYRE654

XYZURY01

XYZPO901

and many others

In this example, there are many parts belonging to the XYZ family, but rather than process all of the parts, our Web transaction processes the first 10 and displays them to the end user. Then the end user decides if he or she wants to see more; if so, the display process takes up where the last one left off. In such a manner, all of the parts in the family may ultimately be displayed; but for any one transaction, only a few are displayed. The Web designer has set it up so a transaction that otherwise would have required many I/Os is broken into a series of transactions, each of which consumes only a few I/Os.

Furthermore, though the entire sequence of transactions consumes many systems resources, because it is broken up, the system can intersperse other transactions between the execution of the long-running transaction, thus maintaining a high performance level at the Web site.

## Managing the Web Site Workday

Likewise, the workday at the Web site can be divided, in this case, in accordance with performance requirements throughout the day. The high-performance part of the day—typically, the morning and afternoon hours—is reserved for running a large number of transactions. During the night and/or during the weekend, the Web system is dedicated to doing the maintenance activities of the system, which generally require that the system be shut down and/or that long sequential runs against a lot of data be completed without interruption.

That said, the e-business often faces a unique challenge. Because of the global appeal and reach of the Web, setting maintenance periods is more difficult: There is rarely a time that somewhere in the world it's not a high-performance period. Nevertheless, generally, peak periods of activity can be determined, thus worked around.

Enter again the monitor. One approach to maneuvering around the problem of worldwide, constant activity is to divide the databases geographically, generally into the Americas, Asia and the Pacific Rim, and Africa/Europe. Doing so accommodates the various time zones more efficiently. When the Asia/Pacific segment is in full operation, maintenance activity is being done in the Americas.

## Capacity Planning and Management

Capacity planning includes Central Processing Unit (CPU) power, connectivity, bandwidth, and storage planning. Capacity planning and management can also help ensure good performance of the e-business system. The most effective way plan for capacity is to monitor system activity and do extrapolations based on current trends, factoring in known changes to produce a reasonably accurate picture of growth. Known changes include new functionality and business acquisition.

The primary advantage of capacity planning is that it puts the Web administrator in a position to be proactive in managing systems resources. Capacity planning makes it possible to schedule necessary upgrades to software and hardware, or additions to hardware, as opposed to instituting them on an emergency, reactive, way.

Another proactive management technique is to employ a parallel architecture. A parallel architecture implies the ability to add small units of capacity at all levels without disruption. The value of a parallel architecture is that linear, scalable performance is achievable. With a linear, scalable architecture as the foundation to the Web environment, if, say, hardware capacity doubles, response time can be halved. As the volume of data and the workload grows, taking the parallel approach to hardware becomes more important.

## Managing High Volumes of Data

From a strategic perspective, proper management of high volumes of data is very important to performance. Unmanaged or improperly managed data will quickly clog up the system. Such bottlenecks may occur as a result of:

- Indexes growing large and inefficient.
- Data being forced into contingency space and becoming hard to access. Most databases make provision for limited space acquisition beyond the basic allocation.
- Hashed data colliding. A hash data collision is when two rows have the same key value based upon using an algorithm. The database must stop and resolve this collision by sequencing.
- Sequential searches taking a long time to execute.
- Long chains of data being created.

To prevent these and other similar data bottlenecks, it's a good idea to create a staging area of data, as shown in Figure 6.8. As shown, data enters the system at the Web. But as soon as possible, the data is moved to the data warehouse. As the data ages inside the data warehouse, and its probability of access declines, the data is moved to secondary storage. In this way, a very large volume of data can be stored without damaging the performance of the system.

## Data Marts and Performance

Organizations create data marts for many reasons—often as much political as they are technological—such as

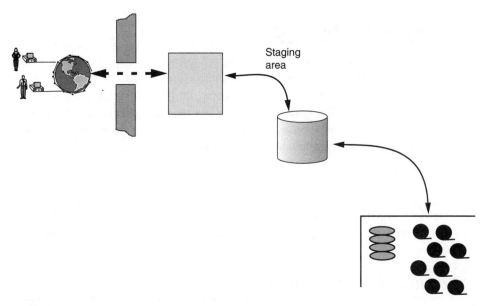

**Figure 6.8**   Moving volumes of data regularly greatly enhances performance.

- Customizing data the way the data mart likes to see it.
- Creating an environment that can be directly controlled by the department owning the data mart.
- Optimizing the processing of the department that owns the data mart.
- Being able to use multidimensional technology, such as OLAP.
- Isolating departmental processing from other processing.

Whatever the political and/or technological reasons for creating a data mart, one overarching effect of doing so is that it improves performance throughout an organization. From the moment of its creation, the benefits begin to accrue. For starters, it is optimized to meet the particular needs of the department that owns it. This improves performance. Second, the system on which the data mart operates is dedicated solely to the needs of the department. This also improves performance. Third, by removing the departmental data and processing from the data warehouse, performance is improved at the data warehouse as well. Distributing processing cycles across multiple processors improves performance across the board.

This is especially important for the e-business environment because the data from the Web finds its way into the data warehouse then into the

## Exploration Warehousing

An exploration warehouse is a facility designed to conduct major statistical analysis needed for data mining and data exploration. Attempting to do statistical analysis on the data warehouse slows the warehouse down; and attempting to do this level of analysis on the data in the Web environment is even more detrimental to performance.

Exploration processing is best done in a dedicated environment, to reduce the burden of processing the data warehouse and on the Web environment.

data marts. By improving performance in the data warehouse and the DBMS, the responsiveness in the Web environment improves.

# Network Performance

One classic cause of performance problems in the Web environment and throughout the corporate information factory is the network. The network of course is the facility through which data flows from one component to another: simply, the faster data flows, the better the response time.

Network performance may be compromised by these factors:

- Bottlenecks
- Workload
- Peak period processing
- Capacity
- Protocols

Like performance issues elsewhere in the Web environment, network performance must be addressed at the design level, at the implementation level, and at the ongoing operational level.

At the design level, the Web designer must assure adequate capacity throughout the network to handle the anticipated workload. To do that, the Web designer must consider all the routes that will be taken, and estimate the amount of traffic that will pass over those routes. After the network has been implemented according to the design, it must be managed and monitored. Because the traffic going across the network is always dynamic, the network monitor must constantly look at the traffic flowing through each node and across each line. Bottlenecks need to be identified and corrected. Computer operations must be kept abreast of the workload that is flowing through the network.

## DBMS Technology and Performance

Too often, the people involved in building an e-business environment treat the selection of the DBMS technology that will be used throughout the environment and the corporate information factory as a given. In some cases, the DBMS technology will have been chosen far in advance. But in most cases, it is possible to select DBMS technology while one or more components of the system are being built. In this case, the goal of the designer is to make sure to select the most powerful DBMS to accommodate site's components. Figure 6.9 illustrates how different DBMS technologies can be used throughout the CIF and the Web environment.

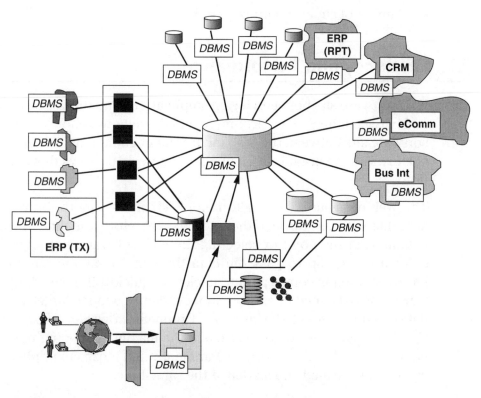

**Figure 6.9**  Efficient database management throughout the CIF.

Obviously, different DBMSs have different capabilities. Some optimize on end-user flexibility and elegance of presentation, others on transaction performance. Still others optimize on the volume of data managed or on the capability to handle data across multiple media. When shopping for an appropriate DBMS technology, consider the following criteria:

- Amount of third-party software that will run on the DBMS
- Cost of the software
- Scalability of the software
- Platforms the software will operate on
- Volume of data the software can manage
- Storage media the software can accommodate
- Possible performance levels
- Complexity of operation
- Type and amount of training required for staff
- Number of support staff required

## ETL Efficiency and Performance

ETL software sits between legacy applications and the data warehouse and between the Web environment and the data warehouse. When ETL software sits between the Web environment and the data warehouse, it is known as the granularity manager. Figure 6.10 shows this configuration.

The Web designer will have to tailor ETL processing to the volume of data that will pass through the interface; therefore, the time to consider volume is at the point of selecting the ETL software, not after. If ETL software is set up to pass the data through a common interface, the interface often becomes a bottleneck very quickly. If, instead, ETL software is programmed to execute independently, a much larger volume of data can flow through the interface. Optimally, however, ETL processing should be parallelized, to ensure that the maximum amount of data can pass through the ETL interface. Parallellization means multiple extracts can be transformed and loaded at the same time.

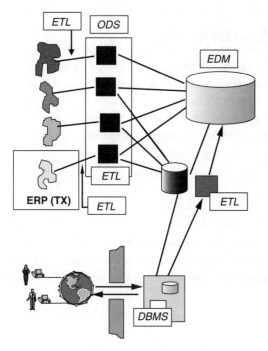

**Figure 6.10** Efficient ETL and granularity manager software.

## Using the Granularity Manager and Snapshots to Improve Performance

Although it is not always possible to do so, creating snapshots, rather than updating data, produces very good performance. A snapshot is a mirror clone of the production system most often created in storage hardware. The system operates much more cleanly, and transaction integrity does not become an issue, because it doesn't have to keep track of what has control of a record at any moment in time.

Taking snapshots does entail a trade-off, however: the number of records created. This is where the granularity manager, whose job it is to filter those records, comes in. To understand how this works, consider the following simple example. In a Web site database is a record for Mary Jones that shows she last logged on to the system on July 29, and purchased home products. Then, on August 2, Mary logged on again, but this time to look at fine art.

## Referential Integrity and Performance

Referential integrity refers to the practice of embodying business rules in data structures. For example, if a zip code is not in the master zip code table, it is invalid and will not be accepted. Referential integrity as a Web site performance enhancer has its place, particularly in transaction processing systems, but it comes with performance trade-offs. This checking requires cycles and time. Among these, referential integrity:

- Supposes there is only one business rule that relates data.

- Is complex to design and administer.

- Does not work well for large amounts of data.

For these reasons, formal referential integrity facilities of the DBMS are not recommended. If it is absolutely necessary to create referential integrity among several data structures, using application code rather than DBMS-supplied code is advisable.

Using update processing, Mary's record in the Web database would be updated to reflect the latest visit date—August 2—and she has an interest in fine arts. Using snapshot processing, the record in the Web would go untouched. Instead, a new record would be added, to make note of Mary's interest in fine art. Now two records exist for Mary Jones. A snapshot has been created; no update to her previous record has been done.

# Other Performance-Enhancing Techniques

A number of other techniques can be implemented to ensure a high level of performance of a data warehouse-enabled Web site. These include

- Moving small amounts of data.
- Using log tapes to monitor performance.
- Generating online reports.
- Creating rolling summary data.
- Physically colocating data.
- Processing data during off-hours.

- Avoiding repeat queries.
- Presequencing transactions.

We'll briefly examine each of these in turn.

## Moving Small Amounts of Data

Throughout the Web/CIF environment, it is wise to move small amounts of data frequently rather than move large amounts of data infrequently. Moving large amounts of data chokes the system, by requiring large resources for handling; moving large amounts of data also causes queues to form, which continue to grow while previous processes in the queue await completion. It is the queues that cause the greatest performance concern.

## Using Log Files

One of the most powerful performance features of the Web environment comes in the form of log files. (The term log "tape" is an eponym. It can actually be a disk file in emulation mode.) Log files are created as a by-product of Web processing. They contain a wealth of information all relating to the processing that has occurred in the Web environment. There are four very good reasons why using the log tape can enhance performance:

- The log file is created in any case, and further use of it comes at no incremental cost to Web processing,
- The log file contains a great deal of detail.
- The log tape can be taken offline for processing.
- Once the log file has been created, it can be moved to a server other than the Web server for processing.

Combined, these reasons make processing against the log file a very smart strategy. In many Web environments, it is the log tape that is used to capture and access clickstream data.

## Generating Online Reports

A simple way to save considerable resources in the Web environment is to generate online reports. Online reports make sense when the organization runs the same report repeatedly. Each time someone requests the same report, considerable system resources are required to generate it. Once a clear pattern of use has been established for any report, it's a good idea to create the report once, and put it online, so that people can access it readily.

## Creating Rolling Summary Data Structures

In some Web environments, there is the possibility of creating what is called *rolling summary data*. Figure 6.11 shows some simple rolling summary files. The tables in the figure contain daily data, weekly data, and monthly data. At the end of each day, a record is created to summarize the activity that has transpired throughout the day. At the end of the week, and at the end of the month, records reflecting those time periods are created.

Rolling summary data is useful, when, for example, a number of people want to see data for a specific period of time. The detailed records do not have to be constantly accessed to create the same data. As such, rolling summary structures of data can save huge amounts of machine processing power. In addition to saving large amounts of machine cycles, rolling summary data can greatly condense data, and therefore save storage space as well.

Rolling summary data is not, however, generally applicable. There are some types of data that do not lend themselves to a rolling summary structure, such as attribute data about the individual (i.e. address). The

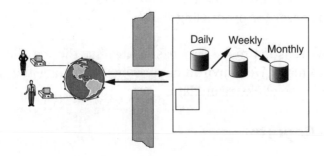

**Figure 6.11**  Implementing rolling summary data structures.

Web designer must ensure that rolling summary structures are useful and applicable before specifying this technique. This can best be done by consulting with the business users.

## Physically Collocating Data

When different types of data are used together regularly, performance can often be enhanced by physically collocating the data—that is, putting it in the same physical block. For example, if three tables contain data that is used together regularly, the Web designer can specify that a single record be created to hold the data types that are accessed at the same time. By doing this, the Web designer optimizes the performance of the system, because only one I/O is needed to access the collocated data, whereas three would be needed to access the data stored if it were stored in separate tables.

The design trade-off to physically collocating data is that it creates redundant data, and system resources are required to create and update the collocated data.

## Off-Hours Processing

To minimize contention for system resources during peak periods of processing in the Web environment, it is advisable—if at all possible—to delay the running of long sequential processes until ample machine resources are available. Performance is greatly enhanced when transactions do not have to compete for resources.

Often, for e-businesses, the sun never sets on the workday—in particular, if it is attracting visitors from around the world. Nevertheless, in any Web environment, processing peaks and valleys can be identified, by careful monitoring. Once the valleys have been identified, they can be relegated as the times to run long-sequence processes.

## Repeat Queries

Queries, like reports, are often run repeatedly. For any query that is run repeatedly, it makes sense to run the query once then post the results online. The Web administrator can determine which queries are being run repeatedly by monitoring the Web environment.

## Presequence Transactions

The optimal way to handle transactions that are going to be run sequentially against data in the Web environment is to presequence the transactions in the database. The effectiveness of this approach depends, of course, on there being a physical sequence to the data stored in the Web databases.

# Educating End Users to Improve Performance

Investing in education for those end users who need to access data in the Web environment can pay handsome dividends to the e-business. Training should, of course, be done prior to turning end users loose to access the data. Topics to address in any end-user training should include:

- Proper use of the tools used to access and analyze Web data
- Definition of the data that should and should not be accessed
- How to structure a call to the database
- Times of day that are best for various activities
- What to expect when issuing a call
- What data resides in the different databases

Education can be in the form of classes or can be informal working sessions with key developers, onsite education seems to be more readily accepted.

# Summary

From this chapter it should be clear that performance must be addressed at all levels of the Web environment: selecting hardware and determining its scalability; indexing data; designing data; defining the workload, monitoring the environment, managing data volume. All these factors and more must be addressed to achieve optimal levels of performance.

Equally important is that performance be built into the system from the beginning, and thereafter constantly be monitored and adjusted. Following is a checklist of standards for building in system performance:

- Access data from the ODS, not the data warehouse.
- Condense data from the data warehouse to the ODS so that it is very efficient to access.
- Create arrays when the data is used together on a frequent basis.
- Merge tables when data is used together on a frequent basis.
- Create redundant data when the same element of data is used in many places.
- Summarize and aggregate data when usage warrants.
- Avoid generating many I/Os in the same transaction.
- Use indexes to create an efficient path to data.
- Monitor data to track what is going on inside the system.
- Enlarge the processor when capacity is depleted.
- Use a parallel architecture for scalable performance enhancement.
- Manage volumes of data based on frequency of access.

# CHAPTER 7

# Data Storage Technologies for E-Business

**E**ffective Internet applications require a storage architecture that is extremely robust. What was operationally acceptable in a brick-and-mortar environment is totally unacceptable in e-commerce. Scheduling downtime for performing backups or system testing is not acceptable in a community of users whose expectations are 24/7, 365-days-a-year availability.

How is it possible to design storage capacity for universal availability? The purpose of this chapter is to answer that question, by examining the issues related to information storage and access where demands for performance and availability cannot be compromised. As with all technology, there is a trade-off between reliability, performance, and cost. This chapter will walk through the relevant factors necessary to make a useable choice.

## The Nature of Data Storage

Data has certain characteristics that affect how it is captured, stored, and made available to users over time. Data is

- Continuous in the real world, but discrete in storage.
- Persistent over time, yet also potentially perishable.
- Valuable only insofar as it can be accessed.

The following sections examine each of these characteristics as they affect system performance.

## Discrete versus Continuous Information

In the real world, information exists as a continuous stream. If we try to emulate what is seen in a device, the information is recorded in "frames," or pictures. When a film is run, the frames are played back at a speed that is faster than the receiver channel provided by the human eye can detect. Thus, the brain perceives the information flow as continuous, meaning that each unit, while discrete, is perceived as continuous.

This illustrates the dilemma of information management: the units in which data is stored are more an accident of history and of manufacturing efficiencies than a natural response to the information continuum. The more continuous and detailed the information is, the more important the capacity and reliability factors become.

## Persistence

Simply put, persistence is existence over a period of time. For information to be of value, it must have persistence. The value of data in an Internet environment is very different from that in a traditional environment. In a traditional operational environment, persistence largely depends on the functional nature of the system. For example, accounts payable, order entry, accounts receivable, and general ledgers all have well-defined time intervals for detailed data. At regular intervals, the data is summarized and reduced in size. Thus, the persistence factor is dictated by functionality and organizational growth, with the bulk of the data persistent in detail for a relatively short period of time, usually from time of capture (T0) to T0 + 90 days. This is described as the *formula of data value.*

Persistence in an e-business data warehousing environment is totally different. There, persistence is dictated by the use of the data for strategic reasons. Most often, in retailing, marketing requirements set the persistence level. Thus, if true trending analysis is performed, 27 months of data, or three repetitive seasons, are required, especially for such staple items as consumer electronics and appliances. Figure 7.1 illustrates the need for three seasons of data for trends analysis with durable products. This long period of detailed data retention varies by industry. In the case of the pharmaceutical industry, where drug interaction is a concern, for analytical reasons, the minimum persistence period is set at 30 years. Once again the formula of data value can be calculated with perhaps less precision but within acceptable known parametric boundaries because of business liability and risk issues associated with people's health.

This new order of magnitude is perhaps somewhat troubling to those who have planned for conventional operational systems; they are still within the realm of size projection by conventional technique (although with much less precision). Figure 7.2 illustrates the relative size differential between a conventionally structured DSS and e-business data warehousing.

Three-Year Trend

Winter
Dec 1999

Winter
Dec 2000

Winter
Dec 2001

Sales

Gas Prices Rise

**Figure 7.1**    Trending analysis and data persistence.

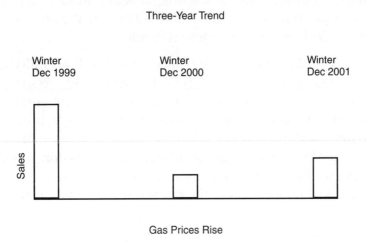

**Expectation of Availability**
**Brick-and-Mortar Business**

Reporting
Detail Traditional
Business

90 Days

Reporting Detail
E-Business DW

810 Days

**Figure 7.2**    Size comparison of traditional DSS and e-business data warehousing.

## Latency

Application latency is the time it takes before the timeliness of the data as returned to the application either impacts the application adversely in performance or loses intrinsic value. An example of negative performance is when the speed of data return physically slows the application to the point at which the wait time is noticeable by users. An example of intrinsic value loss is when a trading research application returns an answer after the active market factors have changed.

There are many forms of latency. There is latency in the code, latency in the operating system, latency in the communication wires, and naturally, latency in the storage. Figure 7.3 illustrates some sources of latency.

Latency is sometimes described as "path length." Path length is usually applied to the total time it takes to transfer data. Traditional mainframe-based tools can measure path length well. However, in the open-system, multiplatform world, this is much more difficult.

Network latency is often measured by "ping" time. The Ping utility sends out a packet to a defined network address. The utility measures the time from when the packet is sent to when an acknowledgment is received. While this is a crude measure of interplatform path length, it does not reflect any intraplatform latency. Further, some utilities that report intraplatform performance actually skew the utilization numbers because of the need to use internal cycles to run the utilities. The more intelligent storage devices, such as the integrated cache disk arrays, use

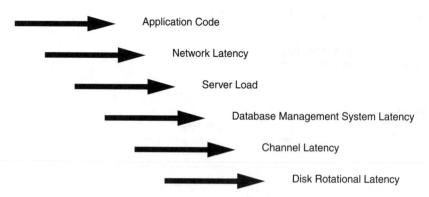

**Figure 7.3**  Sources of latency.

passive monitoring technology to "listen" on the common bus structures for activity. Because the relationship between the bus and the listening device is passive, the listening device uses no cycles that are allocated to productive work. The Integrated Cache Disk Array (ICDA) tends then to report accurately the CPU-to-storage path length or latency. (The ICDA is explained more fully in a later section.)

Unfortunately, there is little accurate reporting of path length in the application side of the open-systems world. Thus, from a 50,000 foot perspective, it is difficult to easily diagnosis where in a complex world the latency is introduced. In the end, the best insurance against latency problems in an e-business environment is to go long on horsepower and long on bandwidth. The hardware-related infrastructure costs represent in reality less than 15 percent of the total e-business investment. Doubling capacity over the predicted level is an insurance approach to business success. That is, typically, manpower is diverted from revenue-generating applications to manage infrastructure change. By overbuilding the initial infrastructure to avoid latency and capacity problems, a longer period of productivity is obtained during the e-business development cycle. This typically results in a faster time-to-market, higher market penetration, and quicker profitability cycle. In e-business, these factors become critical to success.

## Access

Information that is inaccessible is of no value. In order to assure access, the right delivery mechanism must be available. If the "pipe" to store data is too small, the application slows. Likewise, if the pipe to retrieve the data is too small, the customer becomes frustrated. Here, again, the continuum problem surfaces. In the best of all possible worlds, each application should obtain enough capacity, on demand, to maintain optimal performance in both directions. Unfortunately, while storage media has rapidly evolved, the pipes have not developed as rapidly. Changes in the communications infrastructure are slower in coming due to the level of management consensus needed to adopt these changes.

## Storage Capacity and Performance

Once upon a time, there was only one place to store data in a system. Today, large systems use multiple storage devices, and e-businesses typically use a

## Information versus Data

It is the process of aggregation and interpretation that turns data into information. Information derived by aggregation and interpretation has a life of its own. In general, the more aggregated the information, the longer the period of persistence in a brick-and-mortar business. It is assumed that that all of the business value in the atomic data has been extracted and that only summarized data has continuing business value. Thus, point-of-sales (POS) data may not be interesting after several quarters, but weekly sales information will continue to be interesting for longer periods of time. Figure 7.4 illustrates the relationship between aggregation and persistence in data for uses other than exploration and e-business.

It is not clear that the preceding assumption is true in the e-business world. E-businesses are still trying to learn what the real value of data is—and, for that matter, where the line between data and information actually lies. (This subject is more fully explored in Chapters 8 and 9 on information analysis and exploration.)

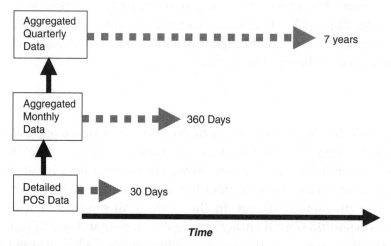

**Figure 7.4**   Aggregation and persistence over time.

mix of devices. These devices have very different characteristics. Some are capable of reconfiguration; others are not. Some are good for delivering a predictable and continuous stream of data; other devices are good for fast small-record recovery. The performance characteristics of such storage "containers" can be identified as shown in Figure 7.5. The concept of storage containers as shown in this figure supports the building of the kind of

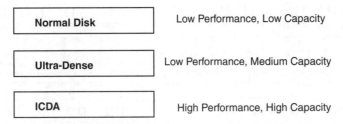

**Figure 7.5** Storage containers and their characteristics.

heterogeneous storage infrastructure common to e-business systems. Using different containers allows data to be sent to a container of appropriate speed or cost so as to assure maximum utility at minimum cost risk.

The following sections will describe hierarchically each basic type of storage container.

# Caching

Cache is nothing more than memory. In a perfect world, all data would exist in memory, and the information would be instantaneously available. But there are a few reasons why this world is not perfect. For one, memory is expensive. Two, the fastest types of memory need power to retain information, although there are other types of memory that retain information without power. Finally, to some degree, information in memory is vulnerable to destruction from a number of sources, most frequently human error. Thus, in our less than perfect reality, cache is a transient area used to speed the flow of information, but it is never the permanent repository of data.

## *Integrated Cache Disk Arrays*

The Integrated Cache Disk Array (ICDA) is largely the invention of the EMC Corporation. In the early 1990s, it was recognized that the time it took a disk to physically rotate and find the relative location of an item of data (referred to as the "locality of reference") caused severe processing delays. An engineer, Moshe Yanai, recognized that inserting a large generic cache between the disk and the host allowed for the buffering of information in and out of disk. But in order to fully leverage the cache, code needed to be written to signal an end-of-channel when data was written to cache instead of to disk. Further, whereas the cache

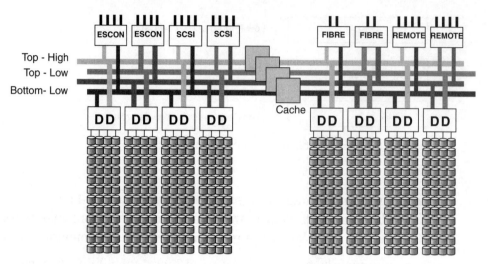

**Figure 7.6** ICDA architecture.

assumed responsibility for signaling an end-of-channel, data integrity became the responsibility of the storage array. This required full redundancy, battery backup, and error recovery. The net result is that the integrated cache disk array offloads substantial processing onto the ICDA and off of the host platform. Figure 7.6 illustrates a typical ICDA architecture.

In an e-commerce environment, the ability to isolate and determine functional requirements is key to scaling. Thus, the principle role of the platform becomes one of applying the business rules and functions while relegating information management to the ICDA. Virtually all very large storage requirements today are handled by the ICDA.

## Controller-Based Rack and Stack Arrays

With controller-based rack-and-stack storage, a single tray of drives is connected to the platforms by two controllers. Figure 7.7 illustrates the rack-and-stack architecture. These controllers are either full processors or are firmware-based devices. In either case, they provide alternate pathing to the data.

Rack-and-stack storage provides a higher degree of reliability than inboard disk, with improved performance. It does not, however, provide the higher-level functionality provided by the ICDA. Thus, typically, the higher-level functions like load balancing and mirror imaging are provided by host-based software, which reduces processing cycles available for use by applications.

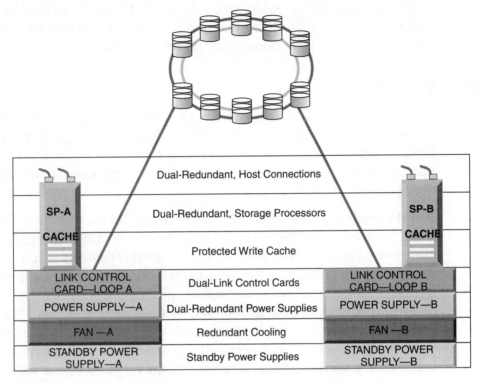

**Figure 7.7** Rack-and-stack architecture.

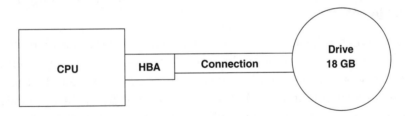

**Figure 7.8** Standard disk architecture.

## Conventional Disks

Conventional disks are usually installed in the server itself. Figure 7.8 illustrates the conventional disk architecture. These disks provide only a minimal level of performance and reliability. In the early development, or proof-of-concept stage, these devices are adequate. The problem is that once an e-application is brought online, reliability and scalability become critical to business operations. Thus, the use of conventional disk technology becomes the system's Achilles' heel. It is very often the high stress of a real-world application that causes a disk to fail, despite it having passed conventional manufacturing tests.

## Ultra-Dense Disks

The latest evolution of disk technology is the ultra-dense disk, which is architecturally similar to conventional disk technology. The driving force behind the use of ultra-dense technology is cost. The data transfer rate of the ultra-dense technology is still in the same range as conventional disks.

To effectively leverage ultra-dense technology in an e-environment, it must be used in an appropriate way. Two very different application classes are the best candidates. The first class is relatively inactive mass storage applications. This includes deep-records retrieval applications, typically associated with document processing (for example, for archival-records retention as required by regulatory agencies). The second class consists of applications that are focused on a predictable stream of data delivery in a sequential order. The common term for this is bit streaming. Bit streaming is most frequently associated with Internet delivery of audio or video services. In both cases, large files are delivered at a fixed rate of delivery. In these cases, the ratio of data volume to transfer rate that is found in ultra-dense technology is very acceptable.

Ultra-dense technology works best with applications that mitigate the size of data stored in comparison to the rate of data usage. High-speed entirely random access is not a viable alternative, because transient utilization spikes will negatively impact the performance profile of the applications. In the first class of applications just referenced, the transfer rate is relatively low compared to the volume of the data. In the second class of application, the transfer rate is fixed, and the access method is sequential. In both classes, high transient utilization rates are avoided, and thus, as a rule, the application is not subjected to peak overloads.

## Optical Storage

Optical technology can serve as either online or near-line storage. It can be used in either permanently mounted drives or in a jukebox arrangement. (Figure 7.9 illustrates the optical technology architecture.)

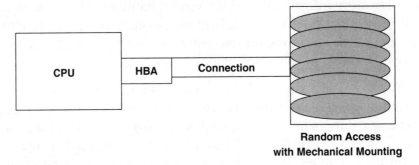

**Figure 7.9** Optical disk jukebox architecture.

Until recently, optical technology was read-only. Currently, read-write media is rapidly becoming the standard. The problem is that the access speed for optical technology is substantially slower than standard magnetic media technology. Further, the jukebox mechanical technology is substantially weaker than the mechanical technology used by tape silos. Applications in e-business require a highly reliable infrastructure capable of withstanding short high-stress periods. Therefore, the usual attraction of optical, high data density at lower cost, is rapidly undermined in an e-commerce environment.

In several cases, Web sites developed originally for optical media have moved content to ultra-dense technology at the same or lower price points, with much higher levels of reliability. In some cases, this has been done by emulation; that is, having the optical devices emulated on ultra-dense magnetic media.

Another consideration is that optical technology has undergone rapid change in both media format and density. Thus, there are widespread issues related to compatibility of both old and new media. This is not the case with magnetic media, which, despite changes in transfer rate and density, remains totally transferable and compatible across old and new media. While optical has found a home in desktop and portable computing, other than as a distribution media, its role in e-business is still questionable.

## Near-Line Storage

By definition, near-line storage is still tape, and is primarily used for archiving. Near-line storage supports procedures and practices that can be used to store information using existing facilities. Thus, when data is rolled off a large data warehouse in an e-commerce environment, the same facilities and procedures used to produce backups can be employed to archive valuable business data.

Near-line storage can be used to store vast amounts of data for long periods of time at reasonable cost; however, it is not a cost panacea. In near-line storage, data is unloaded in sequential format, so it can take longer to perform unload and reload processes. In traditional business, the interval from data creation to in-depth analysis may be long enough to make such reload time requirements inconsequential. But in e-business, the rate of change in the business can be so rapid that such delays will erode the value of the information being analyzed.

A second factor to consider involves the order of magnitude of information that is needed to understand how the customer got to a particular location on the Net. In traditional brick-and-motor business, these patterns of client navigation to a business are well known and highly exploited. In the e-commerce world, new patterns of navigation are invented on an almost daily basis. They include site-to-site linking, search engine linkages, mail-to-site linkages, and a whole new series of linkages based upon the shift from wired to wireless technology.

Now that we've examined the various types of storage technologies, let's look at how they relate to one another in what we call the "storage hierarchy."

# The Fast Pace of Innovation in Storage Technology

In a complex society, the ability to navigate information has transcended the ability to navigate space as a measure of societal competency. As in all aspects of society, need creates the demand for technology innovation. Storage is no exception. For example, current ultra-dense storage technologies for server implementations provides 100- to 1,000-gigabyte units of storage capacity. It can be safely assumed that the 100-gigabyte level will be surpassed within an 18-month interval. The standard disk technology of 73- to 183-gigabyte technologies will jump to the 183- to 500-gigabyte levels in the same time period. In both cases, no new technical breakthroughs are required to hit these new levels.

## The Storage Hierarchy

In the information arena, there is a natural data storage hierarchy. Figure 7.10 illustrates this hierarchy. The lowest tier is near-line storage. The term near-line is, actually, a misnomer, given that unconnected information is in fact "near line." This implies media that requires human interaction to make it available. Clearly, tapes in a manual library fall into this category. However, digital videodisk, digital audio disks, and CD-ROM also fall here as well.

Tier 2 devices take the media and put them into an automated mounting facility. Again audio, video, data disks, and tapes can be managed. The differentiation is the media in an automated facility can be mounted without human intervention, and the mount time is substantially faster. The original objective on tier 1 devices is the cheapest possible media cost at the expense of human cost and time delay. Tier 2 devices provide faster access to information but with a higher capital investment price. The capital investment offsets the high personnel cost associated with near-line. In both tier 1 and tier 2 devices, the slow access times involved dictate essentially large data sets accessed in a sequential order. While disks of various types are capable of random access, the slow mount times involved make random access concerns irrelevant.

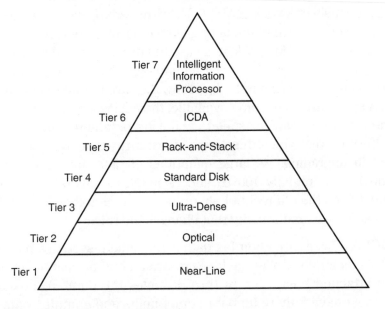

**Figure 7.10**   The storage hierarchy.

Tier 3 devices are continuously mounted data sets. While optical disk devices are capable of performing in this manner, tier 3 devices are usually magnet disk drives that are defined in the industry as JBOD, an acronym for "just a bunch of disks." While capable of either sequential or random access, no optimization takes place. Thus, the speed of the device impedes the speed of the computer to the extent it waits for data to be read or written. The other limitation of JBOD is reliability. Media failure means data loss. Data loss may or may not be an acceptable business risk, based on how transitory the data is. The problem in e-business is that data that at one point is assumed to be transitional can have undiscovered value. Therefore, any data loss may have a negative business impact.

Tier 4 devices elevate the level of reliability. This is usually done in host-based software. Several companies, most notably Veritas, have provided this level of reliability for years. The mirroring or parity checking is accomplished by using the principle of duplexing. Duplexing involves committing data to separate devices before telling the host application that the data is committed. Duplexing is software-based mirroring at the expense of host cycles. It provides reliability but at the expense of application performance on a saturated system.

Tier 5 devices resort to firmware to provide some level of RAID (redundant array of inexpensive disks) protection. While there are many forms of RAID, the highest level is RAID 1. The firmware provides the necessary level of protection without impacting host application performance. Some devices such as the IBM Shark array use full processors, while others, like the Compaq arrays, use firmware technology. These devices are highly reliable and perform efficiently. Typically, they are not upgradeable. Thus, as higher speed drives become available, the necessary bandwidth to support the increased transfer speed cannot be obtained, causing obsolescence. Further, the typical high capacity of array-type systems creates a problem in upgrading. As large quantities of data are concentrated in these devices, minimally 100GB and as much as several terabytes, the movement from the old technology to the new technology is nontrivial. It requires software functionality that changes the rules.

Tier 6 ICDA devices are complex data management systems in their own right. This technology uses cache to return an end-of-channel command to each attached host, then in turn destages the data. To destage the data, it must have fully redundant components and complex data verification technology. Additionally, this level of device has the capability to replicate copies of the data, either internally for enhanced functionality like concurrent backup, or across distance for business continuance. To date, only two companies have technology in this class: EMC and HDS (Hitachi).

Tier 7 devices are at the current top of the hierarchy. These devices incorporate all of the features of tier 6 but add enhanced functionality. This enhanced functionality includes the capability to do high-speed inter-platform data transmission while simultaneously changing data types and values. Such interaction includes the standard EBCDIC-to-ASCII translation, as well as actual value substitution. This is accomplished by leveraging the emulation capability inherent in these devices (necessary to allow for simultaneous connection to disparate hosts), as well as the capability to invoke standard transformation tools through a supplied application-programming interface (API). The next effect is to center the data management issues solely in the tier 7 devices, and free all attached platforms for applications process use only. Currently, only EMC provides products in this class.

## Building Storage Infrastructure

In e-business, storage infrastructure can be built from any of the seven tiers of the storage hierarchy; the key is to understand how to select the appropriate infrastructure for the business architecture. Figure 7.11 illustrates the key factors in making the appropriate decision.

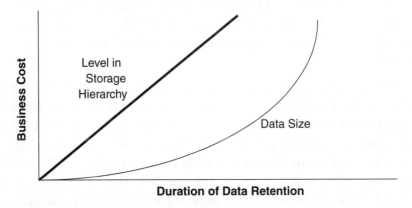

**Figure 7.11**   Factors for selecting containers in storage hierarchy.

In the proof-of-concept stage, any device will work. The criterion of support usually dictates a portable demonstration system for venture capitalist and funding angels. This type of system can run on a disk attached to a laptop. For the sake of speed and simplicity, no elaborate technology is needed. Once the system is online, however, requirements change rapidly. The key issues then are the cost of maintaining large volumes of data, the growth in business functionality, and the value of the data. If the business objective is to minimize labor cost as it relates to infrastructure maintenance, then the proper strategy is to maintain as much information as high in the hierarchy as possible. The reason is not technology. The top-tier devices have the highest capacity and lowest risk of failure, as well as requiring the fewest people to maintain. In reality, the tier 6 and 7 devices transfer the maintenance activity to the provider, thereby freeing internal staff to focus on revenue-generation activity. The tier 7 providers also have near-line technology to transfer data from the arrays at speeds not available at lower levels. This requirement occurs because current technology concentrates in excess of 20 terabytes into a space equivalent to three standard racks. This intense concentration of data requires the capability to remove large quantities to a near-line environment either locally or remotely without platform involvement.

A second consideration is whether the value of data is fully known within a reasonable period of capture. Consider this: many publishers consigned their past issues of magazines to the category of dead information. For years, the industry allowed consumers to recover information on a cost plus basis: if a desired back issue was requested, it was actually photocopied, and an expense fee was charged. In the current Web world, these same publishers are in a race to digitize this same material due to its value as a form of knowledge capital. It is of value, however, only if it is easily accessible online, and thus saleable on demand.

As e-businesspeople become more and more savvy, in terms of exploration warehousing and data mining, new requirements to extract and exploit transient clickstream detail will emerge. The large scale of the data, coupled with the reload speed requirement, dictates against an architecture requiring the use of high-tier devices (6 or 7) to act as a large-scale information cache, surrounded by high-speed near-line devices to load or unload this cache without involving extensive manpower.

## Bricks and Cement Blocks

How do you decide which storage technology to use? One extreme view is take many small units of inexpensive storage ("bricks") and assemble them into a storage matrix. But this can result in problems with reliability. These "bricks" are a commodity product, with a short lifespan. Though testing is better than it was years ago, reliability problems persist with such commodity storage devices. The reason is a sales model that by definition makes the product to a limited profitability model.

Storage manufacturers are increasingly driven to build very large drives, which are much more profitable to them. (The cost of manufacturing an 18GB drive and a 36GB drive are almost identical. From a cost-benefit basis, the 36GB drives spread the cost out over more capacity. Thus, the classic measure of cost per megabyte drives the manufacturer to produce higher and higher capacity drives, driving down consumer price per unit while driving up profitability per unit for the manufacturer.) Very large drives, however, provide a problem from an architectural standpoint; they can easily turn into "cement blocks." The problem is that capacity tends to increase on a technology curve much more rapidly than transfer rate. Transfer rate is highly tied to the speed of the drive. This problem is overcome in the higher levels of the storage hierarchy by logical segmentation (partitioning).

# The Wireless Matrix

Wireless technologies change the nature of storage required for e-business. To be effective, real-time wireless applications require storage that minimizes latency and optimizes storage capacity, along with sufficient processing horsepower to handle increased volumes of data.

For example, consider the development of Global Positioning Systems (GPS). As these systems moved from military to civilian use in the automobile industry, positioning based solely on latitude and longitude became almost meaningless. To bring value to the technology, visual conventions needed to be superimposed over the reference position. The answer was to provide map information, such as highways, routes, and waypoints, in order to achieve success. With the advent of memory modules in the 4Mb to 64Mb range, it became possible to download sufficiently large pieces of maps into a device with the horsepower necessary to dynamically display the application in real time. Today, virtually every automobile manufacturer has begun the process of integrating this technology into their product offerings.

The so-called handshaking between the large data warehouses and the local data-intensive applications has just now begun to occur. The same GPS device continues to dynamically acquire data as to the local position of the vehicle while in use. The same device offers information on restaurants, attractions, and filling stations. This device currently has the capability to upload data via a conventional serial computer interface. Clearly, the systems installed as standard interfaces in the next generation of automobiles will upload this data. The value of this data is incalculable. It will be used for predictive load balancing in a transportation network, a new form of roadside advertising without signs, as well as the much-desired "auto-pilot" for the tired driver. The key lies in time, horsepower, storage, and locality of reference.

Wireless communication moves the locality of reference closer to the real world and the real user. It is impossible at this time to say how large these data stores will be; what can be said is that all that is known now will shift again, and this shift will be an order of magnitude larger than any known paradigm shift to date.

## Summary

Clickstream data in e-business represents a change in the order of magnitude of data management from that of traditional brick-and-mortar businesses. In selecting a storage infrastructure, the total cost of operation and ownership must be examined. While currently there are seven levels to the storage hierarchy, the lower the level, the more labor-intensive the data management problem becomes. If the business model requires the acquisition and retention of large-scale data for primary use and secondary exploration, then the most reasonable solution is to partner with high-tier providers. These providers offset the higher cost of acquisition by assuming more maintenance and technology change risk, and lowering the internal cost of support for handling massive amounts of data. Ultimately, selection of the appropriate storage technology should be based on the business model, not strictly on technology itself.

# CHAPTER 8

# Applications for E-Business

W hen traditional brick-and-mortar businesses add a Web component, analytical applications change. Examining these changes helps to understand the role of information analysis in e-business. That's the purpose of this chapter, to determine which analytical applications remain the same, which change, and which are new to the scene of the Web environment.

## Defining Analytical Applications

Analytical applications provide the first level of conversion of data into usable business information. These applications summarize data by time unit, organizational hierarchy, product hierarchy or geography, in such a way as to provide information for making business decisions. The metaphorical distinction is the difference between a check register and the balance in a checking account. The register tells the account owner about each transaction, but does not tell the account owner anything about his or her current financial position. The account statement tells the owner where the account stands, and whether there is a net cash increase or decrease from the previous period. Analytical applications for e-business are not very different from those used in other businesses. The primary difference arises due to the volatile nature of e-business. For example, while most applications remain the same, the periodicity may be very different. It is worthwhile reviewing the various classic applications and seeing how time affects them in an e-business environment.

## Classic Financial and Operational Reporting

Core business financial reporting functions remain unchanged in an e-business environment. What changes is the time element. All of the traditional structured operations still need to be analyzed, but on a much more frequent schedule. Monthly and quarterly cycles common to brick-and-mortar businesses translate into daily and hourly events in the e-business environment.

This change in periodicity has been observed before. When mortgage rates became highly volatile in the 1980s, mortgage institutions that were used to changing rates on a quarterly basis found themselves in crisis. One of the largest lenders in the United States, which had built a high volume but low rate of product analysis infrastructure, virtually had to close up shop because of its inability to first report, then analyze, and finally act in a highly changeable market place. (At the peak of volatility, rates were changing three times in an eight-hour period.) In a similar fashion, reporting in an e-business environment must accelerate to match the periodicity needed to support timely decision making.

For e-business applications, some traditional architectural techniques for building applications may become liabilities. One of these techniques is often referred to as "the close." Closing designs usually encompass a technique that sums up details and creates a "bucket," or summary, value based upon fixed time intervals. Unfortunately, in e-business, the periodicity of meaningfulness may or may not be known. Figure 8.1 illustrates the rate change in different business modes. Further, Web events may change the value. Examples of this phenomenon can be found in the real world. Events such as the death of Princess Diana or the success of the television show *Big Brother* alter the demand on a particular site on the Web. When a surge in popularity drives large numbers of users to a particular site, the usual measurement scheme such as hits per hour during

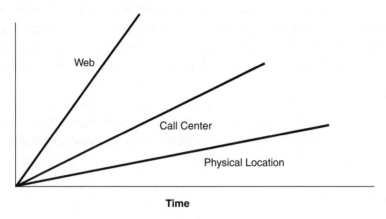

**Figure 8.1** Different rates of change.

a day need to be altered into more meaningful measurements like hits per minute or hits per second.

Further, the reporting scale quickly alters. Instead of being the well-known bimodal curve as is typical or traditional in a brick-and-mortar business, the curve often returns to a traditional two-tailed normal distribution with the distribution centered upon the event time.

Though it's true that, like other businesses, e-businesses only need to report to the financial community quarterly, they do need financial reporting capable of tracking revenue generation and orders taken by hour. The reason for this lies in the balance between revenue and risk in an e-business. In brick-and-mortar businesses, the period to correct a financial problem can reasonably be one or more quarters. In e-business, the customer can find an alternate provider so easily that the customer base can, literally, vote with their fingers in a matter of hours—the next provider is only a click away. Therefore, measures such as revenue per minute or net new customers per hour become meaningful, even necessary, units of reporting.

## Customer-Centric Reporting

Traditional business relies on some degree of interpersonal interaction, such as making personal phone calls, sharing meals, and giving gifts. In e-business, the interaction between the customer and the enterprise is Web-based. Traditional measures such as revenue per customer become business measures, but don't necessarily measure the effectiveness of customer interactions. What are the new measures of customer centricity? These new measures include customer retention, churn, and site time. Customer retention has always been a traditional measure of success in the brick-and-mortar world. How, then, in an e-business environment, is customer retention different? For one thing, the path from the electronic front door to the electronic back door is a very short path. The time is a matter of seconds, and the customers don't stop to impulse buy or browse on the way out. A second issue is how to establish customer intimacy.

## Churn Analysis

Churn analysis is defined as the ability to ascertain how and why customers stay, as opposed to leave, a supplier of goods and services. Customer churn is closely associated with volatile market or business conditions. There is well-known precedent for both. Right after the deregulation of the telecommunications business, the long-distance vendors, including AT&T, MCI and Sprint, experienced churn for the first time. And they weren't prepared for it. Most industry executives were trained in a regulated industry in which the customer was a prisoner of a single supplier. Customers now had virtually unlimited mobility. The issue of customer turnover became a monumental problem. Once it sank in that the cost of new customer acquisition was very expensive, the industry began to actively implement place retention programs.

The same problem exists in the e-business world today. Too few sites manage their customer base on the basis of retention rather than hit rate. The portal sites use an array of services to retain head count. However, few, if any, sites run customer loyalty or customer affinity programs, despite the fact that such programs have proved to be extremely effective in the brick-and-mortar world.

## Customer Intimacy Analysis

Many papers have been published on the issue of customer relationship management (CRM). But when questioned, few managers can define what CRM means. CRM is nothing more than understanding how well an enterprise understands its customers and how well its products and services are tailored to the needs of those customers. The analysis of customer intimacy is based on the ability of the e-business to "listen" to the customer. Listening to the customer essentially means providing a vehicle for the customer to articulate his or her perception of the e-business; associate that information with the e-business-based customer data, external customer data; and score the value of that information. That data then can be scored on the basis of the level of customer involvement with the e-business, as well as the value of the customer to the e-business. This is then used to adjust the amount of resources to allocate to a particular customer.

In a brick-and-mortar environment, resources are viewed in terms of people, time, and money. In an e-business, the resource can be allocated on a secondary processing priority. For example, decisions about using specific data mining tools can be determined based upon a predefined profile. Profiling simply defined is a method to determine what technique is appropriate to the data and the business problem.

## Product-Centric Reporting

In e-business, goods and services need to be categorized in the same manner as they are for traditional brick-and-mortar business. Thus, individual items are typically categorized by stock-keeping number (SKU) and then grouped into meaningful categories that can be analyzed from a business perspective. Thus, the category becomes the fundamental unit of business management.

In essence, each category is a way of compartmentalizing risk. Product managers may add or subtract individual items, but they manage by category. Dissimilar types of products can be homogenized into a category, thereby mitigating the risk of any individual product failure. Further, very different product categories can be compared based on normalized business measures. These measures include percentage growth in revenue, percentage growth in profit, and percentage turnover in SKU.

The concepts of managing the product dimension are well established in the marketing sciences. The key difference in e-business is once again time and volatility. In traditional business, marketing campaigns take months to construct. In kiosking, individual items are carefully selected for display in a physical plant. The intent is almost always *drag-through* or *cross-sell*. In drag-through, items in the same or closely related categories are displayed together. Thus, diapers, baby wipes, and baby lotion are displayed together. Assuming that all three are in a category called "baby supplies" the kiosk raises the probability that an individual who wanted diapers will buy the other products as well. The opposite concept is cross-sell. An example of cross-sell is the kiosk that displays chips and salsa. The salsa is probably in a chips category, while the salsa is usually displayed along with the canned vegetables. Clearly, these two products go together even though the delivery may be by different suppliers and supply chains. In the e-business world, the same pattern exists.

Multiple-product Web sites are typically organized and managed by category lines. This is because the visitor to the Web site usually visualizes product in terms of categories. Thus, an electronic consumer goods site will have categories of "audio," "computers," and "television" because this is how the consumer categorizes the real world. Further subcategories of television could include "HDTV," "wide screen," and "portable."

This is not to say that a single SKU could not or should not appear in multiple categories. In the real world, this happens. Figure 8.2 illustrates how a single SKU can and should belong in more than one category. Further, an item, which is specialized to a particular market, will appear in that category. A recent example of this is the portable television unit. This product is a television that is hung over the back seat of an automobile; children can plug in their various game units to play while the adult is driving. This particular device is not sold in the television or the consumer electronics department. Typically, it is found in the automotive section of a real or virtual store. This is an example of an SKU that is so specialized that the category strength of its specialized market place is more important than its generic category.

In e-business as in a traditional store, the display area—commonly the home page on a Web site—needs to be analyzed on a regular basis. This display area becomes the primary vehicle for high-velocity cross-sell. In

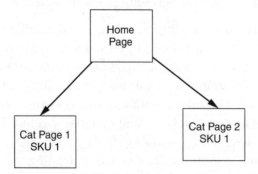

**Figure 8.2** Bill of materials data structure as it applies to Web site structure.

essence, the home page area is the highest-velocity area in the site; and by kiosking, at least two or more major product categories are simultaneously hit. The value of this page to category management cannot be overestimated. Thus, hit ratios and linking must be continuously analyzed in order to assure the maximum business value. The top category page at the site then becomes the critical space for drag-through kiosking. The lead space provides a mechanism to keep the customer within the site subarea. This space again is critical to increasing the product velocity and revenue generation of the site. In the brick-and-mortar metaphor, this is the entrance to each department. Constant analysis is required. In conventional business, the rate of change in this critical area is, at best, weekly. In e-business, these areas need to change, minimally, daily and possibly daily or hourly in a highly volatile e-business—for example, online gaming. In other e-businesses, such as specialized commodity sites, these areas need to vary based upon the personalization algorithm as well as on a time basis.

## Transactional Analysis

Just as in traditional business, the object of the Web site is to generate revenue. The transaction represents the contractual relationship between the consumer and the e-business. The difficulty in e-business is defining what constitutes a transaction. In a classic retail site, the transaction can be an electronically secured order. As most firms go through the transition from brick-and-mortar to click-and-mortar, the nature of a transaction becomes unclear. If a consumer goes to the Web site to shop, but consummates the transaction at a retail location, is that Web site any less important than the retail location in securing the business? Figure 8.3 illustrates the nature of a vector transaction in the new business model. Particularly in retailing, Web site, traditional location, call center, and catalog may all come into play in a single transaction. The complexity of the path to the final transaction is unique to a transformed e-business company.

In traditional retailing, indicators such as coupons, flyers, and retail advertising are measured by immediate short-term transactional impact. Thus, in campaign management, a location is targeted for increased performance, a campaign is begun by either print media or by broadcast, and the transactional impact is measured for the targeted location and/or product for the duration of the campaign. A delta in sales by a

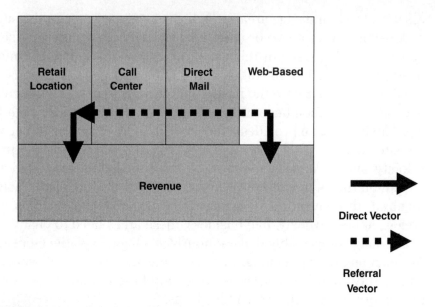

**Figure 8.3** New business model and vector approach.

percentage can then be analyzed on a cost-per-transaction basis. The combination of the velocity of business and the navigational path to the transaction transforms everything known about transactional analysis into a new level of complexity.

This new level of complexity—best called *vector analysis*—falls into the realm of exploration warehousing and out of the realm of classical analysis. Classical analytical applications are based on hypotheses that have been well proven over time. Thus, like axioms in mathematics, it is unnecessary to reprove them continuously. When, however, the path to revenue becomes complex and unpredictable, no axioms are possible. In a world with no axioms, the new axioms must be uncovered or—more properly—discovered. This discovery requires an exploration approach as opposed to an analytical approach. This discovery approach is the province of exploration warehousing.

## Analyzing Information-Only Web Sites

A large number of business Web sites offer few or no products for sale. These sites are primarily designed to attract the "right type" of individual for purposes of target marketing. The site derives its revenue by advertising and referral. The referral is typically by means of linking, but in some cases it is by traditional list preparation.

In these informational sites, the definition of a transaction differs from those in sales-focused sites. Typically, the transaction involves capturing critical information about the customer. If sufficient information is obtained to identify the customer, then a "transaction" has been completed. Sufficient information means that the data is of marketing use to a partner. The value of this information is contractual, set by the capture site and the end business partner that needs the value. The transfer of information on a contractual basis is what provides the revenue flow based on data.

Advertising revenue flow is based on the business-to-business value ascribed to the site based upon consensus of the community of interest. In short, the population of interest votes with their fingers, and that determines the business value of the site. The analytics of transactional analysis on these pure informational sites are solely based on measurements of site impact.

### Measuring Site Impact

Site review services essentially provide the same level of service as a movie reviewer. That is, they most often provide a rating without the explanation of why. In a brick-and-mortar company, in-store traffic is the fundamental measure of potential. You cannot derive revenue and profit from a customer, nor even sell to the customer, unless you get the customer into the store. In an e-business, the measure of store traffic is the "page hit." Particularly, the home page hit is the critical measure, since the home page is the hub of interaction between the company and its customers. Therefore, most Web sites, with the exception of limited service sites, have evolved into a design that is home page-centric.

## Internal Site Navigational Analysis

Once a potential customer enters an e-business site, the objective becomes complex. In a conventional store, the objective is simply to get the customer to buy and, if possible, add to the shopping basket. In a brick-and-mortar store, it is a reasonable expectation that if an individual enters the store he or she will buy. Though comparison shopping may occur in a store with products in the low- to mid-cost range, there is

## Multimedia Web Site Solutions

Several e-businesses have recognized that the future holds a multimedia solution. One such company, Millennium Telesis of New Jersey, has integrated Web site and call center technology with an icon that can be embedded on a page that calls a live operator and pushes that Web page to the operator. By recognizing the limits of a single technology, this approach moves to a more humanistic interaction that better meets the customer's expectations for service.

a higher degree of certainty that the shopper will buy if he or she finds the desired product. The challenge then is to add to the shopping cart by either cross-sell or drag-through.

In e-business, these phenomena still exist; however, the assumptions about buying behavior may be very different. For example, a visit to a site does not guarantee a sale. In observation, the exact opposite is true. In most business-to-customer (B2C) sites, the vast majority of hits are informational. The presumption of intent to purchase is simply not true. This changes the fundamental approach to customer understanding in e-business.

Further, in the sales process, a step takes place in all sales methodologies called *qualification*. During qualification, a salesperson ascertains basic requirements of setting up a sale. Is the customer looking for the product? What is the customer's time frame? Does the customer have money? Is feature/function part of the deciding factor? What obstacles exist to stop the acquisition from going forward? In e-business, the ability to qualify customers is limited. If the same sales process were followed in an e-business as in a traditional business, the required amount of interaction would undermine the essential drive of the e-customer—that drive being immediate gratification.

In e-business, then, the qualification process is inductive, and must be nonintrusive. How then can intent to purchase be measured? The answer lies in how well the customer can be retained at the Web site, since the longer the customer stays at the site, the more likely he or she is to make a purchase.

# Site Hang Time: Establishing Site Efficiency Baseline

As long as instant gratification is the driving force in e-business, time is the best measure of customer satisfaction. As long as a customer remains at a site, he or she is a potential customer. Just as page hit analysis is the indicator of "customers in the store," site hang time analysis is a critical analytical application for determining why customers stay in the store. There are plenty of reasons for hang time, which are not necessarily good reasons for customers to return to the site. These reasons include insufficient horsepower that negatively affects page response, poor infrastructure design, poor page design, and inadequate connection bandwidth to the Web.

These types of problems are all classified as *nonproductive path length*. Productive path length is the time it takes to return information, including execution of code and retrieval of data. The ratio of productive time to nonproductive time is a measure of efficiency in architectural design, not of user satisfaction and interest. Productivity analysis is necessary to establish a baseline number, to then determine the real customer-based concerns. Without this baseline number, it becomes impossible to do causal analysis on real customer concerns. Once the baseline is established, attention can be turned into how the site interacts with the customer. Baselines are established by testing in an unstressed environment.

(Note: In the world of B2C, the game is capturing and gratifying customers. In the game of business-to-business (B2B), the concern is accelerating a business process. This is more in line with the objectives of typical online transactional processing systems. For example, an effective B2B system might be designed to cut a business process from days to an hour by leading the user through a set of detailed questions.)

## Content-Based Internal Site Analysis

Once the customer is captured at the e-business site, it becomes interesting to examine how the customer interacts with the site. The customer may continue to "hang" at the site because the information he or she seeks can be found there. Or the customer may continue to stay at the site because the site links to information the customer needs; the "home" site can then be thought of as a nest of internal and external links.

When content is the reason the customer remains at the site, the number and duration of page hits becomes the unit of analysis. This analysis has two different results. One result has an operational impact on the infrastructure environment. If certain content pages have a long period of "residence" with frequent hits, these pages become candidates to be made cache-resident to speed up the entire site. The second piece of the analysis is content-driven. If the page experiences a long duration above and beyond the baseline analysis, then it can be assumed that the page has an intrinsically high content value. In content analysis, it becomes necessary to answer questions about what the content is and who is interested in it. It is the process of answering who, what, and why questions that is the interesting analysis. For the first time, the information worker enters the world of causal analysis to determine the attributes of the individuals who are exploring the site. (Chapter 9 provides in-depth coverage of the exploration of Web sites.)

Often, when there are discussions about content analysis, the problem of identifying the customer becomes an issue. While Web pages can easily be categorized by content, the visitor to the site is only identified by his or her IP address or by identification provided to the Web site via a registration process. This problem of proper identification is often viewed as insurmountable by the developer. The problem of net identification is neither insurmountable nor unknown to people who have worked in the world of "soft" or marketing data for years. A technique called soft linking is used to associate individuals into households in marketing data with acceptable levels of usability.

## Visit versus Buy Analysis

The measure of revenue takes many forms. One crude measure is revenue generation by visit. This requires tying an order to a site visit. To evaluate this data, the cookie becomes all-important. Secondary questions immediately emanate from the first question. Did the customer buy on the first visit? How many times did he or she visit before buying? What was the length of time he or she spent at the site before buying?

# Summary

Most e-business analysis is structurally identical to that for brick-and-mortar enterprises. In fact, it can be said that there is an equivalent to each and every function found in conventional business analysis. What differs is the time factor. In e-business, the rate of change is much faster than that for traditional business models. Thus, the speed and complexity of analysis must match the velocity of e-business interactions.

# CHAPTER 9

# Exploration in E-Commerce

**W**hat is meant by exploration in e-business? As laid out in the earlier work, *Exploration Warehousing* (Inmon, Terdeman, and Imhoff, John Wiley & Sons, 2000), exploration involves building an environment where information discovery can take place. In this environment, ideas are turned into hypotheses for testing. If a particular hypothesis pans out, then data mining techniques can be used to confirm its value for decision making.

This chapter examines how exploration in e-business differs from exploration in a brick-and-mortar company. Before we begin, however, it is important to point out that exploration is an evolving discipline, and while some practices are well accepted, others are subject to debate. Therefore, the ground we walk upon here is far from solid.

## Time

The speed of change in the e-business environment dictates a concomitant change in behavior in the utilization of information. In the traditional brick-and-mortar company, time is defined in terms of business process. Periods of time are viewed in terms of reporting periods. Thus, sales per week, sales per quarter, and sales per year are the time periods understood by traditional businesses. For these businesses, the focus of exploration is on reducing costs or improving sales within a conventional reporting period.

In e-business, the exact opposite is true! E-businesses are very sensitive to the impact of individual events, therefore exploration must focus on much shorter units of time if decision making is to be effective.

The event-driven nature of e-businesses is reflected by such phenomena as companies that launch a television event in order to promote a web event. A parallel to this exists in the telecommunications industry. For years, AT&T has maintained a wall of large-scale information screens in its Network Operating Center (NOC) in New Jersey. The screens graphically depict the switches and lines interconnected into the telephone network. In addition, other screens depict the data associated with stress loads at various points. The most interesting screens, however, carry standard broadcast information from a well-known news network. Why? The answer lies in the real world, not in the technology infrastructure. Events like an earthquake in Japan cause a worldwide load shift in demand. The seconds of time that the broadcast information provides enables the shifting of resources ahead of the load peaking.

In the real world, all forms of communication, including the Web, react to events in a similar manner. Today, media events such as movies and concerts have corresponding Web sites that support the sales and marketing efforts. The loading on these sites can only be managed by watching the external indicators of interest in the event being promoted. In the next section, we will look at how operational exploration can be used to ensure that sufficient resources are available to meet demand, thereby ensuring that the full revenue potential is realized.

## Operational Exploration

The need to align resources with demand in e-business follows a model that became very well known in the early days of industrialization. This model was formulated in the discipline of operations research. In operational research, time and motion are married to yield a result that is desired or known. The mechanics of operations research involve observation, analysis, and, finally, optimization. Typically, the desired outcome was defined in terms of time efficiency in order to maximize production and minimize cost. This is not very different in an e-business environment. Operational exploration involves the process of determining the potential parameters necessary to modify the infrastructure of the e-business plant to accommodate dynamic changes in the business.

This process can, however, be complicated in the web environment by the fact that many e-businesses are in a continual state of transformation. Think, for example, how some traditional phone companies have transformed themselves to become Internet service providers. Or how Amazon.com moved from being a bookseller to a seller of more general merchandise, including music and electronics.

As these enterprises transit through this journey, they are generally guided by a business plan. This strategic business plan is only a guideline, not a measurement of the journey. But often the journey will take the enterprise to an unanticipated way station. A case in point was the breakup of AT&T. While the ostensible breakup was a growth and manageability issue, clearly the long-lines division was intended to be a communications company.

## Classical Business Value and Exploration

Typically, in traditional business, exploration follows one of three areas of interest: customer, product, and transaction. In exploration, the explorer looks past the traditional analysis to test for new sources of business value. Often, the method is to subdivide the data within a dimension. Thus, a large slice of data may come from one of the three areas of interest or even a combination of areas. In general, exploration depends on empirical observation. In essence, the explorer has to have "a nose" for data.

As the data becomes more and more complex, the likelihood of success from casual observation decreases dramatically. In order to derive value from a casually observed phenomenon, the explorer moves to data mining techniques to ensure the integrity of the finding. In classical business analysis, the roles of exploration and mining are well-known and defined processes. The complexity of multiple paths to revenue and multiple revenue sources, sometimes called channels, may require a new model for exploration in e-business. Figure 9.1 illustrates a vector approach to viewing traditional and e-business.

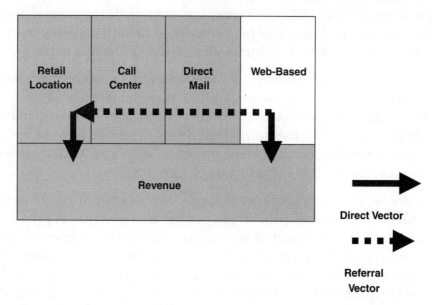

**Figure 9.1**  The vector model across channels.

## The Importance of Approach

In the previous chapter on analytical applications stemming from e-business, a conclusion was reached that the navigational path to revenue may or may not be defined by a traditional transaction. Further, the path by which a customer causes revenue generation may be as critical as the actual revenue transaction itself. Most of the literature to date analyzes the approach to the web transaction. Questions involve the link to the site, the clicks at the site, and the profile of the transactor. But in this new world, the customer may arrive at the "airport" at one of multiple runways. Moreover, the customer may do a series of "touch and go," near, and landings. Figure 9.2 illustrates a "touch and go" vector approach. The approach path or "vector" is as important as the actual landing. In shortening the approach vector, the time to revenue can be shortened.

A second issue is the profile of the customer. Little is known about how customers use the various channels. Do they see something in the broadcast arena and then go to the Web for information? Do they circle back to the traditional store to handle the goods? Do they really buy the best price, or is the price tempered by distance? All these questions are topics of exploration, for the true patterns are unknown.

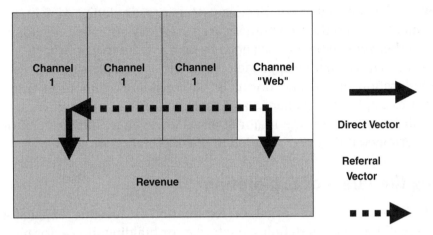

**Figure 9.2** The "touch and go" approach.

## Trust, but Verify

In understanding how to construct an exploration model, it is necessary to transcend both traditional analyses and data mining paradigms. In data mining, the target of mining is usually defined as deep and narrow. This deep and narrow requirement causes a constriction about the quality of data. In exploration, particularly in e-business, the focus of analysis is often broad (i.e., across dimensions or domains), therefore the quality of data need not be at the same level. Further, because exploration is a hypothesis formation process, the data need not be without error. (In fact, the data can contain errors and still yield value.) The key is to understand that between the hypothesis formation in exploration, and taking business action verification needs to take place. Verification can sometimes be done by classical analytical processes or by data mining.

It would be imprudent to take action without verification. Many of the failures in business positioning on the Web occur because entrepreneurs rush forward on intuitive feeling, bad data, or assumption, without going through a verification step. On the other hand, there are those that wait too long before uncovering a change, and make verification their life's work. The right positioning is a happy medium between assurance and action in a timely fashion.

## Constructing the Model

The construction of an exploration model in e-business is not an intuitive process. In traditional business, an inductive approach to business analysis is used, but this approach tends to limit the scope of activity to what can be observed. Because e-businesses don't exist in a single dimension, and their customers are extremely complex and adaptive in their behavior, e-businesses need to take a deductive approach to exploration. The deductive approach is holistic, encompassing aspects of the exploration that would normally be considered remote or incidental. For example, minor channels of revenue can have a significant, though indirect, impact on the major sources of revenue, but this can only be determined if they are included in the exploration process.

## Defining the Target of Exploration

If, for example, the target of exploration is revenue expansion and recognition, then in defining the target for building the vector model, all revenue sources must be considered. This could include direct sales revenue, channel sales revenue, and competitive revenue. What is competitive revenue? It is that revenue that was referred to after a competitor interaction with the enterprise under examination. Most enterprises focus exclusively on lost revenue without understanding fully the how and why of loss. Once again, the issue becomes the buyer's behavioral pattern. If a buyer circles over a site but decides to land at a competitor's site, there is often a reason. It is well known that there are differential buying patterns based upon socioeconomic factors. Further, there are differential patterns of behavior based upon transportation patterns. The Internet has radically disturbed the differential buying behavior based upon communications patterns. Old communication patterns were well understood in marketing, based upon direct mail, broadcast, and print media, as well as direct sales. All these patterns were slow. The communication speed in the Internet is immediate. It is extremely easy to overlook a pattern in the crush of web-based information. It is even easier to negate its value in channel centricity.

## Defining the Approach Pattern

Figure 9.3 illustrates some of the possible approach patterns to the targeted area of interest, in this case revenue. (We refer to these components as the *vector sphere*.)

Many dot-coms leverage traditional broadcast media, television most specifically, to establish their brand identity. They may also depend on print media, word of mouth, direct mail, referral, virtual links, and personal contact—all are components of the vector sphere. It is not enough

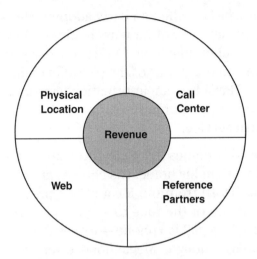

**Figure 9.3**  Some of the components of the vector sphere.

to look at the world in terms of tight pairings of cause and effect; the entire vector sphere must be considered. In the case of the e-business site, the tie to the broadcast media yields little or no direct revenue by providing an "approach path" to the real revenue generation tie.

Continuing with our airplane metaphor, at an airport, the air traffic controller determines the plane's approach based on demand and air space. In e-business, it is the potential customer who determines the approach. The e-business can widen the runway, provide incentives, increase interest, and remove sales obstacles, but in the end, the consumer determines the approach patterns. In the end, each customer is different and is motivated differently. In vector-based explorations, these behavioral patterns are tested for. To see how this works, let's now look at an example of one customer's experience in the world of communications.

## A Hypothetical E-Tailing Case Study

Mr. Harold is a 53-year-old family man involved in the high-tech computer industry. Like many of the baby boomers, the telephone company he grew up with was a monolith (which we'll call Megaphone), and he stayed with Megaphone partly because it was the path of least resistance, but also because Megaphone had become a cultural icon, like Coca-Cola, Harley-Davidson, and Marilyn Monroe. What would make Mr. Harold leave one of his beloved cultural icons and change to a new communications provider?

For one thing, Mr. Harold is what is called an early adopter. He is comfortable with, and sees the advantages of, new technology. He was an early user of the automatic teller machine (ATM), an early user of portable computers, and even an early user of the personal digital assistant (PDA) technology. Mr. Harold is an information consumer, and therefore wishes to leverage the value of information at all times. Price is less of an issue for him than service.

As time progresses, Mr. Harold becomes increasingly aware of the need for increased Internet bandwidth in his home. His choices are threefold: cable, digital subscriber line (DSL) from the local phone provider, and satellite service. He is very aware of the race to service his city neighborhood. The local provider—let's call it Vphone—arrives first with service and support. Interestingly enough, Megaphone offers the same service, but at twice the price of Vphone. Further, Vphone provides the physical link into Mr. Harold's house. Mr. Harold quickly realizes that Megaphone adds no value other than its brand name; Vphone is the key provider, and so he orders DSL service from Vphone.

Mr. Harold also has wireless cellular service from Megaphone for exactly the same reasons he maintained his long distance service with the company. Mr. Harold decides to upgrade his service, and as part of the package with Megaphone receives a new cellular phone. Quickly, Mr. Harold finds that the phone is defective. Mr. Harold's business requires frequent contact with others on a timely basis. Cellular service is critical to his business performance. Dealing with Megaphone is difficult. It requires multiple phone calls, during which representatives seem to try at every turn not to accommodate the caller. The phone has a value of $50. Mr. Harold on average does $1,500 to $3,000 a year in business with Megaphone. Megaphone does not get it! Eventually, however, Megaphone sends a replacement phone to Mr. Harold; but it turns out that this is a "refurbished" phone. It, too, is defective. Mr. Harold calls Megaphone with a proviso that this time the phone must be new. He explains the problem, the consequences, and the cost and frustration. The Megaphone staff responds that they cannot help him. Mr. Harold cancels his cellular service, his wife's cellular service, and his long distance with Megaphone—a total in excess of $5,000 per year. Mr. Harold calls Vphone, and within 10 minutes, it has captured all of Mr. Harold's business. A short ride to the Vphone store and all is well: Mr. Harold has a new phone, new service, and is a happy customer.

# Initial Contacts and Linkage

Let's look at what went wrong for Megaphone and right for Vphone. Both Vphone and Megaphone had contacts with Mr. Harold. Vphone had his local service; Megaphone had both long distance and cellular service for Mr. Harold and his wife. Both companies had adequate information based upon zip code to identify the socioeconomic status of Mr. Harold, so as to determine whether he was a subject for target marketing. If any company has an edge, it was Megaphone. It should have been able to determine that it had a multiple-person household with at least three or more services—a perfect target for cross-selling. (The object in cross-sell is to leverage the existing customer base to add more revenue.) Clearly, Megaphone had done little or no exploration on the existing customer base to determine customer value in the retail market space.

Let's now look at the approach vector for Mr. Harold (see Figure 9.4). The first "fly over," or vector approach, to Vphone occurred at the Vphone DSL Web site. Vphone requires the consumer to input both zip code and telephone number information to determine whether DSL is available for that customer. Though Vphone missed an opportunity to dynamically link the potential for new business and existing business at the Web site, it did capture the e-mail address to use in marketing—but in a very traditional manner, principally with follow-up e-mails on the availability of DSL service. The second opportunity for dynamic linking came when Mr. Harold remembered that Vphone offered cellular service. This came from personal referrals as well as from the home page of Vphone's Web site. Again, because of the stovepipe nature of the Web site data, a cross-sell opportunity was missed. At the same time, Mrs. Harold had gone to the very same site to determine what types of cellular instruments were available. Another opportunity missed. By this time, Mr. and Mrs. Harold have visited the Vphone site from three different virtual identities: Mr. Harold's DSL ID, Mr. Harold's work ID, and Mrs. Harold's work ID. The failure to understand the process of exploration prolonged the time to sale by weeks.

After canceling his service with Megaphone, Mr. Harold returned to the Vphone site again. Obtaining the location of the nearest local store, he called to find out how fast service could be activated. When told, Mr. Harold immediately went to the store to obtain service. The sales concluded.

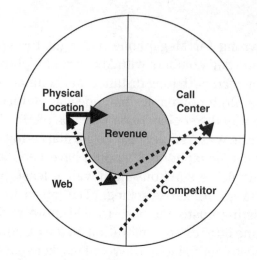

**Figure 9.4** A case study of vector approach.

Now let us turn to a vector interpretation to define how exploration could have either found new value or sped the time to revenue in this case example. (Had Megaphone performed the same analysis, the odds are high that it could have taken pre-emptive action to avoid the churn problem. And remember that churn is expensive—in the telco industry, the cost of retaining a customer is much less than the cost of acquiring a new customer.)

What are the concepts appropriate to exploration in e-business, to help to identify and alleviate the churn problem as identified in this example? The key is soft or inferential linkage.

## Inferential Linkage

In e-business exploration, "approximately right" is right enough. The process of exploration does not require the same level of discipline necessary in analytical data acquisition. For example, in web mining, much effort is placed on defining a "cookie," a unique address, so as to positively identify the customer. But such positive identification is not necessary for hypothesis formation; it's only needed for supposition. The technique of relating data that might or might not be accurate is called *sparsely populating indexes*. Figure 9.5 illustrates inferential linkage for Mr. Harold's household for exploration purposes. With this technique, a table is built based upon multiple index entry points, with the

| Name | Phone | Address | Add Link | Phone Link |
|------|-------|---------|----------|------------|
| Mr. Harold | (212) 111-1234 | 93 Ave | Junior | Mrs. Harold |
| | | | | |

**Figure 9.5** The importance of inferential linkage.

understanding that it is very likely that there may be many indices, but in most cases entries may only be linked two at a time (i.e., a dyadic entry). When a new dyadic entry on two indexes finds an existing entry for a pair, interesting things are observed. Let's apply this technique to the case example.

If Megaphone had built a dyadic entry for Mr. Harold's address and cell phone, the company would have had the base on which to do exploration across lines of business. Further, by adding a paired entry for long distance and address, Megaphone would have linked long-distance value to cell phone value and established an inferential link. Why is this an inferential link? Without hard account number linkage numbers, the analyst cannot absolutely be certain that the individual is the same on both accounts. Also, there is the issue of Mrs. Harold's account. Here, once again, the soft linkage of address would have provided an indication of a second cellular phone and a projected value. What if Mr. Harold's billing address had been his office address? When individuals apply for cellular service, a home phone, a business phone, a business address, and a home address are almost always required information for service.

As you can see, there are multiple sources for creating sparsely populated index tables. Unfortunately, many firms, in their quest for "hard" linkages, overlook these soft linkage sources. Let us now look at this example from the Vphone side of the problem.

When Mr. Harold entered the Vphone Web site to learn about its DSL service, he was required to enter his phone number to find out whether DSL service was available in his area. At that point in time, Vphone had Mr.

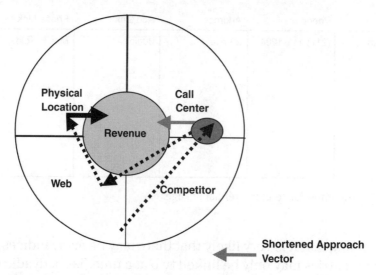

**Figure 9.6** Shortening the vector approach.

Harold's phone number and e-mail address. If this information had been added to the existing local service information, and the request for DSL information added to the zip information, Mr. Harold should have been profiled as a high-tech user. Clearly, this type of user would be a natural candidate for target marketing. Interestingly enough, while Vphone advertised cellular service on the same home page, no attempt was made to solicit any other classic cross-sell products. Effective use of exploration technique would have identified Mr. Harold as a "high-value" customer. Identifying the "fly over" or long approach path could have enabled proactive action at either the Web site or at the call center, to shorten the approach vector. Figure 9.6 illustrates a shortening of the vector approach to revenue.

## Ascertaining Customer Value in Exploration

In classical analysis, the value of a customer is based on his or her actual contractual value to the enterprise. This is certainly useful for calculating revenue yield and profitability for the firm. But does this type of activity have value when trying to find new opportunities through exploration? The answer is, probably not. For purposes of exploration, an estimated value maybe as meaningful as a calculated value. The reason for this is timeliness. If an estimated value can be derived from known parametrical data, then the timeliness of a meaningful result may be of more use than an actual value. In the case example, if Mr. Harold's base service is $90 a month for cellular access, a projected value of $1,200 a month is certainly adequate for exploration value. Whether Mr. Harold actually does $1,200 or $2,000 a year in business with Megaphone does not materially change the problem.

## Householding in E-Business

How important is an estimation of net value to a click-and-mortar business? The answer is self evident: Very important! The relationship between Mr. and Mrs. Harold's accounts becomes an issue in calculating the value of the economic unit. This process of placing an economic value on an economic unit is known as *householding*.

Under householding, separate economic units are aggregated into a single entity—it is assumed that the individual units act or interact as an organic whole. The family is the most familiar unit of householding. In retail banking, the concept of the economic unit of the household is well established. Systems often provide "hard" or "tight" linkages between members of a single family. Usually, this is done by explicit information such as Social Security numbers in trust accounts or by linking accounts for minimal balance reasons. Other accounts are linked "loosely" by inferential information.

The most common technique is proprietary to the Harte Hanks firm. While the totality of the technique is considered a trade secret, it is commonly held that a portion of the technique involves normalizing the common address terms and abbreviations for items such as street, then using a combination of zip code plus the first 22 digits of the address coupled with name.

At least one major retail bank developed its own major householding algorithm. Unfortunately, this particular technique did not take into account an ethnically developed housing unit, and more than 100 separate families were householded together. In the case of analytical analysis, only hard links are acceptable because the results are typically subject to audit and inspection. In the case of target marketing, householding by address is a well-accepted technique.

Another problem found in a banking analysis has to do with whether the behavior occurs during the day or at night. In the analysis, it was found that, for customer convenience, most accounts were located near the person's business address, rather than the residential location. When socioeconomic data by zip code was applied, strange skewing occurred. When the data was corrected for nighttime address (i.e., home address), the socioeconomic data became meaningful. Just as soft linkages between accounts become meaningful in target marketing, soft linkages by address are meaningful in exploration.

# Differential Address Linkage in Exploration

The use of address as a soft linkage becomes critical not only to house-holding but also as a vector factor of approach in exploration analysis. Remember in the example that Mrs. Harold made the visit to Vphone's Web site to ascertain the availability of cellular packages for Mr. Harold. If the householding had been done by means of the sparsely constructed indexes, the linkage would have become clear between Mr. Harold's work identity, Mrs. Harold's work identity, and their joint household identity. Further, most work identities contain the domain identification of the work holder.

There are other types of households, such as households of identity or common interest. While some affinity groups are not readily identifiable in this way, many others are. Indeed, the domain name owners of commercial and nonprofit organizations are matters of public record. It is thus possible to establish soft linkages between an Internet service provider (ISP) and work-based identities. How then can we link these individual events into a potentially meaningful chain? One possibly it is to view each of the events in time sequence to see if there is a causal chain.

## Events and Time

In the case study, Mr. and Mrs. Harold accessed various channels of information from different locations in time sequence. In each case, the channel moved the customer one step closer to revenue. It is also possible that different customers engage in very different approach patterns. The time sequence of each event is the chain to revenue. Time re-enters the exploration analysis not only as the length of the vector, but also as the sequencer of events as well. This is uniquely different from other types of analysis that assume association or causality in sequence but only on a paired level. The vector model accounts for multiple time sequences of varied length. The major caveat is that no mathematical technique can be applied, for there is no interval level measurement that is universal for measuring either the strength or length of the vectors. Thus, at best, only a hypothesis of causal behavior can be obtained.

But this is exactly the point, this is what exploration is about: A hypothesis, not a confirmed factual analysis. For analysis, much more stringent criteria must be applied. Exploration is a starting point, and where analysis cannot take place, at least an indicator of value.

# Summary

Exploration in e-business allows for new approaches for knowledge discovery. It enables the discovery of how people behave across sales channels. It enables the discovery of new business value. Exploration, most of all, enables the formation of new hypotheses, which can be validated. Exploration does not, however, provide conclusive proof of an idea. For conclusive proof, traditional analytical techniques such as data mining must be applied.

This chapter also demonstrated that use of the vector approach model can be a viable method of detecting the changing patterns that occur in the click-and-mortar world. Because of the fast-paced nature of e-business, traditional analysis often can't yield results quickly enough to be of use for decision making, especially if the infrastructure is weak. Unless vast amounts of information can be moved from the transactional environment to the data warehousing environment, and on to an analytical environment rapidly, any discovery may be too late to be of business value. In many cases, this type of well-integrated infrastructure has not been built. Instead, what is found is a patchwork system. In such environments, exploration techniques maybe the only way to discover value in a timely fashion.

# CHAPTER 10

# Adapting to Changes in Your E-Business

E-business customers expect instant responses to their queries. Time frames for procurement and implementation processes continue to shrink, even though companies are faced with dwindling human resources. To reconfigure an e-business requires an integrated view of the resources supporting the e-business and its performance.

Of course, for businesses unable or unwilling to build them, there are time-sharing technologies available, such as application service providers (ASPs), to provide the complex technology suites. This permutation is especially interesting since it must connect to multiple internal information systems without forcing changes in those systems. E-business initiatives require corporate information resources throughout the enterprise; they cannot be segregated from the rest of the enterprise and apportioned exclusive resources, or they will fail. Traditional computer operations tend to view the e-business side as non-mission-critical. Integration requires careful position and guidance to ensure integrity between old and new technologies. Figure 10.1 illustrates the point that integration is required to prevent these losses.

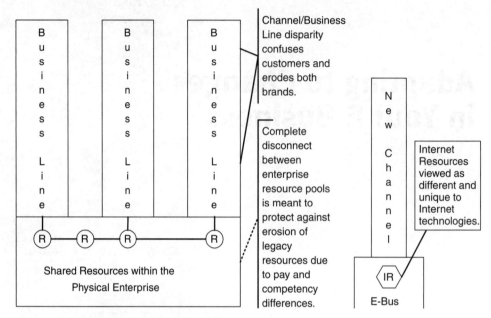

**Figure 10.1** Segregated e-business failure.

By adopting these ASP services, it is possible to forestall some of the issues attendant to e-business. The ASP quickly provides the company with a Web presence and a means of transacting business online. However, the back-end processing requirements are met only at the surface level; little time or attention is spent on long-term integration. And because integration is not the initial focus of those overwhelmed by the task of establishing an e-business presence, they are confronted with it later, after they've had some success with their Web site. Examining the e-business presence as it relates to other business change issues is useful.

## Branding Dilution and Loss

The first attempts of many brick-and-mortar businesses to establish a Web presence were made in completely separate, as opposed to integrated, environments. As a result, many failed. Business analysts quickly dissected those early e-business experiences, and concluded that the separation of Web and physical channels to the point of exclusivity was a mistake.

Basic branding theory teaches the importance of respecting and maintaining the consistent presence of a brand. Treating the dot-com version of a business brand as separate and exclusive offers little incentive to try it. The only way to meaningfully leverage the value of the physical brand electronically is to establish the electronic brand as an organic outgrowth of the existing physical success. Distinctions are much more easily made once the electronic brand extension is realized. These distinctions include special e-commerce marketing and offerings not available in traditional channels.

Launching the electronic brand as an exclusive offering is warranted only when the electronic brand is sufficiently new and different—and then it requires a greater investment. An example of this is BarnesAndNoble.com. The entire way of doing business is different. But in most cases, an integrated view of e-business initiatives is necessary to support healthy brand growth and development.

## Requirements for E-Business Agility

Agility in e-business is the ability to constantly adjust and change.

## Mobilization

Mobilizing e-business resources requires:

- An understanding of customer preferences and usage patterns
- A strategy for aggregating customer attention across distinct channels

Customer preferences constantly evolve based on economic circumstances and available alternatives. When the e-business infrastructure is positioned so as to leave delivery formats and timing as open as possible, strategies may be devised and executed with maximum margin for change. In contrast, when the e-business infrastructure is limited by a constrained infrastructure, it becomes necessary to constantly revisit the e-business application's development cycle. This includes hard-coding presentation layer dynamics because the infrastructure is not flexible enough to utilize XML, or because other methods to reformat content based on delivery are certain death.

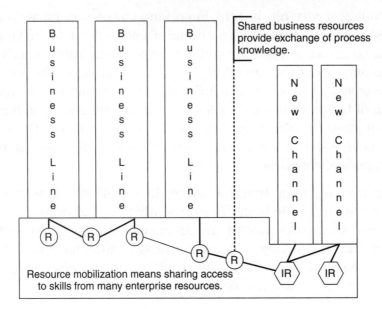

**Figure 10.2** Mobilized resources.

Supporting the mobility of corporate information resources requires flexibility and scalability. This can be achieved by a flexible infrastructure. Figure 10.2 illustrates the integrated view of e-business that supports resource mobility.

Making the jump from an integrated, mobile resource set to a responsive resource set is the next challenge of e-business agility.

## Responsiveness

E-business agility is about making information resources responsive to two types of feedback. The first is status and control responsiveness. Tracking the status, and controlling the progress, of ongoing initiatives requires constant information updates. Information assets must be positioned to respond to varying demands, such as rapid increases in Web site activity. Tracking the results of an e-business initiative can require several subject areas to be integrated and available for analysis. It can also require varying degrees of frequency and granularity. Exploration and mining activities are often required to support analysis of usage patterns and adoption rates.

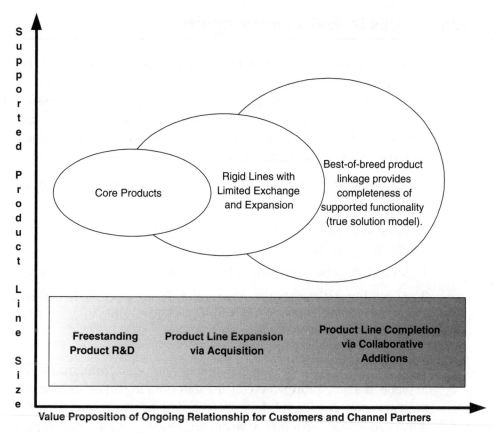

Supported Product Line Size

Core Products

Rigid Lines with Limited Exchange and Expansion

Best-of-breed product linkage provides completeness of supported functionality (true solution model).

**Freestanding Product R&D**

**Product Line Expansion via Acquisition**

**Product Line Completion via Collaborative Additions**

**Value Proposition of Ongoing Relationship for Customers and Channel Partners**

**Figure 10.3** Vendor collaboration increases market value.

The second form of feedback is broader, and occurs over longer time horizons. Management must track the overall efficacy of their initiatives to determine the "fit" of the initiatives to their intended purpose. Serious consideration must also be given to the ongoing validity of the intended purpose and scope. E-business economics and markets change so rapidly that even a six-month project can be imperiled by the dynamics of the marketplace. Figure 10.3 adds important feedback, measurement, and prioritization capabilities to the integrated view of e-business.

Chapters 1 through 9 identified the critical issues facing e-businesses, along with many ways to utilize corporate information assets to provide solutions. The balance of this chapter examines the forces and issues driving e-business, in order to identify a means of supporting information technology professionals with business-based reasoning for e-business agility measures and methods.

# Challenges to E-Business Agility

Learning, knowing, and executing are the key activities required of anyone who hopes to develop an agile e-business. Knowing which technologies to use and when to use them is difficult, because classic business measures fail to indicate the efficacy of planned investments in information technology. Investing in information assets requires the same skills and discipline as physical plant investment has always required.

Three steps are involved in establishing a foundation for e-business agility:

1. Classifying information assets, and evaluating their performance characteristics.

2. Identifying the current and future value of information flows.

3. Assembling a corporate information factory (CIF) design that can accommodate current needs yet remain flexible enough to adjust for future needs.

Executing on knowledge requires that the proper information technology be in place. It also requires recognizing that creating an enterprise information infrastructure cannot be done in so-called Internet time. This is precisely why corporations around the world are renewing their interest in enterprise architecture planning as a means of ensuring that proper information assets are in place before attempting to fulfill e-business requirements.

Distinguishing between learning activities and outcomes is imperative in the process of capturing outcomes and making them available to the enterprise. It is equally important to distinguish learning from training and instruction. Mistaking skill and task-level improvements, which follow directly from training exercises, for broader behavioral shifts associated with learning experiences has been the fatal flaw of many corporate training programs. The critical dimensions of learning must be present if any behavioral change and growth is possible.

## The Incalculable Advantages of E-Business Agility

Few companies try to quantify data warehousing success levels, robustness of the CIF, competency levels of information technology staff, and organizational ability to adapt to e-business challenges; these assets are

## Enterprise Architecture Status

The status of enterprise architecture and major enterprise initiatives must be considered carefully when exploring e-business initiatives. Agility is often tested at the outset of e-business initiatives, as technical and business resources are already fully absorbed by ongoing enterprise initiatives. Many business improvement and infrastructure initiatives require sustained executive commitment; hence, they rapidly exhaust internal attention as well as budgets for external resources.

How the enterprise architecture is laid sets the stage for an e-business success—or failure. E-business agility relies upon a solid foundation of information infrastructure and management recognition of the value of information assets to the enterprise. Firms with a solid—that is, scalable—information infrastructure are better positioned for e-business success. Resource mobility and responsiveness require an infrastructure that supports rapid reallocation of key technical and business resources.

not indicated in published financial statements. The reason is that there is a lack of cohesive metrics to apply to such subjective areas. Therefore, the primary motivation for analyzing any of these areas is, simply, the growing desire to identify a central integration point for management reporting and analysis support.

The data warehouse should be designed to satisfy the need for enhanced enterprise performance. Properly executed data warehouses provide key business advantages that are not obvious to the external observer. Preparing for and executing a data warehouse project requires a careful analysis of the impacts on resources and business outcomes. The business outcomes can be projected by those business units whose data will be integrated and accumulated. For example, one major international energy concern was able to justify its global data warehouse project on the basis of "moving the margin." The executive sponsor—quite properly—projected an improvement in the enterprise profit margin once the information was integrated and accumulated for analysis, and identified improvements to corporate performance.

## Hallmarks of E-Business Initiatives

E-business initiatives are designed, approved, and implemented based upon "new economy" expectations. These are driven by the intense desire for immediate gratification, by the "we need to be on the Web now" demand. That translates to: put the procurement system online now, and report on all of the success it breeds and costs it reduces; get the order entry and configuration systems online immediately, so we can quantify the revenue increase. More specifically, these need-it-now hallmarks often include:

- Providing immediate gratification to the corporate sponsor.
- Answering security and privacy concerns.
- Supplying often hard-to-estimate growth rates.
- Using comparatively new and sometimes exotic technologies.
- Responding to shortages of internal technical resources.
- Coping with uncertainty about capital allocation schemes.

## Old Economy versus New Economy

These vexing conditions find their roots in the new economy versus old economy debate. New economy technology pitches heightened management expectations (although, recently, it seems the investment community has largely settled this argument by returning technology stock valuations to earth). The differences between economic schools of thought are most evident in the metrics they use to measure activity. Table 10.1 provides examples of this disparity.

**Table 10.1** Economic Metrics

| METRIC | OLD ECONOMY EXAMPLE | NEW ECONOMY EXAMPLE |
|---|---|---|
| Periodic | Monthly, Quarterly, Annual | Seconds, Hours, Days |
| Cyclic | Business, Industry and Investment Cycles | Technology Cycles, Transaction Cycles |
| Logical | Line or Division | Channels |
| Geographic | Region, District | Time Zone |
| Physical | Same Store | Web to Store connections Locational computing |
| Relational | Account | Customer, Partner |
| Collaborative | Specified Supplier | Potential Partner |

The differences in periodic measures illustrate the accelerated pace of e-business; cyclic measures indicate the rapid pace of change in technology, because these changes constantly offer new channel capabilities for customer interaction. Transaction cycles, too, are an important measure in e-business because they indicate the rate at which Web site activity is converted into revenue. Logical distinctions are being made more along channel lines than along arbitrary line or division categories; and the 24/7 nature of e-business erases or redraws former geographical boundaries. Likewise, time zones are an important challenge to processing requirements since close of business processes (occurring in different time zones) must accommodate daily business reporting needs.

### Locational Delivery

Physical measures are similar at one level: the locational aspect of product delivery. Same store sales remain a key measure of retail success. The e-business counterpart is becoming the web-to-store connection.

E-businesses that can link their online shoppers to available click-and-mortar inventory are experiencing high levels of success. CompUSA is a good example. Online shoppers can search through thousands of products on the company's Web site; once they find what they are looking for, they can determine whether the product is in inventory in a conveniently located store. All shoppers have to do is type in their zip code to find stores within a given geographical range, along with the stock status of the desired item.

Locational computing has broader applications as well. Using embedded network technology, wireless service providers and Web service aggregators are teaming up to provide contextually meaningful updates to Web-enabled shoppers in real time. The first applications for this can be seen in the travel and rental car industries. Locational computing will afford "Web drivers" the opportunity to identify updated sale and stock information at retail outlets within a specified range of their current (and constantly updated) location; it will also give them driving instructions to the nearest store that has the item they want to purchase.

As an extension to this capability, a brick-and-mortar retail business will be able to lure customers off the streets using a constantly updated, personal billboard in their cars. That retailer will enjoy the competitive edge of being able to reach customers en route—and of knowing which customers it acquired in that manner. Imagine the interest on the part of restaurant and other food-related businesses alone.

Business and economic cycles have long controlled the pendulum swing between spin-offs and mergers. Consolidation waves wash over various industries due to the forces of economy of scale, regulatory, and technology activities. The rapid-fire pace of e-business does not always allow time for business consolidation or even formal alliance. Therefore, the trend in e-business, particularly in the B2B space, will continue to be toward loose collaborations and peer-level partnerships. Filling the spaces in product lines, service offerings, and geographic coverage (think time zone) is not a mergers and acquisitions process. It is a matter of engaging in a rapid succession of relationships that yield gap-closing results without encumbering the assets of the enterprise. Indeed, corporate performance must rely upon corporate collaboration skills. We call this the *collaboration coefficient.*

### The Collaboration Coefficient

The collaboration coefficient is a measure of an organization's "speed limits." An enterprise can fill gaps in its product and service lines in three basic ways:

- Research and development
- Merger and acquisition
- Collaboration and partnership

Companies typically engage in combinations of these behaviors, although many establish a preferred method and rely upon it for most of their needs. That said, a hybrid model, which constantly considers alternatives and allows for flexible choices, often fares better in highly competitive e-business markets.

Research and development is well known in the pharmaceutical business. Mergers and acquisitions in the computer industry are well understood, such as IBM's acquisition of Lotus Notes. An example of the partnership approach can be found in the software industry. Informix Software recently completed a prolonged series of acquisitions that resulted in multiple product lines. The firm reconfigured its lines into two distinct areas, and spun off a separate company to specialize in information asset management. Pete Fiore, president of the newly created Ascential Software describes his company's mission as: "Providing the means to pull together large amounts of disparate information, enhance its value, and deliver it in usable formats to the people who need it when they need it." Ascential Software's corporate parent, Informix Software, is aware of the challenge its new creation faces, which is why Informix President and C.E.O. Peter Gyenes is adamant about the power of partnerships. Gyenes has specified the prerequisites to a competitive collaboration coefficient for Informix Software in this way:

- A partnership must provide an equal and balanced value proposition.
- A partnership requires dedicated management on each side.
- Partners must view each other as "friends of the family" and act accordingly.

Ascential Software satisfies its customers' needs by carefully selecting and engaging partners that can add to the overall value of the combined offering. The company is careful to avoid the "not invented here" pitfall that prevents rapid product line evolution. The company is also open to collaboration with customers and user groups that present important suggestions for product enhancements.

E-business agility requires this kind of corporate flexibility. Mobility and responsiveness of corporate resources are often accomplished in concert with trusted partners. Identifying these partnerships and the appropriate level of reliance upon them distinguishes successful e-businesses from their competitors. Even competitors are finding ways to collaborate on product and service offerings. Standards setting groups continue to sort through the difficult issues relating to product interaction. The creation of the Uniform Discovery and Description Integration Project (UDDI) is an example of these industry collaborations. Firms contribute significant resources that would otherwise be spent in competitive practices, to ensure that customers have access to products from various members in many different combinations. Imagine bringing more than 100 vendors together to provide these resources, and to agree to compromises in order to resolve product interaction issues.

**Table 10.2** Levels of Profitability

| LEVEL | TYPE | PURPOSE |
|---|---|---|
| Enterprise | Aggregate | Financial Accounting |
| Market/Country | Aggregate | Financial Accounting |
| Region | Aggregate | Management Accounting |
| District | Aggregate | Management Accounting |
| Store | Local consolidation | Management Accounting |
| Product Line | Output-based Consolidation | Profitability Analysis |
| Product/SKU | Output-based Consolidation | Profitability Analysis |
| Account | Input-based Consolidation | Profitability Analysis |
| Customer | Input-based Consolidation | Profitability Analysis |

# Corporate Performance: Levels of Profitability

Profitability analysis, based upon the success levels of product lines, has developed into a critical means of supporting resource allocation decisions. Corporate profit analysis is conducted at many levels. Financial accounting has a long and rich tradition of providing comparable, consistent, and coherent indications of corporate health and growth. Management accounting has extended external reporting measures with internal cost and other performance indicators for all levels of management.

Profitability measures have expanded in e-business to encompass nontraditional business imperatives. The shift from output-based consolidation associated with products to the input (demand)-based consolidation that drives account and customer profit analysis is critical to e-business agility. This is predicated on the highly relational focus of e-business: e-business benefits even more from profitable relationships than physical business. The reason is the relatively rapid speed of change in the e-business immediately impacts profitability. Thus, understanding the demand patterns of varying types of relationships over time has become critical to e-business growth. This evolution is summarized in Table 10.2.

## Relational Profitability

As customer relationship management (CRM) gives way to customer profitability management (CPM), the link between relationships and profitability becomes more apparent. This is much more than extending some control over relationship dynamics to select customers and partners. It has more to do with viewing the enterprise in terms of its relationships, as opposed to controlling those relationships. Profitability is often charted as a vertical ascent, constantly rising with no apparent ending point. The presumption seems to be that velocity can be achieved and maintained. The opposite is often more illustrative of the lengths to which modern firms go to develop and expand profitability. Profits are increasingly used as a measure of the depth of commitment a firm has to its relationships and the success of those relationships.

Transaction-based profitability is a reflection of specialization. Extremely specialized goods and services could be managed as individual profit producers. This trend is repeated in the electronic world as a trade-off between richness and reach. "Richness" is defined as extension content or choice. In either the physical or electronic world, there is little room for richness. Consumers have a limited appetite for an array of luxury automobiles just as they have for rich connection points. There is often a practical limit of three to five selections for first-tier products and providers. Attention spans are the real targets of rich Web sites. The Web site visit experience must be one worth repeating.

Mining the depths of customer relationships is becoming the new paradigm by financial and technical management in e-business. The stages of e-business evolution include:

1. Transactional

2. Relational

3. Life cycle

Relationship metrics have been limited to viewing a relationship in terms of transaction cycles. This limitation has been prompted by the precept that relationships are linear in form, that is, with finite beginnings and endings, with interim milestones, or transactions. This view is giving way to the expanded notion of the customer life cycle. The leaders in CRM now focus on the circular form of transaction cycles as a way to describe the iterative nature of these relationships. The idea is that customers progress through a predictable and, if successful, repeated cycle of transactional activities. The real success of relationship management will flow from understanding how to connect these

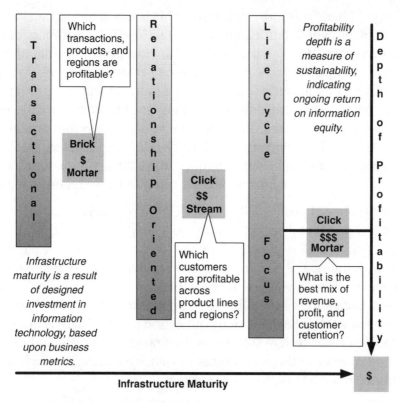

**Figure 10.4** Profitability depths by channel.

repeated transaction cycles throughout the lifetime of the customer relationship. This is not predicated exclusively on "purchase successes." It is, rather, an exercise in mining deeper veins of profit. Figure 10.4 illustrates this evolution toward deeper profitability.

Just as some companies, such as Progressive Insurance, have learned the virtue and value of providing information on competitive alternatives to their own offerings, other e-businesses must identify their ongoing value proposition. Amazon.com now enjoys a move to profitability in its domestic book sales unit, due to the fact that its enhanced value proposition no longer requires it to sell at below market prices. Customers return to the site in response to the personalized information provided. Those return visits spell loyalty, disproving the notion that loyalty is predicated on the success of each purchase. Computer Discount Warehouse (CDW.com) also understands the notion of customer loyalty. Its take on customer loyalty is that *it must remain loyal* to its customers. It achieves this by making it as easy as possible for customers to enjoy nonvolume-related discounts, and access to very rich product information.

These are three examples of e-businesses that understand how to mobilize their corporate information resources to provide true responsiveness to their customers. These companies clearly benefit from this agility. But how can an enterprise ensure these benefits? The answer requires a disciplined approach to the application of corporate information assets to profitability.

## Enterprise Profitability

Enterprise application integration (EAI) offers enterprise-level success without significant investment in infrastructure. The advent of enterprise resource planning (ERP) software promised the integrated management of all transactional activities. Automation of supply-and-demand chains, and resource allocation based upon this automation, were the central themes of global adoption of these programs. At some point, however, it became obvious that not all source systems could fit (neatly or otherwise) into the ERP envelope. Meanwhile, CRM applications and protocols have started to be adopted organizationally. CRM promises a unified view of customer relationships with an eye toward that elusive goal of customer profitability. The obvious combination of these products should yield enterprise profitability management, right?

Some problems have developed that undermine this trend. ERP grew out of MRP (manufacturing resource planning), a production line management system geared toward just-in-time inventory management. This was extremely useful in managing inventory and logistical loads. The bias toward reduced or nonexistent inventory levels freed up huge capital resources for business growth. It also created the basis for what would become "safe to promise" dates for customer order processing in ERP, and established minimum pipeline levels to prevent stock-outs on critical items. Enabling these ERP programs for Web access and electronic order processing kept them in the mainstream of corporate technology adoption.

Concurrent adoption of CRM presented some difficulties for both camps. CRM is concerned with unifying customer contact data and providing intelligence for the enterprise to use in deciding which products to offer to each customer through which channels at what times. CRM ultimately offers the enterprise the capability to identify customer profitability, so that "smart to promise" dates and prices can be determined for each customer. The result is one system, ERP, endeavoring to tell us when to commit to customer orders, and another system, CRM, telling us whether to commit to these orders.

Additionally, there are very serious differences between the way ERP and CRM applications view enterprise relationships. Reconciling these differences consumes significant technical and business resources. Once again, the tendency to reduce all enterprise behavior to a set of discrete applications leaves something to be desired.

# Managing Information Assets for Corporate Performance

Information asset management is an outgrowth of various information engineering and information architecture efforts. It is generally embodied in a limited, product-based message. The general idea is that product-based functionality aids in the construction, management, and distribution of information. The "asset" level is generic to all corporate information.

Vendors dedicating themselves to this approach have made the first step toward tying investments in their products and processes to corporate performance. A more evolved understanding points to classifying information assets in a way that supports derivation of a return on these assets. The real key to understanding information asset value from a financial viewpoint is the relationship between project-based spending and business impact.

The problem with traditional project-based spending is that it seeks to quantify results as a direct result of the project. This is akin to saying that events equal consequences. There is always a translation or execution layer involved when events take place. Interpreting results requires inference and context; results are viewed against selected metrics and within a corporate or technical context. Projects are not completed serially; they are parallel in nature, and often span changing economic and business cycles. These factors require a reconsideration of project impact evaluation. This expanded view of corporate information assets leads to proper alignments of financial and information performance.

# Valuing Corporate Information Assets: The CIF Scorecard

The CIF Scorecard is intended for enterprise use; it supports a financially expansive view of information assets and their management for aggressive returns. These assets are understood to be critical to corporate performance. The goal of the CIF Scorecard is to align these assets with their respective contributions to profitability and balance-sheet growth. Initial application of the CIF Scorecard for business customers has already provided meaningful inducement to sponsoring executives to reconsider their project scope and purpose in light of enterprise use of corporate information assets. Product-line analysis using the CIF Scorecard is changing the way vendors think about solving customer problems.

The CIF Scorecard is focused on both sides of the technology fence—the buying and implementation side and the producing and selling side. The ultimate goal of the methodology is to connect the best possible sources to appropriate uses. Matching up products, services, and customers is the ultimate goal. The intermediate target is matching these products and services to customer projects. The long-term success is attained through understanding the customer's enterprise architectural goals and commitments, and matching these to product lines capable of directly supporting those goals. Product-level matches are often limited to indirectly supporting the project requirements without satisfying the larger needs of the enterprise architecture. These products often undermine the contributions of the CIF to corporate performance because they require redundant financial and human resource utilization.

A new view of corporate information assets is needed. This must be accompanied by an appropriate measurement system for investing in these assets. This is the real challenge of the CIF Scorecard: to uncover and evaluate complex corporate information assets whose value is not currently reflected in financial statements. This is the only way to safeguard corporate investments in information technology. Evaluation of returns on these investments must be done in a completely different way. Total cost of ownership is one example of the need for this new valuation methodology. Quantifying the total cost of a technical resource should not be different from measuring costs associated with other physical resources. Real estate and other production-related facilities are often valued, or monetized, over a usage base. Activity-based accounting continues to enjoy popularity among value-based managers because it helps to identify underutilized assets and to weed out unnecessary carrying costs. Information technology can be accounted for using a variant of activity-based costing: total cost of usage. This activity-based measure tracks actual usage patterns for infrastructure components, and allocates costs over those usage patterns.

A complete description of the CIF Scorecard process is beyond the scope of this publication, the purpose of introducing it here is to provide a working example of emerging methods to support e-business agility. More information can be found at www.billinmon.com.

# Summary

E-business agility is the product of a carefully planned and executed information infrastructure. It is the ability to mobilize and respond to immediate as well as long-term challenges presented by e-business opportunities. The changes brought on by elements of the new economy have permanently affected information technology investment views and patterns. The era of big-iron investing is slowly giving way to an expanded view of where the value is in information technology. E-business forces improved data integration, accumulation, and analysis. The same skills needed to support enterprise growth in the physical world are required in the electronic universe.

The information infrastructure must now support massive growth trends in both the sources and uses of corporate information. Key infrastructure components must be viewed and managed as corporate information assets, particularly data warehouses and operational data stores. E-business agility means making these and related resources available to meet constantly changing demands. It also means adapting these assets to support the daily processing requirements of users, not just applications. As Internet access becomes nearly ubiquitous, users generate a daily electronic routine based on this access. This routine creates demand patterns for all types of information, transaction support, and interaction that rely on corporate information assets. The extent of this evolution is not yet known; the process is just beginning. Long-term infrastructure and architecture planning must take into account this trend toward mobilization and dispersion of users.

Finally, corporate information assets must be classified, measured, and improved based upon financial measures related to corporate performance. Envisioning the corporate information factory as an information portfolio is a useful first step. E-business agility allows information technology to translate technical realities into business impacts, and then formulate technical strategies to absorb these business impacts. E-business agility provides the enterprise with superior competitive positioning, which is sustainable in the face of change.

## Where Do We Go from Here

Current trends in old economy sectors bode very well for new economy participants. Energy markets are just beginning their transition to deregulated marketplaces, with notable and painful results. The difficulties inherent in efficient energy storage continue to drive local and regional production facilities. Geographic anomalies in production and utilization will continue to support electronic trading of energy interests. These forces are being felt in a range of countries, from developing to superpowers. Brokering and transmitting energy interests with extremely short-life use requires high-speed information analysis and exchange. Telecommunications is rapidly moving to the Web via IP telephony and optical networks. Rich, integrated, and even interactive media sets are fast becoming the order of the day. Handheld digital cameras using DVD media for recording accelerate consumer interest in editing, sorting, and exchanging very dense media content.

The trend toward mapping disparate data storage formats and location will intensify. IFS from Oracle and SharePoint Server from Microsoft are the beginning of a next generation of information-mapping products. The need to index, search, and navigate across file systems and geographies makes this functionality a necessity for e-business users. Information highways are beginning to look like their concrete counterparts; improvements are often outpaced before they are complete. Consolidations and mergers continue unabated on a truly global scale. Each business integration requires at least several to as many as thousands of systems integrations. Consider the plight of globally competitive integrated airlines or financial institutions. It is often easier to integrate balance sheets than it is to integrate business systems. Companies with strong competencies in data warehouse-centric CIF frameworks are poised to emerge from business combinations with a decisive advantage. Immediacy, consistency, and clarity are real business benefits that drive profitability in e-business.

# Glossary

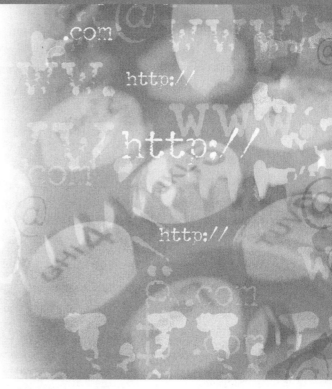

**access**   the operation of seeking, reading, or writing data on a storage unit.

**access method**   a technique used to transfer a physical record from or to a mass storage device.

**access mode**   a technique whereby a specific logical record is obtained from or placed onto a file assigned to a mass storage device.

**access pattern**   the general sequence by which the data structure is accessed (such as from tuple to tuple, from record to record, from segment to segment, and so on).

**access plan**   the control structure produced during program preparation and used by a database manager to process SQL statements during application execution.

**access time**   the time interval between the instant an instruction initiates a request for data and the instant the first of the data satisfying the request is delivered. Note that there is a difference—sometimes large—between the time data is first delivered and the time when *all* the data is delivered.

**accuracy**   a qualitative assessment of freedom from error or a quantitative measure of the magnitude of error, expressed as a function of relative error.

**active data dictionary**   a data dictionary that is the sole source for an application program insofar as meta data is concerned.

**activity**   1. the lowest-level function on an activity chart (sometimes called the "atomic level"); 2. a logical description of a function performed by an enterprise; 3. a procedure (automated or not) designed for the fulfillment of an activity.

**activity ratio**   the fraction of records in a database that have activity or are otherwise accessed in a given period of time or in a given batch run.

**address**   an identification (a number, name, storage location, byte offset, and so on) for a location where data is stored.

**addressing**   the means of assigning data to storage locations and locating the data upon subsequent retrieval on the basis of the key of the data.

**ad hoc processing**   one-time-only, casual access and manipulation of data on parameters never before used.

**afterimage**   the snapshot of data placed on a log upon the completion of a transaction.

**agent of change**   a motivating force large enough not to be denied—usually the aging of systems, changes in technology, radical changes in requirements, and so on.

**AIX**   Advanced Interactive eXecutive; IBM's version of the UNIX operating system.

**algorithm**   a set of statements organized to solve a problem in a finite number of steps.

**alias**   an alternative label used to refer to a data element.

**alphabetic**   a representation of data using letters—upper- and/or lowercase—only.

**alphanumeric**   a representation of data using numbers and/or letters and punctuation.

**alternative storage**   an extension to the data warehouse that enables vast amounts of infrequently used, dormant data to be stored and accessed economically. *See also* Secondary Storage.

**analytical processing**   the usage of the computer to produce an analysis for management decisions, usually involving trend analysis, drill-down analysis, demographic analysis, profiling, and so on.

**ANSI**   American National Standards Institute. A covering by which sets industrial standards.

**anticipatory staging**   the technique of moving blocks of data from one storage device to another with a shorter access time, in anticipation of their being needed by a program in execution or a program soon to go into execution.

**API (application program interface)**   the common set of parameters needed to connect the communications between programs.

**application**   a group of algorithms and data interlinked to support an organizational requirement.

**application blocking of data**   the grouping into the same physical unit of storage multiple occurrences of data controlled at the application level.

**application database**   a collection of data organized to support a specific application.

**archival database**   a collection of data of a historical nature. As a rule, archival data cannot be updated. Each unit of archival data is related to a moment in time now passed.

**area**   in network databases, a named collection of records that can contain occurrences of one or more record types. A record type can occur in more than one area.

**artifact**   a design technique used to represent referential integrity in the DSS environment.

**artificial intelligence**   the capability of a system to perform functions typically associated with human intelligence and reasoning.

**association**   a relationship between two entities that is represented in a data model.

**associative storage**   1. a storage device whose records are identified by a specific part of their contents rather than their name or physical position in the database; 2. content-addressable memory. See also *parallel search storage*.

**atomic**   1. data stored in a data warehouse; 2. the lowest level of process analysis.

**atomic database**   a database made up of primarily atomic data; a data warehouse; a DSS foundation database.

**atomicity**   the property wherein a group of actions is invisible to other actions executing concurrently, yielding the effect of serial execution. It is recoverable with successful completion (commit) or total backout (rollback) of previous changes associated with that group.

**atomic-level data**   data with the lowest level of granularity. Atomic-level data sits in a data warehouse and is time-variant (accurate as of some moment in time now passed).

**attribute**   a property that can assume values for entities or relationships. Entities can be assigned several attributes (such as a tuple in a relationship consists of values). Some systems also allow relationships to have attributes as well.

**audit trail**   data that is available to trace activity, usually update activity.

**authorization identifier**   a character string that designates a set of privilege descriptors.

**availability**   a measure of the reliability of a system, indicating the fraction of time the system is up and available divided by the amount of time the system should be up and available. Note that there is a difference between a piece of hardware being available and the systems running on that hardware also being available.

**backend processor**   a database machine or an intelligent disk controller.

**back up** (verb)   to restore the database to its state at some previous moment in time.

**backup** (noun)   a file serving as a basis for backing up a database. Usually a snapshot of a database at some previous moment in time.

**Backus-Naur Form (BNF)**   a metalanguage used to specify or describe the syntax of a language. In BNF, each symbol on the left side of the forms can be replaced by the symbol strings on the right side of the forms to develop sentences in the grammar of the defined language. *Normal form* is synonymous with Backus.

**backward recovery**   a recovery technique that restores a database to an earlier state by applying previous images.

**base relation**   a relation that is not derivable from other relations in the database.

**batch**   computer environment in which programs (usually long-running, sequentially oriented) access data exclusively; user interaction is not allowed while the activity is occurring.

**batch environment**   a sequentially dominated mode of processing; in batch, input is collected and stored for later processing. Once collected, the batch input is transacted sequentially against one or more databases.

**batch window**   the time at which the online system is available for batch or sequential processing. The batch window occurs during nonpeak processing hours.

**before image**   a snapshot of a record prior to an update, usually placed on an activity log.

**bill of materials**   a listing of the parts used in a manufacturing process, along with the relation of one part to another insofar as assembly of the final product is concerned. The bill of materials is a classical recursive structure.

**binary element**   a constituent element of data that exists as either of two values or states—either true or false, or one or zero.

**binary search**   a dichotomizing search with steps where the sets of remaining items are partitioned into two equal parts.

**bind**   1. to assign a value to a data element, variable, or parameter; 2. the attachment of a data definition to a program prior to the execution of the program.

**binding time**   the moment when the data description known to the dictionary is assigned to or bound to the procedural code.

**bit ([b]inary dig[it])**   the lowest level of storage. A bit can be in a 1 state or a 0 state.

**bit map**   a specialized form of an index indicating the existence or nonexistence of a condition for a group of blocks or records. Bit maps are expensive to build and maintain, but provide very fast comparison and access facilities.

**block**   1. a basic unit of structuring storage; 2. the physical unit of transport and storage. A block usually contains one or more records (or contains the space for one or more records). In some DBMSs, a block is called a page.

**blocking**   combining of two or more physical records so that they are physically colocated. The result of their physical colocation is that the records can be accessed and fetched by execution of a single machine instruction.

**block splitting**   the data management activity whereby data in a filled block is written into two unfilled blocks, leaving space for future insertions and updates in the two partially filled blocks.

**B-tree**   a binary storage structure and access method that maintains order in a database by continually dividing possible choices into two equal parts and re-establishing pointers to the respective sets, while not allowing more than two levels of difference to exist concurrently.

**buffer**   an area of storage that holds data temporarily in main memory while data is being transmitted, received, read, or written. A buffer is often used to compensate for the differences in the timing of the transmission and execution of devices. Buffers are used in terminals, peripheral devices, storage units, and CPUs.

**bus**   the hardware connection that allows data to flow from one component to another (such as from the CPU to the line printer).

**business intelligence**   represents those systems that help companies understand what makes the wheels of the corporation turn, and to help predict the future impact of current decisions. These systems place a key role in strategic planning process of the corporation. Systems that exemplify business intelligence include medical research, customer profiling, market basket analysis, customer contact analysis, market segmentation, scoring, product profitability, and inventory movement.

**business management**  those systems needed to effectively manage actions resulting from the business intelligence gained. If business intelligence helps companies understand *what* makes the wheels of the corporation turn, business management helps *direct* the wheels as the business landscape changes. To a large extent, these systems augment, extend, and eventually displace capabilities provided by business operations. Systems that exemplify business management include product management, campaign management, inventory management, resource management, and customer information management.

**business operations**  represents those systems that run the day-to-day business. These systems have traditionally made up the legacy environment and provided a competitive advantage by automating manual business processes to gain economies of scale and speed to market. Systems that exemplify business operations include accounts payable, accounts receivable, billing, order processing, compensation, and lead list generation.

**byte**  a basic unit of storage—made up of eight bits.

**C**  a programming language. Highly associated with Unix systems and extensively used in e-commerce.

**cache**  a buffer usually built and maintained at the device level. Retrieving data out of a cache is much quicker than retrieving data out of a cylinder.

**call**  to invoke the execution of a module.

**canonical model**  a data model that represents the inherent structure of data without regard to its individual use or hardware or software implementation.

**cardinality (of a relation)**  the number of tuples (rows) in a relation. *See also* degree (of a relation).

**CASE (Computer Aided Software Engineering)**  a package that helps write computer programs more rapidly.

**catalog**  a directory of all files available to the computer.

**chain**  an organization where records or other items of data are strung together.

**chain list**  a list where the items cannot be located in sequence, but where each item contains an identifier (pointer) for finding the next item.

**channel**  a subsystem for input to and output from the computer. Data from storage units, for example, flows into the computer by way of a channel.

**character**  a member of the standard set of elements used to represent data in the database.

**character type**  the characters that can represent the value of an attribute.

**checkpoint**  an identified snapshot of the database, or a point at which the transactions against the database have been frozen or have been quiesced. A recovery point in a processing sequence that guarantees path integrity.

**checkpoint/restart**  a means of restarting a program at some point other than the beginning—for example, when a failure or interruption has occurred. $N$ checkpoints may be used at intervals throughout an application program. At each of these points, sufficient information is stored to permit the program to be restored to the moment when the checkpoint was established.

**child**   a unit of data existing in a 1:*n* relationship with another unit of data called a parent, where the parent must exist before the child can exist, but the parent can exist even when no child unit of data exists.

**CICS (Customer Information Control System)**   an IBM teleprocessing monitor.

**CIO (chief information officer)**   the manager of all the information processing functions in an organization.

**circular file (queue)**   an organization of data where a finite number of units of data are allocated. Data is then loaded into those units. Upon reaching the end of the allocated units, new data is written over older data at the beginning of the queue. Sometimes called a *wrap-around* queue.

**claimed block**   a second or subsequent physical block of data designated to store table data, after the originally allocated block has run out of space.

**class (of entities)**   all possible entities held by a given proposition.

**CLDS**   the facetious name of the system development life cycle of analytical, DSS systems. CLDS is so named because it is the reverse of the name of the classical systems development life cycle—SDLC.

**cluster**   1. in teradata, a group of physical devices controlled by the same AMP; 2. in DB2 and Oracle, the practice of physically colocating data in the same block based on its content.

**cluster key**   the key around which data is clustered in a block (DB2/Oracle).

**coalesce**   to combine two or more sets of items into a single set.

**COBOL (COmmon Business Oriented Language)**   computer language for the business world. A very common language.

**CODASYL model**   a network database model that was originally defined by the Database Task Group (DBTG) of the COnference on DAta SYstem Language (CODASYL) organization.

**code**   1. to represent data or a computer program in a form that can be accepted by a data processor; 2. to transform data so that it cannot be understood by anyone who does not have the algorithm necessary to decode the data prior to presentation (sometimes called *encode*).

**collision**   the event that occurs when two or more records of data are assigned to the same physical location. Collisions are associated with randomizers or hashers.

**column**   a vertical table wherein values are selected from the same domain. A row is made up of one or more columns.

**command**   1. the specification of an activity by the programmer; 2. the actual execution of the specification.

**commit**   a condition raised by the programmer signaling to the DBMS that all update activity done by the program should be executed against a database. Prior to the commit, all update activity can be rolled back or cancelled with no adverse effects on the contents of the database.

**commit protocol**   an algorithm to ensure that a transaction is successfully completed.

**commonality of data**   similar or identical data that occurs in different applications or systems. The recognition and management of commonality of data is one of the foundations of conceptual and physical database design.

**communication network**   the collection of transmission facilities, network processors, and so on, which provides for data movement among terminals and information processors.

**compaction**   a technique for reducing the number of bits required to represent data without losing the contents of the data. With compaction, repetitive data is represented very concisely.

**component**   a data item or array of data items whose component type defines a collection of occurrences with the same data type.

**compound index**   an index spanning multiple columns.

**concatenate**   to link or connect two strings of characters, generally for the purpose of using them as a single value.

**conceptual schema**   a consistent collection of data structures expressing the data needs of the organization. This schema is a comprehensive, base-level, and logical description of the environment where an organization exists, free of physical structure and application system considerations.

**concurrent operations**   activities executed simultaneously or during the same time interval.

**condensation**   the process of reducing the volume of data managed without reducing the logical consistency of the data. Condensation is essentially different from compaction.

**connect**   to forge a relationship between two entities, particularly in a network system.

**connector**   a symbol used to indicate that one occurrence of data has a relationship to another occurrence of data. Connectors are used in conceptual database design, and can be implemented hierarchically, relationally, in an inverted fashion, or by a network.

**content addressable memory**   a main storage area that can be addressed by the contents of the data in the memory, as opposed to conventional location addressable memory.

**contention**   the condition that occurs when two or more programs try to access the same data simultaneously.

**continuous time span data**   data organized so that a continuous definition of data over a period of time is represented by one or more records.

**control character**   a character whose occurrence in a particular context initiates, modifies, or stops an operation.

**control database**   a utilitarian database containing data not directly related to the application being built. Typical control databases are audit databases, terminal databases, security databases, and so on.

**cooperative processing**   the capability to distribute resources (programs, files, and databases) across the network.

**coordinator**   the two-phase commit protocol defines one database management system as coordinator for the commit process. The coordinator is responsible for communicating with the other database manager involved in a unit of work.

**corporate information factory (CIF)**   the physical embodiment of the information ecosystem. The CIF was first introduced by W. H. Inmon in the early 1980s.

**CPU (central processing unit)**   the part of the computer that carries out instructions.

**CPU-bound** the state of processing wherein the computer cannot produce more output, because the CPU portion of the processor is being used at 100 percent capacity. When the computer is CPU-bound, typically the memory and storage processing units are less than 100 percent utilized. With modern DBMSs, it is much more likely that the computer is I/O-bound, rather than CPU-bound.

**CSP (Cross System Product)** an IBM application generator.

**CUA (Common User Access)** specifies the ways in which the user interface to systems will be constructed.

**current value data** data whose accuracy is valid as of the moment of execution, as opposed to time-variant data.

**cursor** 1. an indicator that designates a current position on a screen; 2. a system facility that allows the programmer to thumb from one record to the next after the system has retrieved a set of records.

**cursor stability** an option that enables data to move under the cursor. Once the program has used the data examined by the cursor, it is released. As opposed to repeatable read.

**cylinder** the storage area of a Direct Access Storage Device (DASD) that can be read without movement of the arm. The term originated with disk files, in which a cylinder consisted of one track on each disk surface so that each of these tracks could have a read/write head positioned over it simultaneously.

**DASD** *See* direct access storage device.

**data** a recording of facts, concepts, or instructions on a storage medium for communication, retrieval, and processing by automatic means and presentation as information that is understandable by human beings.

**data administrator (DA)** the individual or organization responsible for the specification, acquisition, and maintenance of data management software, and the design, validation, and security of files or databases. The data model and the data dictionary are usually the responsibility of the DA.

**data aggregate** a collection of data items.

**database** a collection of interrelated data stored (often with controlled, limited redundancy) according to a schema. A database can serve single or multiple applications.

**database administrator (DBA)** the organizational function charged with the day-to-day monitoring and care of the databases. The DBA is more closely associated with physical database design than the DA.

**database key** a unique value that exists for each record in a database. The value is often indexed, although it can be randomized or hashed.

**database machine** a dedicated-purpose computer that provides data access and management through total control of the access method, physical storage, and data organization. Often called a *backend processor.* Data is usually managed in parallel by a database machine.

**database management system (DBMS)** a computer-based software system used to establish and manage data.

**database record** a physical root and all of its dependents (in IMS).

**DatacomDB**  a database management system created by Computer Associates, Inc.

**data definition**  the specification of the data entities, their attributes, and their relationships in a coherent database structure to create a schema.

**data definition language (DDL)**  the language used to define the database schema and additional data features that allows the DBMS to generate and manage the internal tables, indexes, buffers, and storage necessary for database processing. Also called a *data description language.*

**data description language**  *See* data definition language.

**data dictionary**  a software tool for recording the definition of data, the relationship of one category of data to another, the attributes and keys of groups of data, and so forth.

**data division (COBOL)**  the section of a COBOL program that consists of entries used to define the nature and characteristics of the data to be processed by the program.

**data-driven development**  the approach to development that centers around identifying the commonality of data through a data model and building programs that have a broader scope than the immediate application. Data-driven development differs from traditional application-oriented development, which is generally process-driven.

**data-driven process**  a process whose resource consumption depends on the data by which it operates. For example, a hierarchical root has a dependent. For one occurrence, there are two dependents for the root. For another occurrence of the root, there may be 1,000 occurrences of the dependent. The same program that accesses the root and all its dependents will use very different amounts of resources when operating against the two roots, although the code will be exactly the same.

**data element**  1. an attribute of an entity; 2. a uniquely named and well-defined category of data that consists of data items, and that is included in the record of an activity.

**data engineering**  the planning and building of data structures according to accepted mathematical models on the basis of the inherent characteristics of the data itself, and independent of hardware and software systems. *See also* information engineering.

**data independence**  the property of being able to modify the overall logical and physical structure of data without changing any of the application code supporting the data.

**data item**  a discrete representation having the properties that define the data element to which it belongs. *See also* data element.

**data item set (dis)**  a grouping of data items, each of which directly relates to the key of the grouping of data in which the data items reside. The data item set is found in the midlevel model.

**data manipulation language (DML)**  1. a programming language that is supported by a DBMS and used to access a database; 2. language constructs added to a higher-order language (such as COBOL) for the purpose of database manipulation.

**data mart**  contains data from the data warehouse tailored to support the specific analytical requirements of a given business unit. This business unit could be defined to be as broad as a division or as narrow as a department.

**data mining warehouse**  a sister component to the exploration warehouse. In early stages, a single exploration warehouse is sufficient to support the needs of explorers and miners. As time goes on, the miners need their own environment—the data mining warehouse. The exploration warehouse helps explorers find and interpret patterns and make assertions and hypotheses, whereas the data mining warehouse helps miners validate assertions and hypotheses.

**data model**   1. the logical data structures, including operations and constraints provided by a DBMS for effective database processing; 2. the system used for the representation of data (such as the ERD or relational model).

**data record**   an identifiable set of data values treated as a unit, an occurrence of a schema in a database, or a collection of atomic data items describing a specific object, event, or tuple.

**data security**   the protection of the data in a database against unauthorized disclosure, alteration, or destruction. There are different levels of security.

**data set**   a named collection of logically related data items, arranged in a prescribed manner, and described by control information, to which the programming systems has access.

**data storage description language (DSDL)**   a language to define the organization of stored data in terms of an operating system and device-independent storage environment. *See also* device media control language.

**data structure**   a logical relationship among data elements that is designed to support specific data manipulation functions (such as trees, lists, and tables).

**data type**   the definition of a set of representable values that is primitive and without meaningful logical subdivisions.

**data view**   *See* user view.

**data volatility**   the rate of change of the contents of data.

**data warehouse**   a collection of integrated subject-oriented databases designed to support the DSS function, where each unit of data is relevant to some moment in time. The data warehouse contains atomic data and lightly summarized data.

**data warehouse administrator (DWA)**   represents the organization responsible for managing the data warehouse environment.

**DB2**   a database management system created by IBM.

**DB/DC**   database/data communications.

**DBMS language interface (DB I/O module)**   software that applications invoke in order to access a database. The module in turn has direct access with the DBMS. Standard enforcement and standard error checking are often features of an I/O module.

**deadlock**   *See* deadly embrace.

**deadly embrace**   the event that occurs when transaction A desires to access data currently protected by transaction B, while at the same time transaction B desires to access data that is currently being protected by transaction A. The deadly embrace condition is a serious impediment to performance.

**decision support system (DSS)**   a system used to support managerial decisions. Usually, DSS involves the analysis of many units of data in a heuristic fashion. As a rule, DSS processing does not involve the update of data.

**decompaction**   the opposite of compaction. Once data is stored in a compacted form, it must be decompacted to be used.

**decryption**   the opposite of encryption. Once data is stored in an encrypted fashion, it must be decrypted to be used.

**degree (of a relation)**   the number of attributes or columns of a relation. *See also* cardinality of a relation.

**delimiter**   a flag, symbol, or convention used to mark the boundaries of a record, field, or other unit of storage.

**demand staging**   the movement of blocks of data from one storage device to another device with a shorter access time, when programs request the blocks, and the blocks are not already in the faster access storage.

**denormalization**   the technique of placing normalized data in a physical location that optimizes the performance of the system.

**derived data**   data whose existence depends on two or more occurrences of a major subject of the enterprise.

**derived data element**   a data element that is not necessarily stored, but that can be generated when needed (such as age as of the current date and date of birth).

**derived relation**   a relation that can be obtained from previously defined relations by applying some sequence of retrieval and derivation operations (such as a table that is the combination of others and some projections). *See also* virtual relation.

**design review**   the quality assurance process where all aspects of a system are reviewed publicly prior to the striking of code.

**device media control language (DMCL)**   a language used to define the mapping of the data onto the physical storage media. *See also* data storage description language.

**direct access**   retrieval or storage of data by reference to its location on a volume. The access mechanism goes directly to the data in question, as is generally required with online use of data. Also called *random access* or *hashed access*.

**direct access storage device (DASD)**   a data storage unit wherein data can be accessed directly without having to progress through a serial file such as a magnetic tape file. A disk unit is a direct access storage device.

**directory**   a table specifying the relationships between items of data. Sometimes it is a table or index giving the addresses of data.

**distributed catalog**   a distributed catalog is needed to achieve site autonomy. The catalog at each site maintains information about objects in the local databases. The distributed catalog keeps information on replicated and distributed tables stored at that site and on remote tables located at another site that cannot be accessed locally.

**distributed database**   a database controlled by a central DBMS, but where the storage devices are geographically dispersed or not attached to the same processor. *See also* parallel I/O.

**distributed environment**   a set of related data processing systems, where each system has the capacity to operate autonomously, but where applications can execute at multiple sites. Some of the systems may be connected with teleprocessing links into a network in which each system is a node.

**distributed free space**   space left empty at intervals in a data layout, to permit the insertion of new data.

**distributed request**   a transaction across multiple nodes.

**distributed unit of work**   the work done by a transaction that operates against multiple nodes.

**division**   an operation that partitions a relation on the basis of the contents of data found in the relation.

**DL/1**   IBM's Data Language One, used for describing logical and physical data structures.

**domain**   the set of legal values from which actual values are derived for an attribute or a data element.

**download**   the stripping of data from one database to another, based on the content of data found in the first database.

**drill-down analysis**   the type of analysis whereby examination of a summary number leads to the exploration of the components of the sum.

**DSS application data mart**   similar to a departmental data mart in form but different in terms of breadth of user community. Whereas the departmental data mart supports only a department/division within a company, the DSS application data mart supports all users of a particular analytic application. As a result, the user community can span many departments/divisions. Business domains where these analytic applications are common include customer relationship management (CRM) and enterprise resource planning (ERP).

**dual database**   the practice of separating high-performance, transaction-oriented data from decision support data.

**dual database management systems**   the practice of using multiple database management systems to control different aspects of the database environment.

**dumb terminal**   a device used to interact directly with the end user, where all processing is done on a remote computer. A dumb terminal acts as a device that gathers data and displays data only.

**dynamic SQL**   SQL statements that are prepared and executed within a program, while the program is executing. In dynamic SQL, the SQL source is contained in host language variables rather than being coded into the application program.

**dynamic storage allocation**   a technique whereby the storage areas assigned to computer programs are determined during processing.

**dynamic subset of data**   a subset of data selected by a program and operated on only by the program, and released by the program once it ceases execution.

**EDI (Electronic Data Interchange)**   a process by which bills, payments, and orders are exchanged electronically.

**EIS (Executive Information Systems)**   systems designed for the top executives, featuring drill-down analysis and trend analysis.

**embedded pointer**   a record pointer (that is, a means of internally linking related records) that is not available to an external index or directory. Embedded pointers are used to reduce search times, but also require maintenance overhead.

**encoding**   a shortening or abbreviation of the physical representation of a data value (such as male = "M", female = "F").

**encryption**   the transformation of data from a recognizable form to a form unrecognizable without the algorithm used for the encryption. Encryption is usually done for the purpose of security.

**enterprise**   the generic term for the company, corporation, agency, or business unit. Usually associated with data modeling.

**entity**   a person, place, or thing of interest to the data modeler at the highest level of abstraction.

**entity-relationship attribute (ERA) model**   a data model that defines entities, the relationship between the entities, and the attributes that have values to describe the properties of entities and/or relationships.

**entity-relationship diagram (ERD)**   a high-level data model—the schematic showing all the entities within the scope of integration and the direct relationship between those entities.

**event**   a signal that an activity of significance has occurred. An event is noted by the information system.

**event discrete data**   data relating to the measurement or description of an event.

**expert system**   a system that captures and automates the usage of human experience and intelligence.

**exploration warehouse**   an ad hoc environment intended to offload complex and unpredictable query activity from the data warehouse. Unlike the data mart, which supports a user community that asks relatively simple and predictable types of questions (the farmer), questions asked by the user community of the exploration warehouse (the explorer and miner) can be characterized as complex and unpredictable. The type of analysis performed is statistical in nature and used to do such things as forecast inventory and create models to segment customers and detect fraud.

**extent**   1. a list of unsigned integers that specifies an array; 2. a physical unit of disk storage attached to a data set after the initial allocation of data has been made.

**external data**   1. data originating from other than the operational systems of a corporation; 2. data residing outside the central processing complex.

**external schema**   a logical description of a user's method of organizing and structuring data. Some attributes or relationships can be omitted from the corresponding conceptual schema or can be renamed or otherwise transformed. *See also* view.

**external world**   environment in which business and commerce take place. The external world consists of transaction producers and information consumers. Without the external world, there would be no need for the corporate information factory.

**extract**   the process of selecting data from one environment and transporting it to another environment.

**field**   *See* data item.

**file**   a set of related records treated as a unit and stored under a single logical file name.

**first in, first out (FIFO)**   a fundamental ordering of processing in a queue.

**first in, last out (FILO)**   a standard order of processing in a stack.

**flag**   an indicator or character that signals the occurrence of some condition.

**flat file**   a collection of records containing no data aggregates, nested repeated data items, or groups of data items.

**floppy disk**   a device for storing data on a personal computer.

**foreign key**   an attribute that is not a primary key in a relational system, but whose values are the values of the primary key of another relation.

**format**   the arrangement or layout of data in or on a data medium or in a program definition.

**forward recovery**   a recovery technique that restores a database by reapplying all transactions using a before image from a specified point in time to a copy of the database taken at that moment in time.

**fourth-generation language**   language or technology designed to allow the end user unfettered access to data.

**functional decomposition**   the division of operations into hierarchical functions (that is, activities) that form the basis for procedures.

**granularity**   the level of detail contained in a unit of data. The more detail there is, the lower the level of granularity. The less detail there is, the higher the level of granularity.

**graphic**   a symbol produced on a screen representing an object or a process in the real world.

**hash**   to convert the value of the key of a record into a location on disk.

**hash total**   a total of the values of one or more fields, used for the purposes of auditability and control.

**header record or header table**   a record containing common, constant, or identifying information for a group of records that follow.

**heuristic**   the mode of analysis in which the next step is determined by the results of the current step of analysis. Used for decision support processing.

**hierarchical model**   a data model providing a tree structure for relating data elements or groups of data elements. Each node in the structure represents a group of data elements or a record type. There can be only one root node at the start of the hierarchical structure.

**hit**   an occurrence of data that satisfies some search criteria.

**hit ratio**   a measure of the number of records in a file expected to be accessed in a given run. Usually expressed as a percentage—the number of input transactions/number of records in the file $\times$ 100 = hit ratio.

**homonyms**   identical names that refer to different attributes.

**horizontal distribution**   the splitting of a table across different sites by rows. With horizontal distribution, rows of a single table reside at different sites in a distributed database network.

**host**   the processor receiving and processing a transaction.

**Huffman code**   a code for data compaction in which frequently used characters are encoded with fewer bits than infrequently used characters.

**IDMS** a network DBMS from Computer Associates, Inc.

**IEEE (Institute of Electrical and Electronics Engineers)** a governing body that certifies electrical engineers.

**image copy** a procedure in which a database is physically copied to another medium for the purposes of backup.

**IMS (Information Management System)** an operational DBMS by IBM.

**index** the portion of the storage structure maintained to provide efficient access to a record when its index key item is known.

**index chains** chains of data within an index.

**indexed sequential access method (ISAM)** a file structure and access method in which records can be processed sequentially (such as in order or by key) or by directly looking up their locations on a table, thus making it unnecessary to process previously inserted records.

**index point** a hardware reference mark on a disk or drum used for timing purposes.

**indirect addressing** any method of specifying or locating a record through calculation (such as by locating a record through the scan of an index).

**information** data that human beings assimilate and evaluate to solve problems or make decisions.

**information center** the organizational unit charged with identifying and accessing information needed in DSS processing.

**information ecosystem** a comprehensive information solution that complements traditional business intelligence (i.e., analytics) with capabilities to deliver business management (customer care, account consolidation, and so on). This allows companies to capitalize on a changing business landscape characterized by customer relationships and customized product delivery.

**information engineering (IE)** the discipline of creating a data-driven development environment.

**input/output (I/O)** the means by which data is stored and/or retrieved on DASD. I/O is measured in milliseconds (mechanical speeds), whereas computer processing is measured in nanoseconds (electronic speeds).

**instances** a set of values representing a specific entity belonging to a particular entity type. A single value is also the instance of a data item.

**integration and transformation (I & T) layers** a software component of the corporate information factory, which is responsible for collecting, integrating, transforming, and moving data from the applications to the data warehouse and ODS, and from the data warehouse to the data marts, exploration warehouse, and data mining warehouse.

**integrity** the property of a database that ensures that the data contained in the database is as accurate and consistent as possible.

**intelligent database** a database that contains shared logic as well as shared data, and automatically invokes that logic when the data is accessed. Logic, constraints, and controls relating to the use of the data are represented in an intelligent data model.

**interactive**   a mode of processing that combines some of the characteristics of online transaction processing and batch processing. In interactive processing, the end user interacts with data over which he or she has exclusive control. In addition, the end user can initiate background activity to be run against the data.

**interleaved data**   data from different tables mixed into a simple table space, where there is commonality of physical colocation based on a common key value.

**internal schema**   the schema that describes logical structures of the data and the physical media over which physical storage is mapped.

**interpretive**   a mode of data manipulation in which the commands to the DBMS are translated as the user enters them (as opposed to the programmed mode of process manipulation).

**intersection data**   data that is associated with the junction of two or more record types or entities, but which has no meaning when disassociated with any records or entities forming the junction.

**inverted file**   a file structure that uses an inverted index, where entries are grouped according to the content of the key being referenced. Inverted files provide for the fast, spontaneous searching of files.

**inverted index**   an index structure organized by means of a nonunique key to speed the search for data by content.

**inverted list**   a list organized around a secondary index instead of around a primary key.

**I/O (input/output operation)**   Input/output operations are the key to performance because they operate at mechanical speeds, not at electronic speeds.

**I/O-bound**   the point after which no more processing can be done because the I/O subsystem is saturated.

**ISAM**   *See* indexed sequential access method.

**"is a type of"**   an analytical tool used in abstracting data during the process of conceptual database design (for example, a Cocker Spaniel is a type of dog).

**ISDN (Integrated Services Digital Network)**   a telecommunications technology that enables companies to transfer data and voice through the same phone lines.

**ISO (International Standards Organization)**   an organization that governs international standards.

**item**   *See* data item.

**item type**   a classification of an item according to its domain, generally in a gross sense.

**iterative analysis**   the mode of processing in which the next step of processing depends on the results obtained by the existing step in execution; also known as heuristic processing.

**JAD (joint application design)**   an organization of people—usually end users—to create and refine application system requirements.

**join**   an operation that takes two relations as operands and produces a new relation by concatenating the tuples and matching the corresponding columns when a stated condition holds between the two.

**judgment sample**   a sample of data where the sample is accepted or rejected for the sample based on one or more parameters.

**junction**   from the network environment, an occurrence of data that has two or more parent segments. For example, an order for supplies must have a supplier parent and a part parent.

**justify**   to adjust the value representation in a character field to the right or to the left, ignoring blanks encountered.

**keeplist**   a sequence of database keys maintained by the DBMS for the duration of the session.

**key**   a data item or combination of data items used to identify or locate a record instance (or other similar data groupings).

**key, primary**   a unique attribute used to identify a single record in a database.

**key, secondary**   a non-unique attribute used to identify a class of records in a database.

**key compression**   a technique for reducing the number of bits in keys; used in making indexes occupy less space.

**label**   a set of symbols used to identify or describe an item, record, message, or file. Occasionally, a label may be the same as the address of the record in storage.

**language**   a set of characters, conventions, and rules used to convey information, and consisting of syntax and semantics.

**latency**   the time taken by a DASD device to position the read arm over the physical storage medium. For general purposes, average latency time is used.

**least frequently used (LFU)**   a replacement strategy whereby new data must replace existing data in an area of storage; the least frequently used items are replaced.

**least recently used (LRU)**   a replacement strategy whereby new data must replace existing data in an area of storage; the least recently used items are replaced.

**level of abstraction**   the level of abstraction appropriate to a dimension. The level of abstraction that is appropriate is entirely dependent on the ultimate user of the system.

**line**   the hardware by which data flows to or from the processor. Lines typically go to terminals, printers, and other processors.

**line polling**   the activity of the teleprocessing monitor during which different lines are queried to determine whether they have data and/or transactions that need to be transmitted.

**line time**   the length of time required for a transaction to go either from the terminal to the processor or the processor to the terminal. Typically, line time is the single largest component of online response time.

**linkage**   the ability to relate one unit of data to another.

**linked list**   the set of records in which each record contains a pointer to the next record on the list. *See also* chain.

**list**   an ordered set of data items.

**living sample**   a representative database typically used for heuristic statistical analytical processing in place of a large database. Periodically, the very large database is selectively stripped of data so that the resulting living sample database represents a cross-section of the very large database at some moment in time.

**load**   to insert data values into a database that was previously empty.

**locality of processing**   in a distributed database, the design of processing so that the remote access of data is eliminated or reduced substantively.

**local site support**   within a distributed unit of work, a local site update allows a process to perform SQL update statements referring to the local site.

**local transaction**   in a distributed DBMS, a transaction that requires reference only to data that is stored at the site where the transaction originated.

**lockup**   the event that occurs when an update is done to a database record, and the transaction has not yet reached a commit point. The online transaction needs to prevent other transactions from accessing the data while the update is occurring.

**log**   a journal of activity.

**logging**   the automatic recording of data with regard to the access of the data, the updates to the data, and so on.

**logical representation**   a data view or description that does not depend on a physical storage device or a computer program.

**loss of identity**   when data is brought in from an external source, and the identity of the external source is discarded, a loss of identity occurs. It is common practice with microprocessor data.

**LU6.2 (Logical Unit Type 6.2)**   a peer-to-peer data stream with a network operating system for program-to-program communication. LU6.2 allows midrange machines to talk to one another without the involvement of the mainframe.

**machine learning**   the capability of a machine to improve its performance automatically, based on past performance.

**magnetic tape**   1. the storage medium most closely associated with sequential processing; 2. a large ribbon on which magnetic images are stored and retrieved.

**main storage database (MSDB)**   a database that resides entirely in main storage. Such databases are very fast to access but require special handling at the time of update. Another limitation of MSDBs are that they can only manage small amounts of data.

**master file**   a file that holds the system of records for a given set of data (usually bound by an application).

**maximum transaction arrival rate (MTAR)**   the rate of arrival of transactions at the moment of peak period processing.

**message**   1. the data input by the user in the online environment that is used to drive a transaction; 2. the output of a transaction.

**meta data**   1. data about data; 2. the description of the structure, content, keys, and indexes of data.

**metalanguage**    a language used to specify other languages.

**metaprocess**    descriptive information about the code or process(es) that act against data.

**microprocessor**    a small processor serving the needs of a single user.

**migration**    the process by which frequently used items of data are moved to more readily accessible areas of storage, and infrequently used items of data are moved to less readily accessible areas of storage.

**mips (million instructions per second)**    the standard measurement of processor speed for minicomputers and mainframe computers.

**mode of operation**    a classification for systems that execute in a similar fashion and share distinctive operational characteristics. Some modes of operation are operational, DSS, online, interactive.

**modulo**    an arithmetic term describing the remainder of a division process; e.g., 10 modulo 7 is 3. Modulo is usually associated with the randomization process.

**MOLAP**    multidimensional online analytical processing supports OLAP using specialized, proprietary multidimensional database technology.

**multilist organization**    a chained file organization in which the chains are divided into fragments, and each fragment is indexed. This organization of data permits faster access to the data.

**multiple key retrieval**    requires data searches on the basis of the values of several key fields (some or all of which are secondary keys).

**MVS (Multiple Virtual Storage)**    IBM's mainline operating system for mainframe processors. There are several extensions of MVS.

**Named Pipes**    the program-to-program protocol with Microsoft's LAN Manager. The Named Pipes API supports intra- and intermachine process-to-process communications.

**natural forms**    the first normal form: data that has been organized into two-dimensional flat files without repeating groups. Second normal form: data that functionally depends on the entire candidate key. Third normal form: data that has had all transitive dependencies on data items other than the candidate key removed. Fourth normal form: data whose candidate key is related to all data items in the record, and that contains no more than one nontrivial multivalued dependency on the candidate key.

**natural join**    a join in which the redundant logic components generated by the join are removed.

**natural language**    a language generally spoken, whose rules are based on current usage and not explicitly defined by grammar.

**navigate**    to steer a course through a database, from record to record, by means of an algorithm that examines the content of data.

**network**    a collection of circuits, data-switching elements, and computing systems. The switching devices in the network are called communication processors. A network provides a configuration for computer systems and communication facilities within which data can be stored and accessed, and within which a DBMS can operate.

**network model**   a data model that provides data relationships on the basis of records and groups of records (that is, sets) in which one record is designated as the set owner, and a single member record can belong to one or more sets.

**nine's complement**   the transformation of a numeric field calculated by subtracting the initial value from a field consisting of all nines.

**node**   a point in the network at which data is switched.

**nonprocedural language**   syntax that directs the computer as to what to do, not how to do it. Typical nonprocedural languages include RAMIS, FOCUS, NOMAD, and SQL.

**normalize**   to decompose complex data structures into natural structures.

**null**   an item or record for which no value currently exists or possibly may ever exist.

**numeric**   a representation using only numbers and the decimal point.

**occurrence**   *See* instances.

**offset pointer**   an indirect pointer. An offset pointer exists inside a block, and the index points to the offset. If data must be moved, only the offset pointer in the block must be altered; the index entry remains untouched.

**OLAP**   online analytical processing is a category of software technology that enables analysts, managers, and executives to perform ad hoc data access and analysis based on its dimensionality. This form of multidimensional analysis provides business insight through fast, consistent, interactive access to a wide variety of possible views of information.

**online storage**   storage devices and storage mediums where data can be accessed in a direct fashion.

**operating system**   software that enables a computer to supervise its own operations and automatically call in programs, routines, languages, and data as needed for continuous operation throughout the execution of different types of jobs.

**operational data**   data used to support the daily processing a company does.

**operations**   the department charged with the running of the computer.

**oper-mart**   a component of the corporate information factory used to support tactical decision making. Similar in form to the data mart, it differs in that its source of data is the operational data store, *not* the data warehouse.

**optical disk**   a storage medium using lasers as opposed to magnetic devices. Optical disk is typically write-only, is much less expensive per byte than magnetic storage, and is highly reliable.

**ORACLE**   a DBMS by ORACLE Corp.

**order**   to place items in an arrangement specified by rules such as numeric or alphabetic order. *See* sort.

**OS/2**   the operating system for IBM's Personal System.

**OSF (Open Software Foundation)**   an organization dedicated to assuring interoperability between manufacturers.

**OSI Open Systems Interconnection overflow**   1. the condition in which a record or a segment cannot be stored in its home address because the address is already occupied. In this case, the data is placed in another location, referred to as overflow; 2. the area of DASD where data is sent when the overflow condition is triggered.

**ownership**   the responsibility of updating operational data.

**padding**   a technique used to fill a field, record, or block with default data (such as blanks or zeros).

**page**   1. a basic unit of data on DASD; 2. a basic unit of storage in main memory.

**page fault**   a program interruption that occurs when a page that is referred to is not in main memory and must be read in from external storage.

**page-fixed**   the state in which programs or data cannot be removed from main storage. Only a limited amount of storage can be page-fixed.

**paging**   in virtual storage systems, the technique of making memory appear to be larger than it really is by transferring blocks (pages) of data or programs into external memory.

**parallel data organization**   an arrangement of data in which the data is spread over independent storage devices and is managed independently.

**parallel I/O**   the process of accessing or storing data on multiple physical data devices.

**parallel search storage**   a storage device in which one or more parts of all storage locations are queried simultaneously for a certain condition or under certain parameters. *See also* associative storage.

**parameter**   an elementary data value used as a criterion for qualification, usually of searches of data or in the control of modules.

**parent**   a unit of data in a 1:$n$ relationship with another unit of data called a child, where the parent can exist independently, but the child cannot exist unless there is a parent.

**parsing**   the algorithm that translates syntax into meaningful machine instructions. Parsing determines the meaning of statements issued in the data manipulation language.

**partition**   a segmentation technique in which data is divided into physically different units. Partitioning can be done at the application or the system level.

**path length**   the number of instructions executed for a given program or instruction.

**peak period**   the time when the most transactions arrive at the computer with the expectation of execution.

**performance**   the length of time from the moment a request is issued until the first of the results of the request are received.

**periodic discrete data**   a measurement or description of data taken at a regular time interval.

**physical representation**   1. the representation and storage of data on a medium such as magnetic storage; 2. the description of data that depends on such physical factors as the length of elements, records, pointers, and so on.

**pipes**   vehicles for passing data from one application to another.

**plex or network structure**   a relationship between records or other groupings of data in which a child record can have more than one parent record.

**plug-compatible manufacturer (PCM)**   a manufacturer of equipment that functionally is identical to that of another manufacturer (usually IBM).

**pointer**   the address of a record, or other groupings of data contained in another record, so that a program may access the former record when it has retrieved the latter record. The address can be absolute, relative, or symbolic, hence the pointer is referred to as absolute, relative, or symbolic.

**pools**   the buffers made available to the online controller.

**populate**   to place occurrences of data values in a previously empty database. *See also* load.

**precision**   the degree of discrimination with which a quantity is stated. For example, a three-digit numeral discriminates among 1,000 possibilities, from 000 to 999.

**precompilation**   the processing of source text prior to compilation. In an SQL environment, SQL statements are replaced with statements that will be recognized by the host language compiler.

**prefix data**   data in a segment or a record used exclusively for system control; usually unavailable to the user.

**primary key**   see *key, primary.*

**primitive data**   data whose existence depends on only a single occurrence of a major subject area of the enterprise.

**privacy**   the prevention of unauthorized access and manipulation of data.

**privilege descriptor**   a persistent object used by a DBMS to enforce constraints on operations.

**problems database**   the component of a DSS application where previously defined decision parameters are stored. A problems database is consulted to review characteristics of past decisions and to determine ways to meet current decision-making needs.

**processor**   the hardware at the center of the execution of computer programs. Generally speaking, processors are divided into three categories—mainframes, minicomputers, and microcomputers.

**processor cycles**   the hardware's internal cycles that drive the computer (such as initiate I/O, perform logic, move data, perform arithmetic functions, and so on).

**production environment**   the environment where operational, high-performance processing is run.

**program**   a set of instructions that tells the computer what to do. Programs are sometimes referred to as applications and/or software.

**program area**   the portion of main memory in which application programs are executed.

**progressive overflow**   a method of handling overflow in a randomly organized file that does not require the use of pointers. An overflow record is stored in the first available space and is retrieved by a forward serial search from the home address.

**projection**   an operation that takes one relation as an operand and returns a second relation that consists of only the selected attributes or columns, with the duplicate rows eliminated.

**proposition**   a statement about entities that asserts or denies that some condition holds for those entities.

**protocol**   the call format used by a teleprocessing monitor.

**punched cards**   an early storage medium on which data and input were stored. Today, punched cards are rare.

**purge data**   the data on or after which a storage area may be overwritten. Used in conjunction with a file label, it is a means of protecting file data until an agreed-upon release date is reached.

**query language**   a language that enables an end user to interact directly with a DBMS to retrieve and possibly modify data managed under the DBMS.

**record**   an aggregation of values of data organized by their relation to a common key.

**record-at-a-time processing**   the access of data a record at a time, a tuple at a time, and so on.

**recovery**   the restoration of the database to an original position or condition, often after major damage to the physical medium.

**redundancy**   the practice of storing more than one occurrence of data. In the case where data can be updated, redundancy poses serious problems. In the case where data is not updated, redundancy is often a valuable and necessary design tool.

**referential integrity**   the facility of a DBMS to ensure the validity of a predefined relationship.

**reorganization**   the process of unloading data in a poorly organized state and reloading the data in a well-organized state. Reorganization in some DBMSs is used to restructure data. Reorganization is often called *reorg* or an *unload/reload* process.

**repeating groups**   a collection of data that can occur several times within a given record occurrence.

**ROLAP**   relational online analytical processing supports OLAP-using techniques that allow multidimensionality to be implemented in a two-dimensional RDBMS. Star join schema is a common database design technique used in this environment.

**rolling summary**   a form of storing archival data where the most recent data has the lowest level of detail stored and the older data has higher levels of detail stored.

**secondary storage**   any form of media that reduces the cost of keeping the vast amount of detailed data available to the data warehouse and CIF.

**scope of integration**   the formal definition of the boundaries of the system being modeled.

**SDLC (System Development Life Cycle)**   the classical operational system development life cycle that typically includes requirements gathering, analysis, design, programming, testing, integration, and implementation. Sometimes called a *waterfall* development life cycle.

**sequential file**   a file in which records are ordered according to the values of one or more key fields. The records can be processed in this sequence starting from the first record in the file, and continuing to the last record in the file.

**serial file**   a sequential file in which the records are physically adjacent, in sequential order.

**set-at-a-time processing** accessing data by groups, each member of which satisfies some selection criteria.

**snapshot** a database dump or the archiving of data as of one moment in time.

**star join schema** a relational database design technique that organizes data around its multi-dimensionality in terms of business dimensions and measurements (a.k.a., facts).

**storage hierarchy** storage units linked to form a storage subsystem, in which some units are fast to access and consume small amounts of storage, but which are expensive, and other units are slow to access and are large, but are inexpensive to store.

**subject database** a database organized around a major subject of the corporation. Classical subject databases are for customer, transaction, product, part, vendor, and so on.

**system log** an audit trail of relevant system events (for example, transaction entries, database changes, and so on).

**system of record** the definitive and singular source of operational data. If data element, abc, has a value of 25 in a database record, but a value of 45 in the system of record, by definition, the first value must be incorrect. The system of record is useful for the management of data redundancy.

**table** a relation that consists of a set of columns with a heading and a set of rows (i.e., tuples).

**time stamping** the practice of tagging each record with some moment in time, usually when the record was created or when the record was passed from one environment to another.

**time-variant data** data whose accuracy is relevant to some moment in time. The three common forms of time-variant data are continuous time span data, event discrete data, and periodic discrete data. *See also* current value data.

**transition data** data possessing both primitive and derived characteristics; usually very sensitive to the running of the business. Typical transition data includes interest rates for a bank, policy rates for an insurance company, retail sale prices for a manufacturer/distributor, and so on.

**trend analysis** the process of looking at homogeneous data over a spectrum of time.

**true archival data** data at the lowest level of granularity in the current level detail database.

**update** to change, add, delete, or replace values in all or selected entries, groups, or attributes stored in a database.

**user** a person or process issuing commands or messages and receiving stimuli from the information system.

# Recommended Reading

## Articles

Adelman, Sid. "The Data Warehouse Database Explosion." *Data Management Review* (December 1996). A very good discussion of why volumes of data are growing as fast as they are in the data warehouse environment, and what can be done about it.

Bair, John. "It's about Time! Supporting Temporal Data in a Warehouse." *INFODB* 10, no. 1 (February 1996). A good discussion of some of the aspects of time-variant data in the DSS/data warehouse environment.

Geiger, Jon. "Data Element Definition." *Data Management Review* (December 1996). A good description of the definitions required in the system of records.

———. "What's in a Name." *Data Management Review* (June 1996). A discussion of the implications of naming structures in the data warehouse environment.

Graham, Stephen, analyst. "The Foundations of Wisdom." IDC Special Report (April 1996). International Data Corp. (Toronto, Canada). The definitive study on the return on investment for the data warehouse as well as the measurement of cost-effectiveness.

———. "The Financial Impact of Data Warehousing." *Data Management Review* (June 1996). A description of the cost-benefit analysis report done by IDC.

Hackney, Doug. "Vendors Are Our Friends." *Data Management Review* (June 1996). Doug Hackney talks about beneficial relationships with vendors.

———. "Data Warehouse Quality, Part I." *Data Management Review* (January 1996). Part one of a description of data warehouse quality.

———. "Data Warehouse Quality, Part II." *Data Management Review* (March 1996). The second part of the discussion on data quality.

Imhoff, Claudia. "End Users: Use 'em or Lose 'em." *Data Management Review* (November 1996). An excellent discussion of the ways to manage the end-user data warehouse effort.

Imhoff, Claudia, and Jon Geiger. "Data Quality in the Data Warehouse." *Data Management Review* (April 1996). Provides insights and guidelines for defining and measuring quality in the data warehouse environment.

Imhoff, Claudia, and Ryan Sousa. "Information Ecosystem—Administration." *Data Management Review* (March 1997). Details the components and techniques used in administering the information ecosystem.

———. "Information Ecosystem—Corporate Information Factory." *Data Management Review* (February 1997). Details the parts and pieces of the Corporate Information Factory as defined by Bill Inmon. In addition, reviews the business relevance of the capabilities produced.

———. "Information Ecosystem—Information Services." *Data Management Review* (May 1997). Discusses how the Information Services interface is used to provide a common navigation interface to the information ecosystem (metadata, data delivery, DSS tools), how this interface facilitates the coordination of people and process, and how it ultimately provides a common knowledge fabric.

———. "Information Ecosystem—Introduction." *Data Management Review* (January 1997). Introduction to the information ecosystem.

———. "Information Ecosystem—People and Process." *Data Management Review* (April 1997). Details suggested organizational structures and roles. Additionally, reviews processes for building, using, and managing the information ecosystem.

Inmon, W.H. "Choosing the Correct Approach to Data Warehousing: 'Big Bang' vs. Iterative." *Data Management Review* (March 1996). A discussion of the proper strategic approach to data warehousing.

———. "Commentary: The Migration Path." *ComputerWorld* (July 29, 1996). A brief description of some of the issues of migrating to the data warehouse.

———. "Cost Justification in the Data Warehouse." *Data Management Review* (June 1996). A discussion of how to justify DSS and the data warehouse on the cost of reporting.

———. "The Data Warehouse and Data Mining." *CACM* 39, no. 11 (November 1996). A description of the relationship between data mining and data warehouse.

———. "Data Warehouse Lays Foundation for Bringing Data Investment Forward." *Application Development Trends* (January 1994). A description of the data warehouse and the relation to legacy systems.

————. "Data Warehouse Security: Encrypting Data." *Data Management Review* (November 1996). A description of some of the challenges of data warehouse security and industrial strength security.

————. "The Future in History." *Data Management Review* (September 1996). A discussion of the value of historical information.

————. "Knowing Your DSS End User: Tourists, Explorers, Farmers." *Data Management Reveiw* (October 1996). A description of the different categories of end users.

————. "Managing the Data Warehouse: The Data Content Card Catalog." *Data Management Reveiw* (December 1996). An introduction to the notion of a data content card catalog, that is, stratification of data content.

————. "Managing the Data Warehouse Environment." *Data Management Review* (February 1996). Defining who the data warehouse administrator is.

————. "Measuring Capacity in the Data Warehouse." *Enterprise Systems Journal* (August 1996). A discussion of how capacity should be measured in the data warehouse and DSS environment.

————. "Monitoring the Data Warehouse Environment." *Data Management Review* (January 1996). What is a data monitor for the data warehouse environment, and why would you need it?

————. "Rethinking Data Relationships for Warehouse Design." *Sybase Server* 5, no. 1 (Spring 1996). A discussion of the issues of data warehouse data relationships.

————. "SAP and the Data Warehouse." *Data Management Reveiw* (July/Aug 1996). A description of why the data warehouse is still needed in the face of SAP.

————. "Security in the Data Warehouse: Data Privatization." *Enterprise Systems Journal* (March 1996). Data warehouse requires a very different approach to security from the traditional VIEW-based approach offered by DBMS vendors.

————. "Summary Data: The New Frontier." *Data Management Review* (May 1996). A description of the different types of summary data, including dynamic summary data and static summary data, lightly summarized data and highly summarized data, and so on.

————. "User Reaction to the Data Warehouse." *Data Management Reveiw* (December 1996). A description of the different user types in data warehousing.

————. "Virtual Data Warehouse: The Snake Oil of the '90s." *Data Management Review* (April 1996). A discussion of the virtual data warehouse and how the concept tries to attach itself to the legitimacy of the data warehouse.

Jordan, Arthur. "Data Warehouse Integrity: How Long and Bumpy the Road?" *Data Management Review* (March 1996). A discussion of the issues of data quality inside the data warehouse.

Lambert, Bob. "Break Old Habits to Define Data Warehousing Requirements." *Data Management Review* (December 1995). A description of how the end user should be approached to determine DSS requirements.

Lambert, Bob. "Data Warehousing Fundamentals: What You Need to Know to Succeed." *Data Management Review* (March 1996). Several significant strategies for data warehousing to guide you through a successful implementation.

Laney, Doug. "Are OLAP and OLTP Like Twins?" *Data Management Reveiw* (December 1996). A comparison of the two environments.

Myer, Andrea. "An Interview with Bill Inmon." *Inside Decisions* (March 1996). An interview discussing the start of data warehousing, the use of data warehousing for competitive advantages, the origins of Prism Solutions, and building the first data warehouse.

Rudin, Ken. "Parallelism in the Database Layer." *Data Management Review* (December 1996). An excellent discussion of the differences between DSS parallelism and OLTP parallelism.

————. "Who Needs Scalable Systems?" *Data Management Review* (November 1996). A good discussion of the issues of scalability in the data warehouse environment.

Swift, Ron. "Creating Value Through a Scalable Data Warehouse Framework." *Data Management Review* (November 1996). A very nice discussion of the data warehousing issues scale.

Tanler, Richard. "Data Warehouses and Data Marts: Choose Your Weapon." *Data Management Review* (February 1996). A description of the differences between data marts and the current-level detail of the data warehouse.

————. "Taking Your Data Warehouse to a New Dimension on the Intranet." *Data Management Review* (May 1996). A discussion of the different components of the data warehouse as they relate to the intranet.

Winsberg, Paul. "Modeling the Data Warehouse and the Data Mart." *INFODB* (June 1996). A description of architecture and modeling as it relates to different types of data warehouses.

Wright, George. "Developing a Data Warehouse." *Data Management Review* (October 1996). A very good discussion of snapshots and the basic structures of data warehouses.

# Books

Brackett, Mike. *The Data Warehouse Challenge* (1996). New York: John Wiley & Sons, Inc.

Devlin, Barry. *Data Warehouse: From Architecture to Implementation* (1997). Reading, MA: Addison-Wesley.

Inmon, W. H. *Building the Data Warehouse*, 2d ed. (1996). New York: John Wiley & Sons, Inc.

Inmon, W. H., Claudia Imhoff, and Greg Battas. *Building the Operational Data Store*, 2nd ed. (1999). New York: John Wiley & Sons, Inc.

Inmon, W. H., Claudia Imhoff, and Ryan Sousa. *Corporate Information Factory, Second Edition* (2001). New York: John Wiley & Sons, Inc.

Inmon, W. H., Claudia Imhoff, and R. H. Terdeman. *Exploration Warehousing: Turning Business Information into Business Opportunity* (2000). New York: John Wiley & Sons, Inc.

Inmon, W. H., John A. Zachman, and Jonathan G. Geiger. *Data Stores, Data Warehousing, and the Zachman Framework* (1997). New York: McGraw-Hill.

Inmon, W. H., J. D. Welch, and Katherine L. Glassey. *Managing the Data Warehouse* (1997). New York: John Wiley & Sons, Inc.

Kimball, Ralph, Laura Reeves, Margy Ross, and Warren Thornthwaite. *The Data Warehouse Lifecycle Toolkit: Expert Methods for Designing, Developing, and Deploying Data Warehouses* (1998). New York: John Wiley & Sons, Inc.

Kimball, Ralph. *The Data Warehouse Toolkit* (1996). New York: John Wiley & Sons, Inc.

Kimball, Ralph, and Richard Merz. *The Data Webhouse Toolkit: Building the Web-Enabled Data Warehouse* (2000). New York: John Wiley & Sons, Inc.

# Index